RESEARCH METHODS FOR SOCIAL WORKERS

LINDA BELL

macmillan education   palgrave

First published 2017 by
PALGRAVE

Palgrave in the UK is an imprint of Macmillan Publishers Limited, registered in England, company number 785998, of 4 Crinan Street, London, N1 9XW.

Palgrave is a global imprint of the above companies and is represented throughout the world.

Palgrave® and Macmillan® are registered trademarks in the United States, the United Kingdom, Europe and other countries.

ISBN 978–1–137–44282–6 paperback

This book is printed on paper suitable for recycling and made from fully managed and sustained forest sources. Logging, pulping and manufacturing processes are expected to conform to the environmental regulations of the country of origin.

A catalogue record for this book is available from the British Library.

A catalog record for this book is available from the Library of Congress.

Printed and bound by CPI Group (UK) Ltd, Croydon, CR0 4YY

RESEARCH METHODS FOR SOCIAL WORKERS

CONTENTS

List of Exercises   viii

List of Figures   ix

Preface   x

Acknowledgements   xii

**1 From social work skills to research skills: What is
    'being research minded'?**   1
Introduction   1
Working towards research mindedness   5
Applying and defining approaches to enquiry in practice   12
Linking research and evaluation to professional development   14
Chapter summary   15
Further reading   16

**2 Understanding published research and research design:
    Scoping and summarising**   17
Introduction: Media and information   17
Assessing knowledge: Thinking about ontology and epistemology   20
Ways of thinking about research design (methodology)   23
Finding appropriate knowledge and publications for reviews   27
Different kinds of review: scoping studies, systematic reviews,
    meta-analyses and 'academic' literature reviews   29
Skills involved in critiquing research literature (critical appraisal) 35
Chapter summary   40
Further reading   40

**3 Dealing with ethics and maintaining professional values
    during research**   41
Introduction: Principles, professional and theoretical issues   41
What is 'research ethics'?   42
Research governance for social work and health researchers
    (including students) in the UK   44
Research processes: Ethical aspects   47
Ethical issues in research practice   49
Chapter summary   58
Further reading   59

**4 Talking and listening: Using 'qualitative' methods to develop
   relationship based approaches to research**   **60**
   Introduction: The importance of relationships in research and social work   60
   Underpinning approaches in qualitative research: Grounded theory,
      ethnography, feminist approaches, phenomenology, case studies and
      'practice-near' research   62
   Key qualitative methods – interviews, observation, focus groups, vignettes/
      scenarios   74
   Chapter summary   85
   Further reading   86

**5 Working with documentary sources and analysing qualitative
   data in social work research**   **87**
   Introduction   87
   Using documents   87
   Obtaining documentary data from observational methods   92
   Preparing to analyse your material – some practical issues   94
   Dealing with 'qualitative' comments produced by respondents on
      questionnaires   97
   Analysing text taken from documents   97
   Selecting, organising and analysing qualitative data: Interviews
      and focus group material   100
   Chapter summary   105
   Further reading   105

**6 It's all about attitude: Ways of capturing and understanding
   measurable data**   **106**
   Introduction   106
   Descriptive survey design (methodology) and methods   108
   Developing and using a questionnaire/attitude measure on 'attitudes to
      research'   115
   Building explanations from quantitative data   117
   'Pre' and 'post' test design – showing whether or not there are changes
      before and after an intervention   120
   Gathering and analysing data from randomised
      controlled trials (RCTs) – a form of experimental design   121
   Chapter summary   125
   Further reading   126

**7 Mixing it up: How to combine research approaches without
   getting into a muddle**   **127**
   Introduction   127
   Some key theoretical issues in relation to 'mixing methods'   128
   Mixing methods during the research process   130
   Examples of research using 'mixed' methods in different ways   132

Practical considerations when deciding whether or not to mix
    methods in a project   137
Chapter summary   139
Further reading   140

**8 Can you innovate? Developing arts-based and visual
   methods for social work research**   **141**
Introduction   141
Researching and using arts-based methods in social work education   143
Methods of data collection, analysis and interpretation in art-based
    research: discussion   150
Chapter summary   152
Further reading   153

**9 What's out there? Using the internet and social media for
   research**   **154**
Introduction   154
Using online methods in social work research   155
Ethical issues in online/digital contexts   156
Examples of online/digital social work research   158
Chapter summary   162
Further reading   163

**10 Becoming a social work researcher: Building confidence
    as well as skills**   **164**
Introduction/Summary   164
Producing a research proposal   166
Outline of headings for a research proposal   169
My final suggestions   172

Glossary of key terms   174
Appendices   183
Notes   206
References   209
Index   224

LIST OF EXERCISES

1.1	Research questions	7
2.1	Key words/ searching	29
3.1	Ethics scenario 1	50
3.1	Ethics scenario 2	50
3.1	Ethics scenario 3	50
4.1	Interview guide (Appendix B)	184
5.1	Field diary	93
6.1	Clinical trials/errors	125
7.1	Project ideas: 'mixed methods'	139
8.1	Photographs/concept of 'family'	152
9.1	How are digital/online methods being used within your own organisation?	162
10.1	Design your own Research	166

Feedback or actual solutions are given in chapters or in Appendix C

Various discussion points are also included for you to consider throughout the text

LIST OF FIGURES

2.1	Characteristics of positivism	24
2.2	Recap: Hypothesis testing	24
2.3	Characteristics of interpretivism or constructionism	25
2.4	Example: Keyword search	28
3.1	Making an Ethics Application – do's and don'ts	46
4.1	Some characteristics of grounded theory	63
4.2	Basic characteristics of ethnography	65
4.3	Interview types	76
4.4	Types of observational research	81
4.5	Methods of data collection in observational work	83
4.6	Focus group diagram	84
5.1	Using documents	88
5.2	Collating data from parenting group records – London borough of X	91
5.3	Transcription types	95
5.4	Constant comparative analysis – process	102
5.5	Reading qualitative data from interviews and texts (adapted from Mason, 1996, p. 109)	103
6.1	Process for design of a questionnaire	110
6.2	Likert scale examples (taken from ATR questionnaire, Papanastasiou, 2005)	115
7.1	Forms of triangulation	130

PREFACE

This is a book primarily about research and how it can be applied by those who have to grapple with all kinds of problem-solving in their day-to-day work. As such, it is intended as a 'one-stop' introduction, covering both reading about research and doing research. As we will see later, we need to be clear about what we mean by 'research'. Critical appreciation of different approaches to research, how to develop skills to begin to carry out your own project, as well as wider aspects of what I would term 'research mindedness' are equally important in my experience. These aspects are all going to be introduced in this volume.

Some other books may focus on one or other of these areas, but my feeling is that because they are all connected, you should at least be aware of this set of connections when approaching an enquiry or problem-solving activity. My own research journey began when, on leaving school, I was employed in a reference library and was encouraged to ask enquirers, 'What exactly is it that you want to find out?' That question remains essential to me today, whether I am talking to student researchers, practitioners or research commissioners. It is not a question that is easily answered, and it requires reflection rather than immediate certainty on both sides. However, my enthusiasm to explore and share this question with others perhaps indicates why my journey has taken me along the paths of research and teaching and also why I wanted to write this book. My academic background in anthropology has also encouraged me to work across the boundaries of the sciences and social sciences, and therefore not to see differing approaches to research as mutually exclusive.

I have aimed this book mainly at social workers and allied health or social care staff, especially qualifying level students with whom I have worked for many years; but it should also be of interest to those of you who are already qualified and/or are working in practice. You may be drawn into various forms of enquiry as part of your work, for example some employers may wish to develop partnerships that allow practitioner researchers, academics and those developing social work or health interventions to work together more effectively; this can be important for both service user outcomes and for staff development (CPD), and requires understanding of how to carry out research or evaluation. I think it is important, for example, to be clear about making a basic distinction between the design of a research project (what I would term its methodology) and the actual techniques or methods used within that design. Perhaps you may also want to start your own personal journey towards a higher or a research degree; once again, I have often shared these kinds of experiences with people like you, and this book is intended to help you start this journey.

Apart from taking an individualised research degree focus, most researchers will find themselves working on projects as part of a team, which I think is one of the most rewarding (if also challenging) aspects of doing research. This aspect should also resonate clearly with professional practitioners such as social workers; you may think you are already used to team working, but I believe you also need to be prepared for research project team work. This kind of collaboration will often incorporate all sorts of people, including users of services, and will cross boundaries, such as those between local authorities and academic institutions, with their differing agendas, timescales and priorities, perhaps leading to extra and unexpected challenges. Collaboration also raises all kinds of issues about the use of self and the ubiquitous emotional aspects of doing research in practice.

I have had to assume through experience that some of you (especially students) will have had no previous exposure to research methods, and I understand that this subject and set of techniques may seem to be very alien to what you thought you were signing up for when you decided to train as a professional practitioner. Added to this, some of you may also have had little previous knowledge of areas such as statistics, so these aspects of research methods may initially seem particularly daunting.

At this point, I would ask you not to put the book down but to consider setting out on an interesting journey from which you will, I am sure, have much to gain, especially as a professional practitioner. I will attempt to define or explain unfamiliar terminology in the glossary and through various exercises and examples, but we first need to start from where you are; those of you who are already familiar with research methods as a subject area should find much to reflect on and perhaps reconsider in these pages, the contents of which have been drawn from my own personal experiences of working alongside students or social work practitioners when doing research, or when teaching or writing about it.

I always try to come as close as I can to facilitating the application of research methods to your area(s) of professional practice – and I would ask you, as social workers or health professionals, to continue to reciprocate! I have always found this collaborative process very rewarding, and I have learnt a lot from all of you. This approach will provide us with the possibility of starting out optimistically and with similar intentions.

ACKNOWLEDGEMENTS

I consider most research is based on collaborative working, and so there are many people who have helped me along the way, and whose support and wisdom I have drawn upon when writing the current book.

Firstly I would like to thank all the students I have worked with, especially those who have attended the BA and MA qualifying level social work programmes at Middlesex University; you continue to give me hope and encouragement for the future. Other students at Middlesex, including those whose dissertations or research degrees I have supervised, have also contributed a great deal to my own understanding of research and research methods.

Colleagues at Middlesex and elsewhere who have researched, supervised or taught methods with me also deserve to be mentioned here, as do those who earlier in my career encouraged me to undertake my own research projects. Special thanks are due to all members of the Qualitative Women's Workshop on Family/Household Research.

I would particularly like to thank: Lesley Adshead, Lucille Allain, Sally Angus, Elaine Atkins, Emma Ball, Bahman Baluch, Jim Barry, Celia Bell, Elisabeth Berg, Maxine Birch, Björn Blom, Nikki Bradley, Julia Brannen, Karen Bryan, Kay Caldwell, Pat Cartney, John Chandler, Carmel Clancy, Christine Cocker, Helen Cosis-Brown, Yvonne Dhooge, Jean Dillon, Andrea Doucet, Souzy Dracopoulou, Paul Dugmore, Karen Duke, Jane Dutton-Kohli, Ros Edwards, Marion Ellison, Jeff Evans, John Foster, Val Gillies, Tony Goodman, Trish Hafford-Letchfield, Sue Hanna, Rosemary Harris, Teresa Harris, Hannah Henry-Smith, Rachel Herring, Helen Hingley-Jones, Lesley Hoggart, Ray Holland, Mina Hyare, Alison Jones, Lesley Jordan, Eleonore Kofman, Ravi Kohli, Lynne Lehane, Sarah Lewis-Brooke, Jane McCarthy, Lynn McDonald, Anastasia Maksymluk, Wilma Mangabeira, Oded Manor, Melanie Mauthner, Natasha Mauthner, Jane Maxim, Claudia Megele, Sue Middleton, Tina Miller, Peter Milligan, Geoff Most, David Nilsson, Maria Appel Nissen, Chaim Noy, Linda Nutt, Sioban O'Farrell-Pearce, David Oliviere, Lesley Oppenheim, Rena Papadopoulos, Elena Papanastasiou, Sian Peer, Alfonso Pezzella, Georgia Philip, Mike Puniskis, Karen Quinn, Katherine Rounce, Louise Ryan, Peter Ryan, Rosemary Sales, Phil Slater, Theresa So, Betsy Thom, Mary Tilki, Aase

Villadsen, Jorunn Vindegg, Margaret Volante, Sandra Wallman, Jodie Ward, Gordon Weller, Colin Whittington, Margaret Whittington.

Many thanks to Louise and all the team at Palgrave for your support.

Last but not least, thanks to my family – David, Tom and Sarah – for their patience and encouragement.

1

FROM SOCIAL WORK SKILLS TO RESEARCH SKILLS: WHAT IS 'BEING RESEARCH MINDED'?

Introduction

Are you a social worker? Are you 'research minded'? What exactly do we mean by 'research minded'?

Research always starts with questions (or so we are told). If you want to explore a topic you are interested in, you will perhaps ask yourself first what has already been written about the topic? Why, when, or where has something, or may something, happen/have happened? And how is this topic relevant to me? Equally important, however, is how am I going to investigate my chosen topic? This process of thinking will lead you to consider more broadly the concepts of knowledge, information and evidence. To quote the eighteenth-century author Samuel Johnson:

> Knowledge is of two kinds. We *know a subject* ourselves, or we know *where we can find information* upon it. (*my italics*)

Johnson, as a learned man, realised that no one could know absolutely everything; even if you think you are an expert in one topic, there will be many others that are partly or perhaps completely outside of your experience and you will have to seek information about them. So knowing where (and how) to look for all that information is just as important as what you (think) you already know. And besides, how exactly did you come to know something in the first place? For social workers, finding and using information is one of the very first, basic skills you will need in your work.

When I have asked social workers or social work students what are some other job skills they think they need, communication skills always come very high on the list. But if we are taking a questioning approach, once again, we ought to ask, what exactly do we mean by communication?

There are many different media involved in communication (e.g. spoken/verbal, aural, written, visual) as well as different ways of doing the communicating: face-to-face, by telephone, using e-mail or various kinds of social media (Facebook, Twitter), written down (e.g. in a letter), or perhaps communication of ideas via literature or art works or photographs. We will address this issue of different media in more detail later in this chapter. At the time of writing this book, most people will be communicating face-to-face with individuals or groups, but sometimes we may find ourselves communicating with machines, with the intention of communicating with an individual person or group 'somewhere' (the age of robotics being not yet fully upon us).

For social workers, do you think the most important people to communicate with are users of social work services? You may answer *yes*, but think of all the other individuals and groups social workers need to communicate with effectively on a day-to-day basis – other professionals (including other social workers) both within your own workplace and elsewhere, members of third sector/voluntary groups, staff in various agencies (from housing to education to police or prison services). All of these people, including the users of services, are important to you as a social worker, or social work student, and so, as we will see, they have important parts to play in social work research and enquiry.

Taking apart a term like 'communication' may seem a pointless exercise, but it allows us to test out for ourselves what taking a questioning approach means. Taking a questioning approach is the most fundamental building block in becoming 'research minded'; in my view:

- ➤ A research minded person does not simply ask 'what information do I need'? Rather, s/he should ask first, why is this the information or perspective that I need to include in my enquiry?

- ➤ Why should I ask these people rather than those people when seeking information or perspectives on something?

- ➤ Have I covered everything I think I need, and can I justify having done so?

- ➤ Asking these questions will help you to develop *problem-solving skills*, which are also essential in professional practice.

As well as aiming for this kind of approach to communication and information seeking, I should try to take up a questioning approach systematically (which we could summarise as 'going from one logical point to another'), but I am only human, after all, and cannot necessarily expect to achieve total comprehensiveness! I need to justify that what I have decided is in some way logical and needs to be included.

Another important point to reflect on is, 'why do I need to carry out my enquiry in the first place?' We have been using the term 'research' to refer to what I am planning to do, but, in fact, 'enquiry' seen more broadly can take different forms. Later in this chapter we will consider some differences between what we are now calling 'research' (e.g. in relation to academic study or to student project work) and 'evaluation', which is another very commonly occurring form of enquiry often used by social workers and other professionals (see e.g. Cree, Jain and Hillen, 2016). Suffice it to say here that these forms of enquiry do overlap and that they use many of the same methods; it is mainly the purposes of each of these forms of enquiry that are different.

This way of thinking about definitions can result in some anomalies. I have sometimes been informed by ethics committees (usually from health settings) that what my master's students are doing is not research, by which it is usually meant the student does not need to obtain formal ethics approval for her/his project. Very often these students will be carrying out some form of evaluative enquiry, perhaps in work settings, and whilst they may be relieved not to need formal ethics approval, I also feel somewhat cheated on their behalf that the committee does not seem to recognise all the very tangible research skills that these students are learning and displaying in order to achieve their master's degree! Enquiry is enquiry, so perhaps this is a more useful concept to adopt?

Next we need to focus on what we are collecting or exploring. I have already said above that we need to examine why we think we need particular form(s) of information. Information is all around us every day, but a basic idea in research or enquiry is that we need to establish what we need in terms of it becoming our data. Data at its simplest is information that we have recorded for a particular purpose. It may simply be 'lifted' from an existing data source, e.g. National Statistics, an article from a journal, or a piece of information from the Internet. Or we may have constructed it ourselves, e.g. by carrying out a survey using an online questionnaire and recording the statistical data produced, by interviewing a sample of participants to produce a series of interview transcripts (accounts), or by taking a photograph or making a video. In every case, we need to be able to record our data in some way so that we can go back later and analyse it as part of our project. As we will see later, if, for example, we are carrying out **observation** as a method, we need to be able to record and verify what we have observed in order to turn our observations into data. It is not usually enough just to experience something; we need to either make notes about it, video it, take photographs or make audio recordings – this provides everyone with evidence that we did not simply make the whole thing up!

One big change that has come about in the past few years is that communication and sharing of information or data have become much more instantaneous, and larger and larger volumes of information are being shared globally, through social media in particular. This also suggests that we all need to develop good *time-management skills*, in order to cope with such demands (and this is surely an essential skill for social work or health practitioners in other contexts). Instantaneous communication may mean that whilst more and more people have a chance to express their opinions, a lot of miscommunication can also occur as people do not always have time to reflect on what is being shared. Communication in these circumstances becomes much more about instant response, often through short, decontextualised comments. Think tanks such as DEMOS have already conducted research into the use of Twitter and have monitored real-time responses to events such as TV programmes. This work suggests that whilst it is possible to monitor large-scale trends in people's behaviour, and various new methodologies are being established to do this, these approaches to enquiry often depend for ethical reasons upon anonymity of participants. Such approaches are also more about **observation** of what is actually happening between people who are already communicating, rather than about asking people to participate in more conventional research approaches such as surveys. This has many implications both for research methods and also for ethical aspects of research.

What I have been trying to do in the introductory section of this chapter is encourage you to think critically about ways in which we address concepts of information and communication. Developing problem-solving, time-management as well as critical-thinking skills is therefore vital, as in professional practice, and becoming involved in research or any form of enquiry will certainly help you to develop all those skills.

I have also tried to briefly introduce some other concepts that are essential for developing our understanding of these basic ideas underlying research. These include issues of **subjectivity**, being systematic and considering the importance of context. I think it is also important to make a basic distinction between the design of a research project (what I would term its '**methodology**') and the actual techniques or **methods** used within that design, as we will see later.

Finally, I have tried to suggest how we need to take account of the social and technological contexts of research and enquiry, which are changing and evolving more and more rapidly. All of these considerations, I would argue, will help you to start developing your own approach to becoming and being research minded.

Working towards research mindedness

Identifying researchable problems and developing research questions

At the beginning of this chapter I stated that 'research always starts with questions', and so following this idea through we ought to now start thinking about how to develop questions that could form the basis of research or some other kind of enquiry (such as **evaluation** or **auditing**). Bearing in mind our earlier discussion of information and communication, a key issue here is how, if you are a social worker or a student, you can be encouraged to identify researchable problems derived from social work practice. How do you know whether something could be focused on in such a way as to make an appropriate research topic?

This process is not easy for most social work students, but in my experience people can and should be encouraged to talk through the issues they encounter in their practice in order to identify something that will become 'researchable'. For example I have often found students who are planning or doing dissertations tell me that they cannot think of a topic to research; when I have prompted them to say 'what is an issue for you at the moment in your work?' (or as my research supervisor once said to me, 'where does your shoe pinch?'), students have said things to me like this:

'One of the real difficulties I am finding in my social work practice at the moment is that a new assessment tool has been introduced, but we don't really know how to use it.'

'I was unsure what to do when I was asked to make a decision about X; I didn't feel I knew enough about [personalisation/domestic violence/adult safeguarding] although my initial gut reaction was to ...'

'My supervisor is very supportive, but I have spoken to others who have had a difficult experience being supervised. This has started me thinking about the relevance of supervision for social workers, especially students.'

Interestingly, when I have suggested that these kinds of topics could be turned into research, many students respond by saying they thought these issues were 'just about practice'; through further discussion they may then begin to realise that this practice focus strengthens their research work and often makes it more relevant to them personally if they have been strongly affected by the issue in question. This immediately raises issues about the ethical dimensions of research projects, which we will be discussing in Chapter 3.

Responses to the above quotes

> The first quote above might suggest for example that the student or practitioner could develop a survey exploring how others have reacted to using the new tool; or perhaps they could carry out an enquiry amongst managers to find out why it was introduced, and whether more training for staff in its use would be a good idea. This project could be based on individual interviews or perhaps involve a focus group (if sufficient staff time is available).

> The second quote might suggest a project simply about the topic in question (personalisation etc.), but may be also involving users of services (if this is permitted ethically); but, equally, this person's experience could be used to explore whether and how social workers may depend on their 'gut reactions' in practice (sometimes called practice wisdom). This more exploratory study would probably be more successful if the student is using qualitative methods such as interviews, rather than using a questionnaire which will limit the participant to making short, decontextualised answers (i.e. using a survey approach, there will not be an opportunity to understand *why* the participant gives the answer they give as there might be in an interview).

> In the third quote, the student has more or less defined her/his own research question about the role/practice of supervision, although they may not have realised this. They would find that quite a lot has already been published in this area, and it would therefore make a useful project for using either primary methods (such as a survey design with questionnaires, in-depth interviews or using social media amongst students) or else perhaps as a (secondary) literature-based review (see Chapter 2).

Bryman (2007) points out, from his own empirical work with social scientists, that in order to develop researchable problems, researchers can sometimes be more concerned about the value of particular kinds of methodological approach (such as 'mixed' methods) than they are about specific research questions:

> ... the 'dictatorship of the research question' stance may not hold sway for some researchers [in] that they may adopt mixed-methods research for tactical reasons, such as the following: to secure funding, to get research published or to gain the attention of policy makers. (Bryman, 2007: 14)

Bryman further suggests that in some circumstances:

> [The idea that] decisions about research methods and approach are subservient to the research questions that guide them – is questionable as a representation of social research practice. (op. cit., p. 18)

Does this mean that we should not be concerned about developing research questions at all? I don't think so. If we look carefully at Bryman's arguments, we can find some interesting evidence showing why he may have drawn this particular conclusion. Evidence is a concept about which we will have more to say later on. But for now, let us consider how Bryman has used supporting evidence in his article to convince us of this argument that the primacy of research questions over methods and approaches is questionable.

Firstly, Bryman bases this view on his interviews with social scientists (who are therefore professional researchers) and who were already using mixed methods approaches to carry out research. In this specific context, and with these particular people, it may well be that they would be more concerned (as he says in his article) to promote the use of **mixed methods** for reasons of funding or policy. Since mixing methods may lead to the pursuit of several research questions at once (one of the strengths of mixed methods approaches, as we will see in later chapters of this book) it is not surprising that a clear, unique research question could be seen as less necessary to these people than it would be if they were taking some other approaches to research. Furthermore, remember these are professional researchers who may have had many years of experience in their fields; as with driving a car or performing any other technical skill, these people may be less concerned with following the 'rules' (at least, as stated in research methods textbooks) and more used to bending them. Remember the old saying, that you need to know what the rules are before you can break them.

Exercise 1.1 **Research Questions**

Having considered whether we need to begin our research or enquiry with research question(s) at all, let us next consider whether there are some questions which cannot be investigated (and therefore could not be answered?). Try these:

1. Does a (specified) education programme about substance use have any effect on young people's understandings about the effects of various substances?

2. Should smoking be allowed in public places?

3. What do social workers think about the Care Act 2014?

Feedback: Question 1

Looking at Question 1 above, you can see we are interested in making a prediction about the effects of a specified programme or intervention on young people. Whereas all research may need to start with a question, a **hypothesis** relates to a particular kind of question, one that involves prediction. For that reason, a hypothesis will need to be specific about what exactly is predicted to happen. Since any hypothesis can only be tentative, research will then be designed to try to test or even falsify this hypothesis, taking into account causal logic relating to identified **variables**. What has caused what?

It is important to remember that, as Bowling has pointed out:

> A hypothesis is usually based upon *theoretical assumptions* (paradigms) about the way things work. (Bowling, 1997, p. 122)

If we were trying to build a project around Question 1, we might therefore predict (in the following **hypothesis**) that:

> Attendance at the (specified) health education programme will lead to increased knowledge about the harmful effects of particular substances amongst young people who attend.

This is a hypothesis which predicts in one direction,[1] i.e. it predicts increased knowledge will result from attendance on this programme. Question 1 could therefore be based upon this tentative hypothesis or prediction. (Given our question, there might be additional hypotheses that we could test in this study, e.g. about other aspects of attenders' understanding.) We may also express our hypotheses as going in either direction (whether or not), and you may also hear the term '**null hypothesis**'; this suggests basically that in statistical terms if the null hypothesis is supported, the intervention will make no difference to the outcome.

You will notice that I am suggesting we should consider that a hypothesis is supported, or not. This is basically because supporting a hypothesis with evidence is seen as only a temporary, contested state, and someone else may come along and test the hypothesis later on to find a different result. So the word 'prove' is not useful here.

The ways in which we design research can thus help us ensure that we can focus precisely on our identified hypothesis/es when carrying out a project which tests the prediction. For example we would also need to specify exactly how such effects on young people could be measured: which methods should we adopt in order to provide appropriate research data (evidence) about young people's understandings? (For more on **hypothesis** testing and its underlying epistemology, see the section 'Way of thinking about research design' in Chapter 2.)

It is possible, as we shall see later, to combine both causal questions (based on hypotheses) and more exploratory or descriptive questions in a single study, and the research design will need to reflect this combination of its aims and objectives.

Feedback: Question 2

Compared to questions based on specific hypotheses of this causal or predictive nature, other research questions may be much more exploratory or descriptive, and, as we shall see, this is quite legitimate in research terms. It all depends on what you are trying to research. However, having an exploratory research aim also implies developing a different kind of research design which does not depend on this 'causal', hypothesis-testing logic.

If we now look at Question 2, we should find something odd happening: it is a trick question! Although apparently inviting us to explore the issue raised, Question 2 also asks us to make a judgement about whether something should or should not be allowed. We can see that, if we explore this question, the answer(s) we get will depend very much on whom we talk to about this issue, and perhaps equally upon our own views on the subject. Having to make an ethical or moral judgement and present rigorous and specific research data simultaneously is what makes this question impossible to answer effectively. There are bound to be differences of opinion revealed in our research data, so how do we know which to present as 'the answer'? (See also Hart, 1998, ch 4, pp. 88–90, on different types of claims, including claims of value.)

This approach also raises a much broader issue about what we mean by being objective or 'neutral' in research. **Objectivity** is a key aim in some research, especially for those doing research based around hypothesis testing. As we shall see later, this is a tricky issue because the concept of objectivity itself can therefore be related to the research paradigm we adopt: if we are adopting causal logic then we would not only try to keep ourselves as neutral as possible, but we would probably also think of our data as 'factual' and 'real'. We can therefore easily imagine that we would need to stand entirely outside that form of data.

But coming back to Question 2, this would need to be modified in order to answer it with research evidence. It would be important to recognise the key significance of both ethics and policy in trying to develop an answerable question. We could for example ask something instead like:

> ➤ What are the views of health professionals about smoking in public places? (We would need to be clear about the sample of people who are participating in this study.)

Feedback: Question 3

In Question 3 we are also interested in opinions and attitudes, but here we have already specified in advance whose views we are representing, which allows us to describe our participants' viewpoints whilst at the same time maintaining a (relatively) neutral approach ourselves, as researchers. Many researchers carrying out exploratory studies and using qualitative approaches do so very much from personal interest, and they may have strong views about the topic they are investigating. But this is all the more reason for them to acknowledge their own **subjectivity** (their viewpoints) as well as being very clear about which attitudes are coming from their research participants or interviewees. In attempting to answer Question 3, the researcher makes very clear whose views are being described and investigated, and so it will be possible to present the results (whatever they are) in ways which can provide effective and accountable research evidence. (For more on **objectivity** and **subjectivity**, see Letherby, Scott and Williams, 2013.)

Question 3 seems to be a question which could be answered, in theory, at any rate. But is this question really specific enough for us to answer? Is it clear what we mean when we say, 'what do social workers think about the Care Act'? Are we asking them to make a judgement about how good (or bad) a piece of legislation they think it is? Once again, we are getting into the realms of value judgements, and so we might need to carefully modify the wording of this question. Would it be better to consider what effects the Care Act might be having on social workers' practice? For example we could ask something like:

> Do social workers working with adults think their practice has been changed by the implementation of the Care Act, 2014? If so, how?

We are also assuming here that, for the purposes of our research, social workers working with adults would be most likely to experience such effects, so these would be appropriate research participants. But another issue here is timing. If a social worker has only recently started working in this field, will they be able to compare working before and after implementation of the Act? Perhaps we need to specify that we therefore wish to speak to social workers with at least 3 years' experience in working with adults? In terms of sampling, we are starting to set appropriate **inclusion or exclusion criteria** for our study.

Discussion Points

Do you think that researchers should never reveal their own opinions in the course of research – is this what is meant by bias?

I have sometimes heard students say they are going to include hypothesis testing in their own projects, but then they suggest something like:

▶

I predict that the Care Act (2014) is going to make a big difference to social work practice.

Do you think this is a credible hypothesis that could be tested?

If so, how? If not, why not?

(See suggestions in Appendix C, Exercises.)

Ten examples of project titles that made successful social work undergraduate or postgraduate dissertations

1 Is dementia care mapping a useful tool for social workers?

2 Using outcome measures in child protection social work

3 Social workers' experiences of working with young people who are leaving the care system

4 How do social workers manage 'endings' when working with young people in care?

5 Working with recovery models in mental health social work practice

6 Challenges and opportunities for social workers when working in partnership

7 Working collaboratively with black and minority ethnic communities in social work

8 Advocacy in child protection/safeguarding

9 Using 'mindfulness' approaches in social work

10 Female involvement in gangs: challenges for social work

Hint: most of these studies were carried out using qualitative research approaches (interviews, focus groups), but number 1 was produced as a secondary study (literature review) and number 3 was carried out as a questionnaire-based survey of social workers in one local authority.

With acknowledgement and thanks to the students involved.

(See also Appendix C.)

For more on different types of research design, see Chapter 2.

For more about developing a research proposal, see Chapter 10.

Applying and defining approaches to enquiry in practice

Evaluation and **auditing** are forms of enquiry that link to research in many ways, even though (as mentioned earlier) this may not always be fully recognised. Compare these definitions of 'research' and 'evaluation' by the same author (Ann Bowling):

> Research is the systematic and rigorous process of enquiry that aims to describe processes and develop explanatory concepts and theories, in order to contribute to a scientific body of knowledge. (Bowling, 1997, p. 14)

> Evaluation is the use of the scientific method, and the rigorous and systematic collection of research data to assess the effectiveness of organisations, services and programmes (e.g. health service interventions) in achieving predefined objectives. (Bowling, 1997, p. 14)

These definitions suggest that basically it is not so much the methods as the purposes of research and evaluation which differ (see e.g. Cree, Jain and Hillen, 2014). For some, such as Shaw (2011), evaluation (particularly qualitative evaluation) should be seen as essentially embedded 'as a dimension of good practice in social work' (p. 1) in all its phases, rather than simply being applied to social work. This stance does, however, seem to imply that in order to do evaluation or enquiry at all in social work, it is necessary to be a practitioner; this is something which is virtually impossible for researchers, such as myself, who regularly walk alongside social workers and other practitioners (including student practitioners) in order to lend our research experience or expertise but without necessarily sharing the professional's role(s), allegiance or identity. However, despite arguing the case here for researchers to become involved in social work evaluation(s), my view is also that professional social worker(s) should surely be part of every successful evaluation team.

Audit is basically a cyclical process in which professional actions are checked against expectations. It will probably be familiar to practising social workers from managerial endeavours with local authority or third sector services and particularly from the NHS (clinical audit). Although some of the same methods for collecting data etc. can be used within audit and evaluation, I mention this process in passing here and would refer you to other publications and information such as the following:

> ➤ Munro (2004) (who argues that audit would be more useful and effective in social work if linked more closely to research methods)

➤ Standards for employers of Social Workers in England www.local.gov. uk/workforce/-/journal_content/56/10180/3511605/ARTICLE (includes link to audit tool, 2014)

According to the two definitions of research and evaluation above, they seem to have very different purposes, but they can involve the application of the same or similar methods of data collection and analysis. However, in the examples of social work project titles I already mentioned earlier, we suggest that use of theory and explanatory concepts would often be mixed in with a focus on the usefulness of those ideas in practice. Indeed, this is most often a requirement of a master's degree in social work, to be able to link theory with practice. But does this mean that students are usually conducting evaluations, not research?

For example in project number 3, 'Social workers' experiences of working with young people who are leaving care', the researcher would have to explore both theory and social policy in relation to young people leaving the care system, as well as investigating social workers' practice in that field, using rigorous research methods. However, this project was not an 'evaluation' because it did not intend to 'assess the effectiveness' of particular services for young people; the intention was rather to explore more broadly the social workers' experiences of such work and their suggestions for good practice.

So project number 3, like the other examples in the list above, is an example of research which is applied to social work issues whilst also contributing to 'a scientific body of knowledge'.

According to Øvretveit, when writing about health evaluations (1998; 2002), there can be different forms of evaluation based on the overall purpose, which he divides into:

➤ experimental evaluation (exploring 'what works?')

➤ economic evaluation (costs and cost effectiveness)

➤ developmental evaluation (including action approaches)

➤ managerial evaluation (concerned with performance measurement and efficiency)

He discusses basic preparatory steps needed to prepare an evaluation (2002, ch 2) which involve assessing its proposed scope; identifying the criteria that will be used to judge the value of the service or programme; establishing who the stakeholders are; and identifying any constraints, particularly the timeframe, resources available and whether any existing data has been collected that should be included.

Linking research and evaluation to professional development

As we can imagine, this basic framework of types and preparatory considerations (above) could also be very useful as a starting point for evaluations in social work/social care. Many social workers may decide that it will be important to get involved in some form of evaluative research work in order to support their own or colleagues' professional development. Later in the book we will consider various project examples, including 'Project D' which has provided direct professional development opportunities for local authority and university-based social work staff. However, there are other ways of using interest in research involvement to develop your professional skills and interests, for example:

> supporting social work students as a practice educator and facilitating their involvement in student projects

> using university, college or work-based courses to contribute towards developing a portfolio of skills or perhaps working towards higher (research) degree work

> involving employers or partners in developing projects that will help to develop policy or facilitate service users' involvement, e.g. forums involved with young people who are leaving care, or with older people in the community.

Given the importance of relationships in social work, you will note that most of the above suggestions would also involve you as a professional using your own self (including your emotional responses) to enable participation in research and in developing your research interests. This approach may seem surprising but, as Dickson-Swift et al. (2009) suggest:

> In acknowledging the importance of emotions in the research process, we must also challenge the dominance of the western philosophical tradition that judges emotions to be the anathema to academic research. (p. 63)

So I would suggest that dealing with our own and others' relationships and emotions can have as important a part to play in all kinds of research as it does in social work or other forms of professional practice. These issues will be taken up as we go through this book and in considering research examples.

Finally, in this chapter we need to consider the concept(s) **reflectivity/reflexivity** which have become commonly used in relation to both social work and research (particularly qualitative research). Social workers (and researchers) are therefore urged to 'be reflexive' (or 'reflective') in almost everything they do. When examining relevant literature, it is clear that these terms not only differ, but have various meanings that can encompass aspects of practice, research, emotional involvement, ethics and values, as well as epistemology. Some authors have their own particular 'take' on reflexivity or reflective practice (see e.g. Holland, 1999; Schon, 1983) whilst others have debated possible overlaps between reflexivity and critical reflection (e.g. D'Cruz, Gillingham and Melendez, 2007). These terms have been used in different ways, such as in social work theory (Holland, 1999), in social work education and ethics (Cartney, 2015) or more broadly in relation to reflexivity and research design/methodology (see e.g. Babones, 2016) and activities such as qualitative data analysis (Mauthner and Doucet, 2003). Sometimes it is hard to work out how you do reflexivity (e.g. when undertaking qualitative data analysis – but see Mauthner and Doucet (2003) for useful guidance here).

In relation to social work, D'Cruz, Gillingham and Melendez (2007, p. 75) have usefully defined three variations of reflexivity that we can make use of in this book. Reflexivity relates to:

1 'an individual's considered response to an immediate context and making choices for further direction'

2 'an individual's self-critical approach that questions how knowledge is generated and, further, how relations of power operate in this process'

3 'the part that emotion plays in social work practice [or in research processes].'

Chapter summary

> This chapter introduced the idea of 'research mindedness' for social workers, linked to ideas about knowledge and communication, problem-solving and critical thinking as well as the social worker's other existing skills, knowledge and values.

> You have been encouraged to identify research problems from social work practice. How do you know whether something could be focused on in such a way as to make an appropriate research topic?

➤ We have discussed how to produce research questions relevant to social work projects.

➤ We have introduced some definitions of 'research', **'evaluation'** and **'audit'**.

➤ We have identified some ways in which you can develop your own interests in research to develop your professional skills, including how as a researcher (just as much as in practice) you need to work with feelings, emotions and relationships.

➤ We have introduced the concept(s) of **reflexivity** and **reflectivity**.

Further reading

Bryman, A (2007) The research question in social research: What is its role?, *International Journal of Social Research Methodology*, 10 (1): 5–20

Bryman, A (2012) *Social Research Methods*, 4th edn, Oxford: Oxford University Press

Øvretveit, J (1998) *Evaluating Health Interventions*, Buckingham: Open University Press

Smith, R (2009) *Doing Social Work Research*, Buckingham: Open University Press (ch 1, 'Drivers, demands and constraints in social work research'; ch 10, 'The value of social work research')

Walliman, N (2005) *Your Research Project: A Step-by-Step Guide for the First-time Researcher*, 2nd edn, London: Sage

Whittaker, A (2012) *Research Skills for Social Work*, 2nd edn, London: Sage

2

UNDERSTANDING PUBLISHED RESEARCH AND RESEARCH DESIGN: SCOPING AND SUMMARISING

Introduction: Media and information

At the start of this book we tried to briefly identify different types of media associated with the information which researchers need to establish their work. In this chapter we will be mainly looking at how to scope and summarise published research; so before we explore this we need to say a little more about the different types of published or unpublished media you may need to use when conducting any form of enquiry.

Researchers today may use a wide variety of existing media/material when conducting research. Social workers may also use a variety of such media in their professional work. These forms of published or unpublished media need to be identified clearly if the knowledge they contain is to be used effectively in various forms of enquiry or research of relevance to social work. These media can include (in addition to published research in academic journals):

➤ articles in magazines or professional publications such as *Community Care* (containing material of a professional nature that is not necessarily based on primary research findings)

➤ newspaper articles

➤ a variety of government publications**, ranging from official publications such as Command papers, official reports produced for Parliament (such as the Annual Report and Accounts of the Health and Care Professions Council) to public consultation documents, policy papers or research reports such as the Department of Health's annual *Health Survey for England*

➤ All England Law Reports (see www.lexisnexis.com)

➢ statistical publications** (e.g. published in the UK by the Office for National Statistics (ONS), by government departments, or by international organisations; see e.g. www.ons.gov.uk/; European Monitoring Centre For Drugs and Drug Addiction: www.emcdda.europa.eu)

➢ other officially published reports by organisations or official bodies such as the Social Care Institute for Excellence (SCIE – www.scie.org.uk), local authorities or by third sector/ voluntary organisations and charities such as the Joseph Rowntree Foundation (JRF – www.jrf.org.uk)

➢ Serious case reviews (including summaries), which can be a useful source of material for some social work research topics. These are already indexed by key word and listed by year at the web address below, but it may be that by scrutinising the review(s), the researcher can identify additional themes of relevance to their own project. See https://www.nspcc.org.uk/search/?query=serious%20case%20revie2016.

➢ visual or digital media officially produced by higher education institutions, government departments, local authorities or third sector/voluntary organisations and charities.

**NOTE: There is a useful search tool for UK government publications, indexed by government department and publications type located online at: www.gov.uk/government/publications.

For a social policy and economic data resource maintained by the ESRC (Research Council), see www.ukdataservice.ac.uk.

Other useful **databases** for social work and health include:

www.careknowledge.com

www.scie-socialcareonline.org.uk

www.ebscohost.com/nursing/products/**cinahl-databases**

(Cumulative Index to Nursing and Allied Health Literature)

In addition to these forms of media, other **'grey' literature** is produced which can include:

➢ professional or regulatory body requirements or policy documents; see e.g. Health and Care Professions Council: http://www.hcpc-uk.org/aboutregistration/theregister/

➢ some research reports, including those co-produced with users of services

➢ unpublished theses or dissertations; see e.g. Electronic Theses Online Service: ethos.bl.uk

➢ data archives (of research material), e.g. those maintained by UK Research Councils

➢ other archival collections, e.g. London Metropolitan Archives, the National Archives (http://discovery.nationalarchives.gov.uk), universities, local Record Offices

➢ unpublished conference papers

➢ unofficial reports or policy documents that are produced by various organisations and including those co-produced with users of services (these may or may not be publically available, sometimes via archival collections in universities etc.; see above)

➢ unpublished material that is distributed either online or in hard copy (including in archival collections, as above) such as written newsletters, leaflets, minutes of meetings, visual or audio material, blogs, tweets, message boards etc..

➢ data archives, including research material intended for reuse/secondary analysis; see e.g. UK Data Archive based at the University of Essex: www.data-archive.ac.uk

A recent book by Kiteley and Stogdon (2014) describes **'grey' literature** as:

> documents that may not have been published through conventional routes, and which may therefore be trickier to find and access. They can be thought to occupy a 'grey area' in comparison to traditional published material. (p. 7)

For social work and social policy research, including evaluations of various kinds, making use of all these forms of media from different sources can only enhance the quality of enquiry in general terms (see e.g. Bornat, Johnson and Reynolds, 2013). However, there may be some drawbacks as well as strengths in making use of less conventionally published media. For example Kiteley and Stogdon (op. cit.), whilst valuing grey literature for potentially being *more up to date and cutting edge* than other publications, list the following potential drawbacks to using it for research purposes (see also Kiteley and Stogdon, 2014, Table 1.1, p. 8).

Grey literature is often:

➢ not peer reviewed and/or may not be checked by an editor, leading to inaccuracies or inconsistency

➢ not indexed or catalogued, e.g. in databases, so it can be difficult to find, especially if only available in hard copy format

➢ where available online, links to grey literature may not be available indefinitely

Overall these points mean that whilst useful, the reliability and validity of grey literature cannot always be guaranteed.

Assessing knowledge: Thinking about ontology and epistemology

How should we assess various forms of knowledge in terms of their usefulness for social work research purposes? In a publication produced some time ago by SCIE, Pawson et al. (2003) suggest we should first ask ourselves these questions about any piece of knowledge of which we want to make use; in doing this, they coined the term 'TAPUPAS' which stands for:

➤	Transparency	Is it open to scrutiny?
➤	Accuracy	Is it well grounded?
➤	Purposivity	Is it fit for purpose?
➤	Utility	Is it fit for use?
➤	Propriety	Is it legal and ethical?
➤	Accessibility	Is it intelligible?
➤	Specificity	Does it meet source-specific standards?

In providing this framework, Pawson et al. give us some useful initial ideas about how we should evaluate different kinds of knowledge that we may want to use. However, as Kiteley and Stodger (2014) point out, there are 'complex issues involved in considering the status and role of knowledge in social care practice' (p. 6).

This list of TAPUPAS criteria does raise some important, wider issues about our potential assumptions. How are we to decide whether something is 'fit for purpose' or intelligible, for instance? We need to consider these (basically philosophical) issues:

➤ the ways we and others view the world, our views about 'being' (what we can define as **ontology**)

➤ what counts as 'knowledge' from different viewpoints (what we can define as **epistemology**)

From these definitions, we can suggest that there will be different ontologies and epistemologies that could underpin our research: for example you may relate to a feminist ontology (way of seeing the world) and therefore seek to understand how a feminist would view knowledge (taking on a feminist epistemology). This could involve, for example, seeking to obtain data consisting of voices of women themselves when doing research; and/or aiming to work *with* women, rather than just doing research *on* women. As Blaikie (2007) further explains:

> An epistemology is a theory of knowledge; it presents a view and a justification for what can be regarded as knowledge – what can be known, and what criteria such knowledge must satisfy in order to be called knowledge rather than beliefs. (pp. 6–7)

Williams (1998) points out (when discussing his own journey from the practical concerns of local politics and trade union work into academic life):

> What became very apparent was that methodological and ideological stances adopted by researchers had very deep and often unacknowledged roots. This observation is not to imply .... that every study of poverty or crime should indulge in philosophical navel gazing, but rather to lament the lack of effective debate between philosophers, social theorists and methodologists. (p. 6)

From our point of view, the problem is not only about a lack of debate. Williams implies that researchers may be producing studies embedded in their assumptions about the world, and the nature of knowledge, but that this is something they do not necessarily acknowledge. Does this really matter? Don't we all have our own personal assumptions which are bound to affect our ways of doing research? We all have our own characteristics, thoughts and perspectives to bring to and share with others when doing research as well as in professional practice. Our experiences and values as well as our sense of identity/ies – including aspects such as social class, ethnicity, gender, disabilities and sexualities etc. – will surely affect how and why we do research. These aspects are related to **subjectivity** and need to be acknowledged, although this may be more straightforward or even expected when carrying out certain kinds of research (such as feminist research). In order to avoid accusations of **bias**, it has often been necessary, for example, for qualitative researchers to be particularly transparent and reflexive about their research methods (both in collecting data and in its analysis) and their motivations. (See e.g. Ribbens and Edwards, 1998; Mauthner and Doucet, 2003.)

As an example, perhaps I am only going to include some people in my research study who are of particular relevance to me, e.g. I may include my own work colleagues; but could this mean I have been biased in the sample of participants I have chosen?

Discussion Point

Have I been biased if I use a purposive sampling approach that allows me to select e.g. members of a staff team where I have been working?

What exactly do you understand by the term **bias**? (See also Appendix D-4: Sampling.)

On the other hand, perhaps you think that research should just be based on *facts* and not on assumptions at all – that research should aim to be *objective* and therefore *unbiased* above all else. But surely it is our way(s) of seeing the world (our ontological assumptions) and what we count as knowledge (our epistemological assumptions) which will affect our answers to any questions about the 'doing' of research, such as the nature of objectivity itself.

For example, we may dispute how far it is possible to ask questions about cause and effect at all in relation to social processes. (This relates to our views about trying to be objective, and if so, how we do that.) We may have different ideas about what is the appropriate kind of relationship between the researcher and those they research with (or should it be on?), and so on. An important aspect of all this, especially for social workers, is to consider how you deal with different theories about individuals or society, and this connects in turn to how you expect to practise as a social worker.

Discussion Point

What do you think is an 'appropriate' relationship between a social worker and a user of services, for example? How might this reflect your views about the nature of society?

How might these views then affect how you plan and carry out research/enquiry with service users?

As we will see below, there are several key methodological questions which go to the heart of how we set up and carry out our research. Furthermore, where research is applied to a particular professional context, such as social work, you can imagine that this context itself will bring about certain assumptions about what you 'should' do, which will also affect research processes.

Ways of thinking about research design (methodology)

From what I have said above, it is important firstly to understand when designing a research project ourselves, or when critically assessing someone else's research, that we need to build on and take account of key and differing ontological and epistemological assumptions. Some key assumptions are compared below and linked to some basic differences in approaches to research design.

In Chapter 1 we already suggested that different kinds of **research questions** we identified (hypotheses or exploratory questions, for example) link up to different kinds of design: in other words, both research questions and research designs reflect differing ontologies and epistemologies. It is very important when starting to think about doing our own projects, or if evaluating other people's research, that we can get a sense of the ways in which taking up differing approaches to research allows us to carry out an enquiry in different ways and for different purposes. It is not just a matter of choosing specific research methods 'off the shelf'; we need to know which shop we are in first! (After all, we wouldn't try to buy cakes from an electrical shop or electrical goods from a baker's.)

Below we consider some very commonly used approaches to research design. These can be considered ideal types or opposing tendencies grounded in certain philosophical principles that researchers have tended to adopt when designing research projects or thinking about what their research results mean.

Positivism

Positivism as an underpinning philosophical concept was first developed in the nineteenth century (the term being coined by Auguste Comte, with the approach being further developed by J.S. Mill and others). It was essentially an approach that attempted to apply scientific principles to the study of human society.

The implications of these principles to underpin research design are that research using a broadly positivist approach needs to involve systematic identification, gathering and recording of observed 'factual' data leading to explanation and theory (a process referred to as **induction**). There is a tendency for researchers to quantify and then to measure data to provide explanations.

There have been a number of critiques of positivism, especially in its original form: some critiques are really modifications of the approach, especially Popper's **'hypothetico-deductive' approach** (see below), whilst others are essentially contrasting approaches coming from those who do not necessarily share positivism's epistemology (e.g. feminist researchers).

'**Unity of the scientific method'** – a belief in 'natural' scientific study of people and society, alongside other sciences (Naturalism)

Phenomenalism – experience is seen as the only reliable basis for scientific knowledge

Nominalism – any abstract concepts used in scientific explanations must also be derived from experience

Atomism – objects of experience are regarded as discrete (separate), and generalisations refer to regularities amongst separate events

General laws – establishing these is the aim of science; individual cases are to be subsumed under laws to provide explanations

Value judgements and normative statements – a positivist approach separates 'facts' and 'values'

(adapted from Blaikie, 2007)

Figure 2.1 Characteristics of positivism

Karl Popper (a critical rationalist) accepts some positivist ideas (especially use of the 'scientific method'), but as a useful modification he suggested the '**hypothetico-deductive**' or 'falsificationist' method of hypothesis testing, which starts with tentative hypotheses which are tested against evidence; this is in contrast to induction, which starts with observation alone.

The hypothesis-testing method of **deduction** is much more useful to many researchers if they want to start out with existing research or theories on which to base their own project: these will form the basis of the hypothesis/es we want to test.

Remember how in Chapter 1 (p. 8) we first introduced the idea of testing an hypothesis?

Question One: Does a (specified) education programme about substance use have any effect on young people's understandings about the effects of various substances?

We suggested that a tentative hypothesis could be in this case:

'Attendance at the (specified) health education programme will lead to increased knowledge about harmful effects of particular substances amongst young people who attend.'

This would be in one direction, i.e. suggesting increased knowledge as a result of participation; our results would show (statistically) if that hypothesis is supported or not.

(A null hypothesis would suggest that attendance at the programme will not demonstrate (statistically) any effects on knowledge acquisition one way or the other.)

Figure 2.2 Recap: Hypothesis testing

Interpretivism and constructionism

One of the key criticisms of positivism is that it has an inadequate view of social reality – an inadequate ontology, in other words. It is a philosophy that cannot account for the ways in which people construct and maintain everyday reality (if we accept that that is what we are all doing). Consequently, many researchers have found that taking underpinning **interpretive** and/or **constructionist** approaches to research instead of 'positivism' will allow them to work with knowledge coming mainly from subjective understandings and the construction of research participants' everyday concepts and meanings. There are many theorists who have contributed to these kinds of philosophical debates (including feminist researchers), but we can summarise the contrasts of these kinds of position with positivism briefly in the following table:

There is a fundamental difference between the contents of the natural sciences and the social sciences.

The social researcher should attempt to understand the subjective meanings of social action **(interpretivism).**

Researching social issues needs an understanding of the social world derived from the ways people construct and maintain everyday social reality in different contexts **(constructionism).**

Pure observation cannot produce theories, since all observation is 'theory laden'.

Social reality is pre-interpreted (in contrast to physical reality).

Research focus tends to be on words and accounts (qualitative data) or visual data rather than on measurement.

(adapted from Blaikie, 1993)

Figure 2.3 Characteristics of interpretivism or constructionism

In order to research everyday meanings using these principles, the social worker or other social researcher must enter everyday social worlds (of their research participants), grasp socially constructed meanings, and then reconstruct and interpret those meanings in terms of social research understandings. On one level the social work researcher is therefore offering a re-description of these everyday accounts. But on another level these 're-descriptions' could sometimes be developed into theories, although the extent to which these theories could be seen as superior to everyday descriptions is open to dispute (see e.g. Blaikie, 2007).

Some researchers have pointed to the unhelpfulness of making too much of the identified splits in research approaches based on these philosophical theories. Some (e.g. Bryman, 2012; Babones, 2016) have proposed ways of 'bringing together' these positivist or constructionist tendencies by mixing both designs and methods. This overall trend towards 'mixing' has increased in recent years, especially with the rise of research in health or social care which often requires a more pragmatic approach to research, for example when conducting evaluations (see also Chapter 7).

However, most researchers will still tend to refer as a sort of shorthand to quantitative as opposed to qualitative research methods. My own preference is to use these terms ('qualitative'/'quantitative') mainly in relation to different kinds of data, as we will find them useful no matter which kind of underlying approach we are using. However, some researchers also point out that it is possible to do research which is generically qualitative, in other words enquiry that takes up a constructivist or interpretive model without further specific labelling. (See below.) Caelli, Ray and Mill (2003) suggest that for generic qualitative research to be done successfully, researchers need to pay attention to the following principles:

➤ the researchers' position(ing)

➤ distinguishing method from methodology

➤ making the researchers' approach to rigour explicit

➤ identifying the researchers' analytic lens.

Later in this chapter we will be considering how to review research based around specific kinds of design that tend to be associated with different kinds of data; for example a basic typology would be:

➤ experimental or explanatory, hypothesis-testing designs (associated with quantitative data measurement/gathering/analysis, either using groups or individual cases) (see also Chapter 6)

➤ Comparative, survey or other descriptive/exploratory designs (often associated with quantitative data gathering /analysis or sometimes with 'mixed' forms of data) (see also Chapter 6)

➤ Qualitative designs, either generically based using an overall **interpretive** or **constructionist** model, or those based on specific approaches that may include **grounded theory, phenomenology, ethnography,** feminist research or some kinds of **case study** (and are usually associated with qualitative data generation/analysis) (see also Chapter 4).

For more reading on underlying principles of research design see:

Blaikie, N (2007) *Approaches to Social Enquiry*, 2nd edn, Cambridge: Polity Press

Bryman, A (2014) *Social Research Methods*, 5th edn, Oxford: Oxford University Press

Grix, J (2010) *The Foundations of Research*, 2nd edn, Basingstoke: Palgrave MacMillan

Finding appropriate knowledge and publications for reviews

Having gained some understanding of research design and its philosophical underpinnings, we must now link this up to the skills needed to achieve your aim of conducting a research project or evaluation. For most projects, literature searching and reviewing are where research begins,[1] in order to provide you with, amongst other things, a suitable theoretical, legislative and/or practice-based background for your social work project before you can begin to think about generating your own data.

Literature searching is therefore a key skill, whatever kind of review you are doing, but exactly what you choose to search for will at least partly depend on the kind of review you are aiming to do (see next section). As noted above, it is important to be able to assess the usefulness of any piece of knowledge once you have identified it, bearing in mind the epistemological and research design issues we already discussed. *The importance of being systematic when searching for material for your review cannot be overstressed.* This means identifying possible sources of literature or other material in a logical way (as it seems to you – and if you are producing a dissertation, you will need explain to the reader how you did this). Always note bibliographic references carefully, taking Walliman's (2005, p. 74) advice.

In terms of the kinds of materials and publications we have already discussed above, there will be various ways of searching for these: for example, you may choose specifically to search for the name of an organisation within a specific database or library catalogue (especially useful for **'grey' literature** of various kinds); if you know the name of an author who has produced research in your field, you may search for that name (this can be particularly useful when searching in large, generic sources of research literature such as Google Scholar or in subject-based journals).

However, probably the most useful approach to searching systematically within any source(s) is to use subject-based **keywords** that will help you to retrieve research-relevant material of various kinds. Here is an example of such a search, to illustrate what I mean:

I chose to search for the single term 'personalisation' within the database Social Care Online (maintained by SCIE). This produced 1523 results which included books, journal articles and digital media produced between 1989 and 2015 (over 1000 of these references were published since 2010).

How do you think I can make best use of this very large number of results?

Figure 2.4 Example: Keyword search

In examining the usefulness of these results according to the TAPUPAS formula (see again the section 'Assessing knowledge', p. 20), I need to consider what my literature review is specifically focusing on. In this case I am interested in social workers' views about the (UK) 'personalisation' agenda when working with older adults:

➤ Are alternative key terms needed? (Did I miss anything that could be important to my review?)

➤ What inclusion/exclusion criteria are needed when I am searching in order to restrict and focus down within this fairly large number of references? For example:

  ➤ by date when published (e.g. since 2000, or since a particular piece of legislation was passed)

  ➤ by place or language: do I need only material written in English, or only published in the UK, in Europe, in the USA?

  ➤ material related to a specific (subject) discipline (e.g. psychology, health, sociology)?

  ➤ material focused on a particular professional group (e.g. of relevance to physiotherapists, social workers etc.)?

To help me focus all this material, the Social Care Online database already indicates for me:

➤ some alternative key terms (as used in this database) – e.g. adult social care, personal budgets

➤ how these publications are spread by date – this is useful for narrowing down the existing references in relation to policy or legislative changes

➤ how these publications are spread by content or type – in this list, 393 items are labelled as 'research', 150 are 'government publications', 120 are 'practice examples' and 50 are 'research reviews'.

Hart (1998) advises the following steps are needed when carrying out a literature search (Table 2.1, p. 32)

➤ Define the topic of interest.

➤ Think about the scope of the topic.

➤ Think about outcomes (why are you undertaking this search?).

➤ Think about housekeeping (how will you record what you identify?).

➤ Plan sources to be searched (e.g. databases, specific journals, guides to literature). Consider consulting library or information staff at this stage.

➤ Work through your list of sources, recording items systematically.

Exercise 2.1 **Key words / searching**

Choose a database (such as Social Care Online) and identify three keywords relevant to your topic of interest. Using the above suggestions, see if you can search for and produce a list of 8–12 relevant publications for your own topic area. Explain why you think these particular publications would be relevant to a review of this topic.

Different kinds of review: Scoping studies, systematic reviews, meta-analyses and 'academic' literature reviews

You need to think carefully about what kind of review you are producing. Many publications contain a review of literature, e.g. a review will be placed towards the start of an academic journal article or a master's dissertation, even though these are based on primary (own) research; or the entire publication or other document, including master's dissertations, may consist of a review (otherwise called 'secondary research'). This latter example may, however, take various forms and will contain different kinds of content depending on whether it is a **'scoping' study**, a **systematic review** or some other kind of review. As an example that is relevant to social work, let us first look at a scoping study carried out by Alan Rushton for SCIE entitled *SCIE Knowledge Review 2: The Adoption of Looked After Children: A Scoping Review of Research.*

In the introduction, Rushton gives us a clear idea about the brief and purpose he had when writing the review. You will see that it was important for him to include a range of material in addition to published research literature and also for him to signpost the reader to other types of publication in doing so:

> Published *research* literature will be the main source of evidence here although practice and policy papers, the results of Department of Health (DoH) inspections and the proliferating websites would need to be included in any comprehensive review. The brief was *not* to write a critical methodological review covering all the contributors to adoption research and examining the merits of individual studies, but to conduct a broad enquiry into the state of knowledge of the field, drawing attention to existing systematic reviews where available and to reflect on their conclusions. In so doing, the review aims to indicate where secure knowledge has been established and where findings are suggestive but not definitive, and to 'scan the horizon' for future research directions. (Rushton, p. 1)

In taking this approach, Rushton is aiming to establish the scope of this field by making use of a wide range of material and also to look ahead to future research possibilities.

This kind of scoping approach may also be useful to social work students, especially those doing masters dissertations (although methodological considerations about the merits or otherwise of individual studies are also important in academic dissertations, as we will see below).

For more on methodology of scoping studies, see:

> ➤ Arksey, H and O'Malley, L (2005) Scoping studies: towards a methodological framework, *International Journal of Social Research Methodology*, 8 (1): 19–32.

Moving on to examine **systematic reviews**, the first consideration is that this term means more than doing a review 'systematically': I have often had to explain this to postgraduate students who want to provide a literature review for their dissertations. A systematic review is usually very focused and comprehensive, will require adherence to a strict protocol, especially if the review is aimed at a specific database (such as the Cochrane Library or Campbell Collaboration[2]), and this kind of review may also be updated regularly (see our example below on 'Screening women for intimate partner violence in healthcare settings').

Although it is important to state how material for any review was found, systematic reviews are more likely to establish very strict **inclusion** and **exclusion criteria**, often based on research publications that use particular methodologies, e.g. randomised controlled trials (RCTs).[3] This means that they are likely to be most relevant to certain research topics, where our research question is aiming to demonstrate exploring whether or not a particular intervention, medication or treatment is effective. This usually means that a hypothesis is being tested in these research studies, as we saw earlier (with an underlying **hypothetico-deductive approach** to research). This does not, of course, rule out the usefulness of systematic reviews to social work but it is noticeable from examining the Cochrane Library database how many more systematic reviews are available for health or medicalised treatments where 'effectiveness' can perhaps more easily be established or measured.

For discussion about including diverse study types in systematic reviews, see:

➤ Harden, A and Thomas, J (2005) Methodological issues in combining diverse study types in systematic reviews, *International Journal of Social Research Methodology*, 8 (3): 257–271

➤ Rutter, D, Francis, J, Coren, E and Fisher, M (2010) *SCIE Systematic Research Reviews: Guidelines*, 2nd edn, London: SCIE

Some researchers, especially in healthcare, will also refer to integrative reviews which summarise previous research and draw overall conclusions from the body of literature on a specific topic. In a well-executed integrative review, criteria for evaluation are carefully applied, but the review may include a wider range of studies than a systematic review on the topic. See, as an example, Papadopoulos and Ali (2015).

This question of 'effectiveness' and 'what works' also goes to the heart of what we mean by evidence-based practice (EBP), and the relevance of this approach to social work and social care has been debated and researched extensively over the past decade. Many authors have pointed out that how social workers use knowledge and evidence has relevance for their professional identity and values as well as to practice per se, and some research is beginning to reveal complexities involved in these processes (see, for example: Bell, Nissen and Vindegg, *forthcoming*). This has led to newer terms, such as 'evidence-informed practice', which try to capture complexities of this situation for social workers and related professionals.

See also:

➤ www.cochranelibrary.com

➤ www.campbellcollaboration.org

For further reading about EBP and related issues, the following are suggested:

> Soydan, H and Palinkas, LA (2014) *Evidence-Based Practice in Social Work: Development of a New Professional Culture*, Abingdon: Routledge

> Gray, M, Plath, D and Webb, SA (2009) *Evidence-Based Social Work: A Critical Stance*, London: Routledge

> Petersen, A and Olsson, J (2015) Calling evidence-based practice into question: acknowledging phronetic knowledge in social work, *British Journal of Social Work*, 45 (5): 1581–1597

> Scurlock-Evans, L and Upton, D (2015) The role and nature of evidence: a systematic review of social workers' evidence-based practice orientation, attitudes and implementation, *Journal of Evidence-Informed Social Work*, 12 (4): 369–399

I have chosen as an example a systematic review from the Cochrane Library (database), below, which is likely to be of interest to social workers:

Example

O'Doherty, L, Hegarty, K, Ramsay, J, Davidson, LL, Feder, G and Taft, A, Screening women for intimate partner violence [IPV] in healthcare settings, *Cochrane Library*,

DOI: 10.1002/14651858.CD007007.pub3F

The third updated version of this systematic review was published in the Cochrane Library in July 2015, the second version having been produced in 2013 and the original review in 2008.

Key objectives for this systematic review are stated as:

To assess the effectiveness of screening for IPV conducted within healthcare settings on identification, referral, re-exposure to violence, and health outcomes for women, and to determine if screening causes any harm.

Methods employed to identify material for this systematic review

In order to update the 2013 version of their review, the authors searched various named **databases** and two trial registers, and also looked at reference lists of articles included in 2013 and relevant websites. Their inclusion criteria covered:

> Randomised or quasi-randomised controlled trials assessing the effectiveness of IPV screening where healthcare professionals either directly screened women face-to-face or were informed of the results of screening questionnaires, as compared with usual care (which could include screening that did not involve a healthcare professional).

Two authors independently assessed risk of any bias in the trials they identified (by statistical means). As a result, they were able to initially include 13 trials (to add to their existing review). These trials had recruited in total 14,959 women from various healthcare settings including primary care, antenatal clinics and other clinic or hospital settings. These studies were mainly located in high-income countries and urban areas. However, the authors report that:

> The overall quality of the body of evidence was low to moderate, mainly due to heterogeneity, risk of bias, and imprecision.

This led to the authors excluding five of these studies and subsequently doing their primary analysis on the remaining eight trials.

Systematic reviews in journals

Sometimes systematic reviews will be published in journals, for example as noted above the review by Scurlock-Evans and Upton (2015) relates specifically to EBP. The following example is a published systematic review of interest to social workers related to work with older people:

> ➢ Craig, C, Chadborn, N, Sands, G, Tuomainen, H and Gladman, J (2015) Systematic review of EASY-care needs assessment for community-dwelling older people, *Age and Ageing*, 44: 559–565, doi: 10.1093/ageing/afv050, downloaded from http://ageing.oxfordjournals.org/ at Middlesex University on September 3, 2015

Here the main objective was to 'to review the evidence of reliability, validity and acceptability of EASY-Care and its appropriateness for assessing the needs of community-dwelling older people'.

For another example relating to phenomenological studies based on interviews with people with intellectual disabilities, see Corby, Taggart and Cousins (2015).

Meta-analysis

This is a form of review that is used only with studies that are said to be 'empirical' (in the sense that they have involved collection of quantitative data). In the case of meta-analysis, analysts wish to go further than merely critically comparing the studies' findings: this approach involves the direct statistical comparison of data from different selected studies, which need to be examining the same constructs and relationships. This means that those findings can then be reproduced or configured across all the studies in a comparable, statistical form.[4]

Academic literature reviews: Some initial 'tips'

As noted earlier, most academic reviews that are included in dissertations or projects will need to be fairly wide ranging and are not usually focused only on certain research methodologies. Once you have identified relevant material for your review it is important to consider:

> ➤ What kinds of research studies have you obtained in methodological terms? This is because, as we will see below, the ways in which you review research-based publications depends partly on their underpinning design or methodology/ies (how the research was carried out). As noted above, meta-analysis (for example) is only suitable for certain kinds of research study.

> ➤ You should always consider the source or producer of your publication, whether or not it is research based. For example, a document or publication produced by a government department is likely to take the current policy line when presenting material, and you need to be aware of this.

> ➤ Be sure to cite all your references accurately; this is very important in academic writing. For authoritative guidance, see e.g. www.**citethemright**online.com/.

> ➤ Take account of the points we already raised about strengths or weaknesses of making use of **'grey' literature** in your review.

> ➤ Most successful literature reviews (especially for academic purposes) will involve synthesis of a number of different publications in a continuous, comparative, narrative chapter or section. However, skills you may be taught as 'critical appraisal skills' (critiquing) will sometimes assume you are critiquing each paper individually. An academic review often reads better if you can take time to work in stages:

> critique key papers individually in note form for your own use, taking in substantive (subject-based) and methodological issues (see next section)

> afterwards, synthesise and compare key strengths and weaknesses across several papers to produce your review, picking up on relevant issues such as sampling or research ethics as you do so.

For more detail on doing a literature review in academic dissertations, see:

> Hart, C (1998) *Doing a Literature Review: Releasing the Social Science Research Imagination*, London: Sage

Skills involved in critiquing research literature (critical appraisal)

Having identified what you think are relevant items for your review, the question now is: how do you make use of these individual items? One of the key issues in carrying out a review is how to read material critically. What does this mean?

There are two fundamental aspects involved in 'critically appraising' research-based publications. They are both important, particularly for students, if you are to learn to critique effectively. Remember also that research critique has nothing to do with 'personal criticism' of the author(s). Some people feel nervous about criticising someone who has (apparently) written something you may think has been so 'well researched'. Apart from the fact that this may not be so, all researchers should be open to having their research findings challenged; this is usually one reason why they find research exciting in the first place.

One aspect of research critique (or critical appraisal) is to look at *the logic of the author's argument itself* and to learn to read critically, to see whether the content of the author's arguments about the research hangs together. At the same time as doing this, the second aspect of critique is to evaluate systematically the methods/methodology by which the researcher has carried out the research. This will allow you to see whether there are strengths and weaknesses in the methods the researcher has adopted and therefore how much weight we should give to the arguments and to the study results that the author put forward. When considering arguments made by researchers, Hart (1998) suggests:

If our objective is to analyse and then evaluate an argument we need some methods for doing so. Whatever method we use it needs so be clear, consistent and systematic. (p. 87)

Based on Toulmin's structure of an argument, Hart suggests, for example, a method involving the following: a claim (an arguable statement); evidence (data used to support the claim); a warrant (an expectation providing the link between evidence and the claim); and, finally, backing which is the context and assumptions we can use to support the validity of the warrant and the evidence. Any of these elements can be challenged. Hart also points out five different kinds of claim that can be put forward based on:

1 fact (the statement can be proven to be true or false, e.g. 'Paris is the present-day capital city of France.')

2 value (a judgement about the value of something, which cannot be proven true or false (see Chapter 1, Question 2 example.)

3 policy (a normative statement made about something that 'ought' to be done.)

4 concept (based on definitions or how language is used.)

5 interpretation (based on how evidence is to be understood.)

For more on argumentation analysis see:

> Hart, C (1998) *Doing a Literature Review: Releasing the Social Science Research Imagination*, London: Sage

> Toulmin, S (1958) *The Uses of Argument*, Cambridge: Cambridge University Press

Methodology and methodological critique

Whilst you are learning to read critically, you will be ready to develop your skills in evaluating methodological aspects of research publications. This second (or methodological) aspect of critique is sometimes neglected, as the impact of the chosen research design and methods upon the results which are presented may not be fully appreciated by the reader. It may seem easier just to concentrate on content ('what the research was about'), but a critique focused largely on content will possibly end up as very descriptive and lack a critical edge. On the other hand, we must obviously evaluate research methodology in the context of the research we are reading about. If, for example, researchers wanted to obtain the views of social workers about how to work successfully with young people who are leaving the care system, which research design should they have chosen? Which methods should they have used, and how successful or weak was the result? For example, a descriptive survey may be a perfectly good research approach in general, but was it a good choice for this particular study? You can see there will be some overlap in our assessment between these two aspects of research critique (subject/content and research methodology), and attention should be paid to both in literature reviews.

Here are some key issues we need to consider when systematically evaluating the methods reported in any piece of primary research literature:

- What are the stated aims and objectives of the study?

- What was/were the research question(s) and (if relevant) the hypothesis/es to be tested?

- What is the overall research design? How is it described, and do you think it is appropriate?

- Was this a mixed study in terms of design and/or type of data gathered? How have the researchers addressed this issue?

- Sampling – who takes part? What happens to those who drop out? (See also Appendix D-4.)

- Why and how were specific methods and instruments used in this research? Are they valid and reliable and/or trustworthy?

- Do the results presented make sense in terms of the original research question(s)? Are they valid and reliable and/or trustworthy?

- Ethics – how was research conducted with participants? What ethical considerations were taken into account?

- (How) does the author address/answer her/his **research question**(s) following the research?

In addition to these key points, we need to look out more specifically for:

- Ethics – was ethical approval obtained?

- Why and how were specific methods and instruments used in this research (such as questionnaires)? (The researchers should present a convincing explanation showing why these were chosen.)

- Validity and reliability of the instruments or methods used – how is this demonstrated or assessed?

- Technical skill should be demonstrated (especially in data collection or analysis).

➤ Other issues: possible generalisability of the results to other settings or populations; possible use made of participant subjectivity/ies.

Different kinds of research design used in research papers will also need to be evaluated according to their own methods, and some of these specific, additional key criteria[5] are indicated below. (See again my typology of designs, in this chapter.) Remember that you are assessing how these criteria are reflected in the publication you are reading; if the researchers have published elsewhere on the same topic or project, you may be interested to read around their work for background/context, but for the purpose of the critique you assess what you can see in front of you. (Some students I have worked with have made things a little harder for themselves by not realising that initially.)

Additional criteria related to specific designs:

If the study is 'explanatory' and based on hypothesis testing, e.g. controlled trials:

Was there an adequate sample size/ was statistical power addressed?

Was randomisation used, and if so, how?

Were control groups used, if appropriate?

Were control and experimental groups (if used) comparable at baseline?

Were the outcome or other measures used valid and appropriate?

Were all participants accounted for at the end of the study?

Were appropriate statistics used for data analysis? How well has this analysis been done?

How are ethical issues dealt with?

If the study is descriptive/exploratory (especially surveys):

Was there an adequate sample size, drawn from which population?

What does the sample represent (i.e. was the sample intended to statistically represent a larger population – a 'probability sample')?

What are we told about the development of the questionnaire (if used)?

►

Was the questionnaire piloted before use? How was validity addressed?

Were appropriate statistics used for data analysis? How well has this analysis been done?

How is non-response to the survey dealt with?

How are ethical issues dealt with?

If the study is descriptive/exploratory (especially qualitative studies):

Was there an adequate sample, drawn from which population?

How does the author(s) deal with the issue of purpose and representativeness in sampling (i.e. what was the purpose of including these particular people in the study)?

What are we told about the researcher(s), their own intentions, background and conduct during the study?

How are ethical issues dealt with?

How did the researcher(s) justify the use of specific research methods?

How is data analysed? How well have the researcher(s) made use (technically) of the 'in-depth' nature of their (qualitative) data?

How are issues of subjectivity and generalisability dealt with?

It is likely that some of the terms used in the above lists of criteria will be unfamiliar to you at this stage. (See the Glossary for further explanations.) You should, however, note above the differences in approach that are required when critiquing research with different kinds of goal (explanatory, exploratory, descriptive).

In particular, do not get confused about particular kinds of methodology being considered 'the best' in all circumstances. All kinds of research need to be carried out rigorously according to their own goals and chosen methods, as noted above. There are also important ethical dimensions to be considered, which we will be addressing in the next chapter (Chapter 3).

For more on literature critique for different research designs, see also the online Critical Appraisal Skills Programme (CASP), which is particularly useful for practitioners, including social workers: www.casp-uk.net/.

Chapter summary

➢ In this chapter we introduced you to different kinds of media, information and publications relevant to social work research and how to search for them.

➢ We introduced the idea of different (but equally useful) types of **ontology** and **epistemology**, and showed how different kinds of research design (**methodology**) are based on these different foundations.

➢ We introduced and discussed different kinds of review: scoping studies, systematic reviews, meta-analyses and 'academic' literature reviews.

➢ You have been shown how to learn skills that will enable you to critically evaluate published research material of various kinds.

Further reading

Aveyard, H (2007) *Doing a Literature Review in Health and Social Care. A Practical Guide*, Berkshire: Open University Press

Cotterell, S (2014) *Dissertations and Project Reports: A Step by Step Guide*, ch 9 'Literature search and review', Basingstoke: Palgrave Macmillan

Dunne, C (2011) The place of the literature review in grounded theory research, *International Journal of Social Research Methodology*, 14 (2): 111–124

Gomm, R and Davies, C (eds) (2000) *Using Evidence in Health and Social Care*, Sage/Open University

Gomm, R, Needham, G and Boullman, A (eds) (2000) *Evaluating Research in Health and Social Care*, London: Sage/Open University

Hart, C (1998) *Doing a Literature Review: Releasing the Social Science Research Imagination*, London: Sage

3

DEALING WITH ETHICS AND MAINTAINING PROFESSIONAL VALUES DURING RESEARCH

Introduction: Principles, professional and theoretical issues

When starting to think about how we can carry out research, ethical aspects soon emerge. For social workers who are used to thinking about ethics and values in their professional practice, this should not come as a surprise, and much has been written over the years on the topic of ethics and values in social work and other professions (see e.g. Bell and Hafford-Letchfield (eds), 2015; Banks, 2010; 2004; 2012; Banks and Gallagher, 2009; Bisman, 2004).

For example, Banks (2004) suggests the term 'professional ethics' means:

> the norms and standards of behaviour of members of specific occupational groups and the ethical issues and dilemmas that arise in their practice. (p. 3)

Some authors have suggested that social work is essentially a 'moral' endeavour (see e.g. Clark, 2006 or Chu, Tsui, and Yan, 2009), which should encourage you to think in terms of some overlap between professional and 'personal' forms of ethics. Whittington and Whittington (2015) further identify that:

> Professional ethics are the active form of professional values. (p. 81)

They see professional values as beliefs about morally good or bad conduct, whereas 'professional ethics' in social work:

> are typically expressed in professional and regulatory codes and provide both guides to expected conduct and standards of accountability. (p. 81)

Others have written that certain types of ethical principles are particularly well suited to underpinning social work practice in different contexts (e.g. Gray, 2010; Hatton, 2001; Lloyd, 2010; Orme, 2002; Papadaki and Papadaki, 2008; Halse and Honey, 2005). Hafford-Letchfield and Bell (Bell and Hafford-Letchfield, 2015, ch 1) provide a brief overview of ethics and values underpinning social work practice, whilst in the same book Dracopoulou (2015) introduces key underpinning theories and principles relevant to applied ethics, that can be used with differing effects in social work or health care: these underpinning principles relate to **Consequentialism**, **Deontology**, **virtue** and **care ethics**, as well as to the framework of four principles (principlism) devised by Beauchamp and Childress that is widely used in health and social care (see Beauchamp and Childress, 2013). Applied ethics is a branch of moral philosophy that allows consideration of dilemmas in practice, and so these various theories and principles will in many ways also be relevant to research practice.

What is 'research ethics'?

I am going to argue here that for social work practitioners, including students, as well as practitioners working in health care or fields such as education, issues around research ethics are likely to be more complex than they are for other researchers operating only in the social or 'pure' sciences. This is because practitioners including social workers must firstly take account of ethics and values associated with their profession or occupation, as noted above. Secondly, doing research can involve a complex balancing act for individuals and research teams, particularly where these are grounded in different professional or occupational responsibilities, actions and even ways of considering research knowledge, which may in turn lead to further dilemmas and tensions during research between team members and with outsiders.

I suggest there are two key aspects to research ethics, which we will discuss below, that are relevant to anyone who is starting to engage in research or other forms of enquiry such as evaluation:

➤ control and regulation of research: including ethics committees, risk assessment, maintaining appropriate standards

➤ research processes: including individual or team responsibilities to 'behave ethically' whilst doing research; ownership of research interests and/or professional interests; self-regulation.

Linking these two main aspects of research ethics, we must add researcher adherence to specific ethical codes, e.g. guidelines produced by organisations such as the British Sociological Association, the Social Research Association or a professional body (e.g. the Nursing & Midwifery Council (NMC), BASW (2012), Health and Care Professions Council (HCPC)).

Control and regulation of research

For most researchers 'on the ground', the most important part of this regulatory aspect of research ethics is how to get appropriate, formal approval to carry out your research project, which we will discuss in more detail below. However, a little background to debates involved in ethics scrutiny and the overall system(s) in place is useful, as it helps to demystify why controls and regulations have been set up in ways that they have been.

Debates about ethics scrutiny

There are still debates in the UK and elsewhere about the basis for, and usefulness of, various forms of ethical regulation and scrutiny. Some researchers (notably Hammersley, 2009) have stated that much current focus on research ethics based around rules and governance is unhelpful to social researchers, whilst others such as Hedgecoe (2008) have instead stressed their usefulness to researchers (though more recently he also illustrates how university research ethics committees can sometimes serve to restrict research that may be 'embarrassing' to the institution (Hedgecoe, 2016). Iphofen (2009) traces the origins of formal research ethics scrutiny back to past unethical medical experiments, including those carried out by the Nazis that were revealed at the Nuremburg trials; as a result, the Nuremburg Code on medical research ethics was produced in 1947. However, Iphofen points out that despite wide dissemination of this Code, some experimentation that we might still regard today as unethical has continued to occur. In an interesting discussion, Iphofen (2009) examines the intentions of formal ethics scrutiny, which he says has grown for good reasons:

> Formalised ethical scrutiny is intended to assist researchers in estimating and balancing risks of harm to participants, researchers and organisations and considering what benefits might accrue to society, individuals, groups, organisations. (p. 145)

But he also suggests that perhaps it has suited some organisations – including universities – to confuse governance with ethics: instead of a concern mainly with ethical dilemmas arising in research, the focus may have shifted towards organisational risk aversion and damage limitation. To this I would add that there may sometimes be an irritating focus on procedure which can sometimes obscure effective ethical scrutiny of research. On the contrary, those undertaking ethics scrutiny should always strive to be transparent, yet, as Iphofen points out, ethics committees do not always behave ethically. In these complex situations, Iphofen recommends that within existing frameworks of research governance, individuals and groups undertaking research ought to be taking up more responsibility/ies for themselves, to strive to behave ethically whilst conducting research. This does not mean ignoring ethics committee decisions, but it does mean seeing their scrutiny as a starting point for researchers, rather than as a complete replacement for individual or team ethical responsibilities.

Research governance for social work and health researchers (including students) in the UK

At the time of writing (2016) we have all become used to the Research Governance Framework (RGF) underpinning ethics scrutiny in the UK for those working in health and social care. However, there are some changes on the horizon, with a replacement for the RGF expected and new powers for ethics review in social work and social care being assumed by the Health Research Authority (HRA); this is replacing the previous authority on ethics review (vested in SCIE). Various enquiries and scoping exercises have recently been looking into social care research and research by students in particular as part of the HRA's developing remit.

The original RGF was set up in 2001 and aimed to set standards, define mechanisms to deliver standards, and describe monitoring and assessment arrangements. A key intention was to improve research quality and to safeguard the public by enhancing ethical and scientific quality. This came in the wake of several clinical research scandals, e.g. the Alder Hey scandal and subsequent public enquiry involving storage of adults' and children's body parts in hospitals, ostensibly for research purposes, without gaining consent from relatives. These events also led to the Human Tissue Act, 2004, which has had a considerable impact on the conduct of clinical research. The RGF was intended to promote good research practice, to reduce any adverse incidents (ensuring lessons were learnt from them) and to prevent poor research performance and misconduct.

Student research has always been seen as a key issue and universities and colleges and their Ethics Committees are therefore seen as important partners in research governance. Health researchers in the UK (including students) now generally apply first to their own university or college ethics committee and then (if advised to do so) online via the Integrated Research Application System (IRAS). This is a single system for applying for permissions and approvals for health based research in the UK (see: www.myresearchproject.org.uk).

You are able to enter information about your project once via this online system, instead of duplicating information on separate application forms. The system uses filters to ensure that data collected and collated is appropriate to the type of study, and is also relevant to approvals required. As a health researcher you would also be well advised, if working in a Health Trust, to contact your Trust's R&D (Research and development) Department before completing the IRAS form, so as to find out whether full ethics approval will be required for your project.

Another useful way to check whether full ethics approval may be required for a 'health' project from IRAS is via the following web link: www.hra-decisiontools.org.uk/ethics/.

University or college students are also advised to check with your institution whether any issues regarding insurance are relevant to the kind of research project you wish to carry out, e.g. in some institutions students are precluded from carrying out randomised controlled trials with patients for insurance reasons.

Whilst originally focused more clearly on health research, the RGF subsequently extended its remit to cover social work and social care research ethics; an RGF implementation plan for social care was produced in 2004 (see Boddy, Boaz, Lupton and Pahl, 2006). These authors have produced a useful discussion in their paper (2006), based on their own research. This explored which activities that are taking place in social care/social work should require independent (ethical) regulation and what can actually be defined as 'research'. Interestingly, they point to a range of different forms of enquiry, not all of which would count as 'research' needing formal ethics scrutiny.

In practice currently, social work students would expect firstly to apply (like health students) for ethics approval for their research project via their university or college ethics committee. In addition, if you are a student, university staff member, local authority social worker or other researcher aiming to carry out research or evaluation in a local authority, you may also expect to apply, where necessary, to local authority ethics panels (currently organised under RGF arrangements), especially within London boroughs.

Unfortunately, health or social work/care applicants may sometimes be put off making ethics applications due to a perception that ethics forms will be long and complicated or that the process of obtaining ethics approval will be long drawn out or adversarial. This should not be the case, if sufficient care is taken when making the application and if support is obtained from student supervisors, fellow researchers and also from the ethics committee itself; there is usually someone who can be approached to answer any queries. Remember that as well as the completed application form you may need to provide additional documentation, including:

➤ an information sheet you have produced for participants

➤ consent form in appropriate format (sometimes committees supply this)

➤ copies of your questionnaire(s) or interview schedule

➤ evidence from someone in authority that you can have access to participants, e.g. a manager (sometimes termed an internal sponsor for local authority ethics purposes)

➤ risk assessment form

Below are some tips for making a (successful) research ethics application to an ethics committee (Figure 3.1).

DO prepare a full and detailed research proposal or 'protocol' – you will then be able to think through more easily any potential ethical dilemmas that could arise during research and share your ideas with others. Students may be required to have their proposal assessed as part of their course; this is helpful as a peer reviewing process, and even if you do not need to submit your full proposal to the committee, you can 'cut and paste' relevant sections onto the ethics form itself. (See also the next section, 'Research processes'.)

DO consult your supervisor fully (if you are a student), or, if you are a social worker, consult knowledgeable colleagues when preparing your application. If you have specific queries, consider approaching the ethics committee for their advice in advance of submitting your application.

DO obtain all the forms you need to use and check how these should be submitted (sometimes the student supervisor is designated as 'principal investigator' and must submit the forms on your behalf).

DON'T be tempted to leave out crucial details (such as how many participants you are aiming for) or just say 'I don't know' to questions on the form -- the scale of your study can usually be estimated whatever (qualitative or quantitative) methodology you are using. (Some questions may, however, be 'not applicable' to your project; this is fine to indicate, as appropriate.)

DON'T submit a form containing spelling mistakes or other errors – this will show your proposed work in a bad light.

Figure 3.1 Making an Ethics Application – do's and don'ts

DO get your (student) supervisor or a colleague who is familiar with the form **to check it** before submission.

DO submit your application on time if there is a deadline; check when the committee meets.

DO respond promptly and appropriately to any feedback the ethics committee sends you after making your application. Consult your supervisor before making any resubmission.

DO approach the committee (or allow your supervisor to do so) **if you are not satisfied** with the committee's response, or **if there is anything in the response you do not understand.**

Figure 3.1 (continued)

Having considered any formal ethics application you may need to make, this brings us to our second key aspect of research ethics – the need for ethical awareness during research processes.

Research processes: Ethical aspects

As Iphofen (2009) has pointed out:

> the ethically aware social researcher ... regardless of the need for formal ethical scrutiny, asks ethical questions of their endeavours from the outset and throughout the process of conducting the research. (p. xi)

This focus on the researcher's own responsibilities in this regard is crucial if you are to be able to take on-board and develop your project in ways that can really take account of research processes as they happen. Applying for formal ethics approval and allowing others to scrutinise your plans is only the start.

In the list below I outline some basic principles which may be applied when carrying out research (see also Robson, 2002). These are underpinning guidelines which ought to be applied in any research by social workers, students or other researchers.

Some basic ethical principles underpinning social research

- ➤ beneficence – 'do no harm' (e.g. physical harm, mental stress)

- ➤ respect for human dignity, self-determination

- ➤ justice, fair treatment

➤   respect for privacy

➤   gaining 'informed' consent

➤   explaining the nature of the research as fully as possible to participants

➤   not withholding benefits from some participants (e.g. when comparing groups)

➤   not coercing people into participating in research

➤   providing additional safeguards to protect the rights of vulnerable subjects

➤   following specific ethical guidance (e.g. from a professional association such as the British Sociological Association, the Royal College of Nursing, the Social Research Association) and/or getting Research Ethics Committee approval

You may be surprised that I have included 'privacy' but not 'right to confidentiality' in the list. This is because confidentiality (and its twin concept 'anonymity') can involve complex issues, especially for those who are professional practitioners. For example I and my academic colleagues would advise a student interviewing someone who discloses something that suggests that a vulnerable person might be at risk to report this issue to a manager or other responsible person; therefore, promising total confidentiality in advance could be problematic, as this might need to be suspended in practice. This approach might seem to violate good research practice, by which we would usually support the notion of confidentiality, but this is one example where research practice and professional practice might potentially come into conflict. In such situations, I would prioritise adherence to professional ethical responsibilities in nearly all cases. In practical terms, these limits of confidentiality or anonymity ought to be spelt out clearly in any participant information sheet.

For a research example covering this issue, see:

➤ Bell, L and Nutt, L (2012) Divided loyalties, divided expectations: research ethics, professional and occupational responsibilities IN Mauthner, M et al., *Ethics in Qualitative Research*, 2nd revised edn, London: Sage

In this example, the authors came to the conclusion that it is often impossible to 'stop being a practitioner' whilst doing research, even if the (social work) researcher (as in this case) attempts to do so. This is especially important when dealing with (unexpected) issues of risk which relate to the practitioner's own professional responsibilities.

This emphasises that practitioners need to consider ethical dilemmas and self-regulate during research; it is not enough simply to rely on prior ethics approval.

We also need to think carefully about ethical dilemmas that may be involved when conducting research using various kinds of research methodology/design. Researchers should carefully examine the approach or approaches being taken for a particular piece of research when we attempt to 'behave ethically'. There are also moral questions to consider. For example some people might consider animal experimentation to be morally wrong; however, it would be possible to argue that a researcher had carried out such an experiment 'ethically', if certain accepted ethical principles are followed. The whole question of working with emotions in research (Dickson-Swift et al., 2009; Hubbard, Backett-Milburn and Kemmer, 2001), for example when considering issues of morality, is a significant one, and this is particularly so for social workers (Mehrotra, 2015), who will also need to work directly with emotions and feelings in their practice (see also Ingram, 2013).

Discussion Points

Should research start with 'moral principles'? What could happen when researchers disagree about morals?

Should we question whether to get involved in a research project at all if we feel uncomfortable or uneasy about the topic involved?

I therefore suggest that during the conduct of research there can be dilemmas in linking research ethics with all or any of the following:

➤ knowledge/epistemology (what is being researched)

➤ methodology (how is research being done)

➤ collaboration (with whom we carry out research).

Ethical issues in research practice

In this section we will firstly present some scenarios, for you to explore the kinds of ethical issues these might raise for researchers. These scenarios relate to what is being researched and with whom the research is being done. Try to think through any dilemmas that may be raised by these examples. Possible solutions will be suggested in Appendix C at the end of this book. However, in most research there may not be a single, clear, right answer and, in fact, problem-solving is a good, basic skill for all researchers (experienced or otherwise) to develop.

Exercise 3.1 **Scenario 1**

A social work lecturer obtains university ethics approval to do a project which involves interviews and focus groups with academic and practice-based colleagues about their social work practice and practice education. These people are not named/identified in the application. What issues does this raise as she starts to prepare for data collection?

Exercise 3.1 **Scenario 2**

Two groups of academics/social work researchers from different countries want to work together on a project about social inequalities which will involve overseas field-work for all parties. There are apparently ethics/governance procedures in place in both places, but these seem to be very different.
What issues does this raise in practice, and how should these be dealt with?

Exercise 3.1 **Scenario 3**

A mixed group of academics and practitioners, from different professional back-grounds in health and social care, meet to prepare a bid for research funding relating to the issue of domestic (intimate partner) violence. They find they have very different ideas about best practice when intending to involve users of services/patients in their project.

At this stage, who will take the role of 'principal investigator' for the project (required by the funding body) has not yet been agreed upon.

What are some of the key ethical and methodological issues they might need to consider in order to prepare a successful bid?

Project examples

In this section I am going to start to describe some actual research project examples in order to illustrate the kinds of ethical issues that were raised in relation to specific methodological designs; where possible, I show how these dilemmas were dealt with in research practice. (These and other project examples will also be included in subsequent chapters – see complete list in Appendix A.)

Project A – Experimental research

In this interesting example, MacDonald and Turner (2005) carried out a randomised controlled trial involving foster carers, aiming to test effectiveness of cognitive-behavioural methods (CBT) in helping the carers to manage children's challenging behaviour. These kinds of experimental projects raise ethical issues over the necessity to try and control what people do. As we will see below, these researchers had to steer their project in certain ways in order to accommodate both methodological and ethical issues. The paper is valuable to researchers for the ways in which the authors provide honest details about these processes and their responses in practice.

Some key ethical issues relevant to this example are:

> ➤ If giving consent, people should know that they may be consenting to alternative treatments, e.g. either the intervention being tested or an alternative (perhaps a placebo in clinical research). Full information needs to be provided about alternatives.

> ➤ Participants have a right to withdraw from the research at any time (although this may also cause practical difficulties during the research process).

In this example, the researchers needed to randomise[1] foster carers into two groups, those receiving the intervention (cognitive-behavioural training) and those in a control group (on a waiting list for the training). This was in order to make sure that both groups were comparable at the beginning of the study (baseline), so any observed changes could be attributed to the training and not to any characteristics of the two groups. The study was done in six local authority areas in England, and staff in those local authorities acted as intermediaries by passing on information leaflets and subsequent questionnaires to carers. (Randomisation into two groups was done separately within each of the six areas.) The researchers had to exclude a few foster carers once questionnaires were returned because those people did not meet the criteria for the study: local authorities had recruited them by mistake. Some foster carers withdrew from the study at this point due to issues about timing or location of the training, but others withdrew once they realised they had been allocated to the control group. The researchers say:

> Control group status is not generally welcomed by people who are already persuaded that they would benefit from a particular intervention. (MacDonald and Turner, 2005, p. 1270)

They describe how they took several steps to:

> 'immunize' participants against disappointment, taking care to explain the
> importance of the control group. (MacDonald and Turner, 2005, p. 1270)

Despite providing written and verbal information on several occasions, as
well as the assurance that (if effective) the training would be made available to control group participants later on, some carers were apparently
aggrieved to have been placed in the control group and they withdrew
from participation in the study. The final overall sample comprised 67
'training group' participants and 50 'controls'; the study was conducted
using 3 different measures[2] and by making a record of the number of
unplanned breakdowns of placements (this 'breakdown' data was obtained
from interviews).

Foster carers in this study did perceive a need for CBT training, and
they showed overall satisfaction with it. However, the researchers state
that contrary to their own expectations, the training programme did not
achieve the majority of its aims. They attributed this to a mixture of methodological and ethical issues:

> ➤ organisational issues impacting upon the strength of the study [as
>   noted above]

> ➤ limitations in the length and effective content of the training
>   programme

> ➤ lack of available support to foster carers allowing them to implement
>   newly-acquired skills. (MacDonald and Turner, 2005, p. 1278)

It is clear from this project example that the researchers did attempt to
follow appropriate ethical guidelines. Participants were made fully aware
that they could be allocated into one of two alternative groups, and, in
the event, they were of course free to withdraw from the study when
they chose. These researchers did not therefore act unethically. However,
we might add here – were the researchers' attempts to 'immunize' their
potential participants against disappointment by providing repeated information in fact counterproductive? Did people feel not only aggrieved to
be part of the control group, but also somewhat coerced to participate?

In addition, a number of measures as well as interviews were used in
this study with both groups, and the researchers report that those in the
training group were also asked to report on a behavioural project showing
their ability, following the training, to analyse behaviour and implement
behaviour change strategies; however, only half the participants completed this project work. This perhaps demonstrates another overlapping

ethical/methodological issue which may be common to experimental studies. If participants are overloaded with various measures and other expectations during research, they may take the path of least resistance and fail to carry out some tasks which are the easiest ones to avoid doing. Typically, keeping a diary or, in this case, producing a report may have been perceived not only as too time consuming for participants (compared to filling in a simple measure) but, as this was something to be carried out by themselves, they were able to choose not to do it. This could have been less problematic for them than for example refusing to meet researchers for an interview. For more on this Project A and its results, see Chapter 6.

For an example of a mixed methods approach also involving experimental work, see also Project R, 'The *Communicate* Project', in Chapter 7.

Project B – A survey of people offered a bereavement counselling service (Bell, 2003)

Turning to an example of cross-sectional **'survey'** methodology, at first sight these kinds of projects may seem relatively unproblematic (ethically), compared to the experimental methodology noted in Project A. Clearly, questionnaire or measure overload might be an issue for participants in surveys as they can be in experimental or mixed methods designs, although a survey methodology will usually involve administering a single **questionnaire**. However, if used in longitudinal studies, administration of questionnaire(s) may be repeated at a later date, and participants ought to be advised of this well in advance.

Some key ethical issues relevant to this project example are:

➤ respect for privacy – how is the questionnaire administered?

➤ providing additional safeguards to protect the rights of vulnerable subjects

➤ how is the questionnaire constructed – whose agenda is being followed?

In Project B, I was asked to carry out a review of a bereavement counselling service being offered by a hospice for family and friends of people who had recently died in the hospice's care. This is clearly a sensitive topic to research, and so I worked closely with a steering group at the hospice, supported by their service user support group. Initially it was suggested that we might interview volunteers about their experiences, but this was considered by the support group to be insensitive for people who had been bereaved relatively recently; they preferred the idea of an anonymous postal survey based on questionnaires, and so this became the chosen methodology. Wording on the questionnaire was carefully considered and agreed with the steering group; ethics approval was secured. Hospice staff approached people they had been in contact with over a period of two years to ask them to participate in the survey and excluded those who were very recently bereaved. They also took charge of sending out and receiving anonymised questionnaires, whilst I analysed the results, discussed these with the team and produced a report. Separating out these tasks ensured that confidentiality as well as anonymity was maintained, since my own involvement with relatives and friends was therefore limited and participants were in contact with individuals they had learnt to trust at all times.

We allowed room on the questionnaire for respondents to make comments about services they were offered, and many did so; I was pleased to see that those responding to our survey included those who had actually taken up the counselling and other services offered as well as those who had declined them. Respondents felt able to disclose reasons why they had not taken up what was offered to them, which provided useful information for the hospice and its supporters.

This evaluative project taught me, as a researcher, a great deal about working collaboratively on a sensitive project and how to present my skills to the team not as an 'expert' but as a facilitator; the most important outcomes were what we learnt to enable the service to go forward, rather than focusing on any more academic goals, yet work had to be done to a highly rigorous standard in academic terms in order to be credible both within and outside the organisation. These lessons are, I feel, sometimes missed in practitioner research.

Project C – Survey of social work and health students using a pre-existing questionnaire:[3] ethical issues (Bell and Clancy, 2013)

Some social work researchers who are employed or studying in universities may think that working with students does not involve many ethical issues. My own social work students have sometimes chosen to work with fellow students in order to reduce the need to have to consider formal ethical issues and due to short timescales for producing their dissertations. However, it should never be assumed that students are just a 'captive audience' for the lecturer or student to plug in to for research purposes without due care and attention.

Some key ethical issues relevant to this example are:

➤ ensuring that participants are not coerced into taking part in research

➤ establishing from the ethics' committee's perspective what is considered to be 'research' and what is considered an appropriate requirement for the course, e.g. as part of student assessment

➤ ensuring that questionnaires are appropriately anonymised

➤ gaining permission to use a pre-existing questionnaire.

In this example we started out with a dual aim:

1. to provide our students with experience in using 'quantitative methods' which could be assessed as part of their research methods course.

2. to provide ourselves with the opportunity to research how masters students were learning about research in this particular course.

A colleague (Dr Carmel Clancy) was able to identify a pre-existing questionnaire (reported in Papanastasiou, 2005) which we felt was ideal for us to use with our students. The author of this paper was then approached for her permission to use her questionnaire with our own students. It is very important if using any pre-existing questionnaire or measure to establish its status:

➤ Do you have permission to use it?

➤ Are there any financial costs or other requirements involved?

➤ Are there any copyright or intellectual property rights to consider?

These may not be considered 'ethical' issues by some researchers, but it is important to be clear on all of these points, as ignoring them could lead to unethical practice.

Although it was clear we wanted to use the analysed data that would be gathered using this questionnaire as part of student assessment, our second aim (above) potentially put this exercise into the realms of 'research'. In order to demonstrate whether or not students had learnt much about quantitative methods, we would of course have evidence in the form of their assessed work: in the event, we were to run workshops with student groups to explain how to do the analysis and produce a report. However, content of the questionnaire also focused on student attitudes to research, and in order to show whether or not there had been any changes in their attitudes, we would have to use a before-and-after design (i.e. using 'pre-course' and 'post-course' questionnaires).

Our university research ethics committee came back with the following requirements for us to follow:

➤ We could use the questionnaire to gather initial (pre-course) data that would be subsequently analysed by students themselves to produce assessed, individual reports. This was seen as part of 'assessment', and so, strictly speaking, student consent was not needed for this.

> However, our idea for a pre-, post-design as part of a research project meant that we needed some way of matching both questionnaires from each individual student; but these needed to be anonymised.

> Furthermore, the ethics committee decided that since the post (follow-up) questionnaire was not required for assessment, this part of the project was 'research' and so students would need to verbally consent to filling in the post-questionnaire; this process had to be voluntary.

Over several years we have been able to run this project with annual cohorts of social work and some health master's level students, following the above ethics guidelines. All students can be asked to complete the Attitudes to Research (ATR) measure at the outset of their course, with inclusion of a 'unique identifier' known only to that student (first three letters of a name plus a year, e.g. of birth or parent's birth) which effectively anonymises their questionnaire. Data from all the students in the annual cohort (typically between 50 and 60 questionnaires) is then entered into SPSS, including the 'unique identifier' as one of the variables. Workshops are then held, including data analysis and production of (assessed) reports. At the start of the next part of the course, these same students are asked if they will voluntarily complete a follow-up questionnaire. They are asked to include their unique identifier so that the follow-up questionnaire can be matched with the pre-course questionnaire. These processes mean that we have been able to run this exercise both as part of the students' assessment and also as a research project which enables us to understand how students' attitudes may affect their learning.

As we will see in Chapter 6, these ethics requirements, though perfectly reasonable from an ethics perspective, do have implications for the research project and its potential results.

For more on Project C, see also our published paper (Bell and Clancy, 2013) and a related paper by Canadian researchers (Morgenshtern et al., 2011) which uses the same ATR scale as part of a somewhat different research design.

Project D – Working with birth mothers who have had children successively removed from their care: an exploratory, qualitative interview-based study

In this recent qualitative project (see Bell et al., 2015), we set out to interview mothers in one local authority who had experienced successive removal of their children into care. The overall intention was to listen to these mothers' experiences so as to influence the development of appropriate social work interventions for these families.

Some key ethical issues relevant to this example are:

> ➤ ensuring that initial access to participants is carried out appropriately

> ➤ ensuring that participants have enough information to give 'informed consent' to participation

> ➤ providing additional safeguards to protect the rights of vulnerable participants

> ➤ observing ethical principles of respect, fair treatment and social justice when conducting interviews.

The project team (including university academics, practising social workers and social work managers in the local authority) worked out that locally there were about 20 mothers whose experiences would be of interest to the project. These women had all previously had more than one child removed from their care, they were still in contact with the local social services and had key workers. We applied for and obtained ethics approval via the university as well as from the local authority Research Governance (ethics) panel, who both approved a carefully worded Participant Information Sheet.

It was decided that the best approach to accessing these women initially was via their key workers, who were the people with whom they were most familiar. One member of our research team who was a practising social worker therefore held briefing sessions to explain the project to these key workers, asking for their help in approaching the mothers (the first task being to motivate these key workers about the project). If key workers managed to obtain a favourable response, then with that mother's permission their contact details were passed on by the key worker to our colleague. She then offered to explain directly to the mother what the research interview would involve, using the approved Participant Information Sheet; this was so that each woman was able to make a fully informed decision whether or not to participate in an interview. Our colleague then also arranged interviews with the researchers at a convenient time and she was also available to introduce mothers to researchers on the day. This whole process was very time consuming and labour intensive, with some cancelled appointments, but it was necessary from an ethics perspective to maintain trust and confidence of both mothers and key workers.

Thinking now about ethical issues involved in how we carried out interviews for this project, it was very important, as with all interviewing, to maintain underlying ethical principles of respect and fair treatment towards interviewees. In this case, the whole project (including the proposed social work intervention) was also concerned with issues of social justice, and so 'hearing the voices' of these women was a key aim which linked our project methodologically to taking a feminist approach (see also Miller and Bell, 2012). We were very aware that participants were also (like all interviewees) first and foremost assisting us with our project; they were asked to give written consent to being interviewed, as would be expected by most ethics committees. In the event, no one objected to their interview being digitally recorded, but had they done so we would have had to take notes (since you should never attempt to record an interview against the wishes of the interviewee). Sometimes interviewees may prefer you to use 'false names' in the interview (as happened in this project), although some research participants may on occasion like their 'real' name to be used. (There may be similar issues about using the 'real' names of organisations/employers.) For another example of participatory action research involving young people leaving care that addresses this issue, see Allain et al. (2011).

Chapter summary

➤ Research, like social work practice, cannot be regarded as value free, and I emphasise this point throughout the book.

➤ This chapter aimed to demystify some common 'ethics' issues relevant to social work researchers. Information was provided about research governance and ethics scrutiny debates.

➤ Links were made between 'research ethics' and 'professional ethics' since these can sometimes be a source of tension or ambiguity.

➤ The chapter offers advice on coping with formal ethics procedures that are sometimes considered a 'minefield' when trying to start up a research project.

➤ You have been encouraged as researchers or student researchers to adopt an 'ethical', problem-solving stance throughout a research or evaluation project, and we presented you with example scenarios to consider.

➤ Ethical issues underlying project examples have been presented, including co-produced or participatory projects.

Further reading

Alderson, P and Morrow, V (2011) *The Ethics of Research with Children and Young People*, Thousand Oaks: Sage

Bell, L and Hafford-Letchfield, T (eds) (2015) *Ethics, Values and Social Work Practice*, Maidenhead: Open University Press/McGraw Hill

Boddy, J, Boaz, A, Lupton, C and Pahl, J (2006) What counts as research? The implications for Research Governance in Social Care, *International Journal of Social Research Methodology*, 9 (4): 317–330

Boulton, M and Parker, M (2007) Introduction: 'Informed Consent in a Changing Environment', *Social Science & Medicine*, 65 (11) (Special Issue): 2187–2198

Hammersley, M (2009) Against the ethicists: on the evils of ethical regulation, *International Journal of Social Research Methodology*, 12 (3): 211–225

Hedgcoe, A (2008) Research ethics review and the sociological research relationship, *Sociology*, 42 (5): 873–886.

Iphofen, R (2009) *Ethical Decision-Making in Social Research: A Practical Guide*, Basingstoke: Palgrave Macmillan

Miller, T and Boulton, M (2007) Changing constructions of informed consent: qualitative research and complex social worlds, *Social Science & Medicine*, 65 (11): 2199–2211

4

TALKING AND LISTENING: USING 'QUALITATIVE' METHODS TO DEVELOP RELATIONSHIP BASED APPROACHES TO RESEARCH

Introduction: The importance of relationships in research and social work

This chapter will discuss, using research examples, how to make best use of various qualitative research approaches and methods that involve directly communicating with others in various contexts: these include your colleagues, managers or other powerful individuals, users of social work or related services and different professionals. You will remember from Chapter 2 (see Figure 2.3, Chapter 2) that if starting from an **'interpretive'** or **'constructionist'** research perspective, we are interested in knowledge coming from everyday concepts and meanings which, we believe, people either hold or have constructed (how important this idea of construction is depends on our view of reality (or **'ontology'**). Human experience is therefore seen, by researchers taking this kind of (qualitative) approach, as a process of interpretation rather than just the sensory, material apprehension of 'facts'.

As well as using a 'generic' approach to using constructionist or interpretive framework(s) for qualitative research, social work and health researchers may use more specific qualitative approaches, which we will discuss below. These can include **grounded theory, ethnography, phenomenology**, use of **case studies** and feminist approaches. Potential methods (techniques) suitable for all these kinds of approaches include **interviews, focus groups**, observational work and methods that are not necessarily directly 'face-to-face' (using phone, texting or Skype, for example). Parallels (and sometimes contrasts) can be drawn between these qualitative research skills and 'relationship based' approaches that social workers will already be familiar with.

In terms of research methods, if you are taking a broadly (generic) interpretive or constructionist approach, focus therefore tends to be on words and accounts (qualitative data), or, more recently, researchers have additionally focused on visual data and/or material from social media which express these everyday concepts (see also Chapters 8 and 9). In many ways, there are parallels to be drawn here with social work practice in which you don't necessarily take on-board everything you hear or see at 'face value'. You always need, as a professional, to be able to interpret what you are seeing or hearing.

We expect people will negotiate together to produce meanings, although the degree to which we imagine they do this consciously again depends upon our specific, differing ways of thinking about social reality. Researchers following different kinds of qualitative approach or working with(in) different subject disciplines or theories may therefore vary in how far they accept this point about deliberate action. These forms of negotiation, or, to use a more recent term which may sometimes apply, 'co-production' (e.g. between professionals and service users) are all underpinned by human relationships. However, Nowicka and Ryan (2015) suggest (in the context of positionalities in migration research) that:

> researchers should give up the idea of any assumed, apriori commonality with their research participants and instead set out to conduct research from a position of uncertainty. We believe that abandoning taken for granted assumptions and embracing a sense of uncertainty in encounters with research participants is a fruitful strategy in enabling migration studies to move beyond methodological groupism.

Once again, you will be aware how important relationships are to social work practice; as part of this awareness you will also recognise that your positionality as well as power dynamics may have an important part to play. You will also perhaps accept the role of the unconscious in these processes. This is just as true for research as it is for social work generally, although 'power' may have different dimensions in different contexts (see e.g. Hafford-Letchfield (2015) on social work and power, or various chapters in Gillies and Lucey (2007) on power and research).

We noted in Chapter 2 that in order to research everyday meanings, the researcher should aim to enter everyday social world(s) of research participants 'in order to grasp the socially constructed meanings, and then reconstruct[s] these meanings in social scientific language' (Blaikie, 1993, p. 96). Researchers carrying out specifically ethnographic, phenomenological or interview-based studies may all vary in the extent to which they expect to immerse themselves in a practical sense in other people's 'everyday social worlds', and also how they can make use, in their own terms, of this 'social scientific language'.

This suggests one important contrast between research and social work: the researcher is most likely to be seeking theoretical understandings and will present these in such 'social scientific' language (although these understandings can also be applied to others' practice or to one's own if you are a practitioner researcher). Practising social workers are usually more interested in translating people's everyday experiences and understandings into action (using some kinds of intervention), as well as in interpreting what they mean in more theoretical terms. I would argue that these subtle contrasts lie at the heart of the longstanding issue for practising social workers of how to link theory with practice and may (perhaps) explain the occasional suspicion that for practitioners, 'research' is somewhat pointless! However, these issues can also place social workers and other practitioner researchers in an interesting and perhaps advantageous position as both insider/outsider researchers. For a different perspective on these issues, Atkinson (2005) has suggested that some research (particularly participatory research) can come to look and feel like social work: it can engender close working relationships and emotional links between researcher and participant(s) and requires a considerable degree of self-awareness and reflexivity as well as requiring openness on the researcher's part.

For researchers in the social work field, policy or other factors may, however, reduce the amount of time available to carry out project field work, which again may limit the kinds of research methods which can be attempted. Political or organisational imperatives may also come into play when social work research is designed or as it is being implemented. All these issues may realistically affect how research (whether broadly qualitative or quantitative) can be done in social work, which may seem far from ideal, but these parameters need to be seen as significant parts of the research process.

In the next section we are moving beyond taking a generic interpretive or constructionist approach to review some underpinning qualitative research approaches that can be useful in social work research, before looking in more detail at specific qualitative research methods.

Underpinning approaches in qualitative research: Grounded theory, ethnography, feminist approaches, phenomenology, case studies and 'practice-near' research

Grounded theory

Grounded theory approaches differ from other qualitative approaches in their emphasis on theory development. Originally developed in the 1960s by Glaser and Strauss (1967) as an (apparently) unified methodology, which would allow 'the discovery of theory from data', these approaches have turned out to be very flexible and have taken different forms (as pointed out by Dey (1999), Charmaz (2006), Clarke (2005) and Oliver (2012). Strauss, afterwards working with Corbin (see Corbin and Strauss, 1990), took the idea of grounded theory forward in a more general direction, suggesting that:

> Grounded theory is a general methodology for developing theory that is grounded in data systematically gathered and analysed. Theory evolves during actual research... through constant interplay between analysis and data collection. (Corbin and Strauss, 1990, p. 158)

Some proponents of grounded theory approach(es) warn against reading too much subject literature/theoretical material before starting research. This *tabula rasa* approach is meant to leave researchers free to develop theory as it emerges, rather than researchers having too many preconceived ideas. However, this way of working has recently been challenged by some (e.g. Dunne, 2011), who discusses the impossibility of coming to a research project without any form of preparation or grounding in earlier subject literature. Some characteristics of grounded theory are indicated below (Figure 4.1).

Some researchers have recently tried to develop grounded theory: for example Charmaz (2006) reinterprets grounded theory methods in a constructionist light, whilst setting her own development of the craft within its broader historical development. Clarke (2005) uses grounded theory as a starting point 'after the postmodern turn' to expand the

---

> ➢ The grounded theory researcher is supposed to start with a general idea of the subject of study rather than with any formally worked out theory to be tested.
>
> ➢ Theoretical sampling allows the grounded theory researcher to focus on useful cases, and to select new cases that would allow the developing theory to be tested until theoretical saturation is reached.
>
> ➢ Constant interplay between data gathering and analysis (known as constant comparative analysis) is a hallmark of grounded theory.
>
> ➢ Dey (1999) suggests that as proposed, grounded theory represents a 'marriage' between quantitative methods (Glaser) and symbolic interactionism. 'Variables' and 'values' are thus replaced in grounded theory with 'categories' and 'properties':
>
>> 'Glaser and Strauss set out to mark a course between the contrasting extremes of impressionistic qualitative studies and rigorous quantitative analysis ... We are told that categories must be sensitizing and analytic, but it is less clear how they can be both' (p. 44).
>
> ➢ Computer-assisted data analysis has, Dey suggests, drawn upon grounded theory with its emphasis on both analytic rigour and 'naturalistic' enquiry.

Figure 4.1 Some characteristics of grounded theory

repertoire of data and methods appropriate to GT to include narratives and visual materials, developing cartographic (map-based) approaches into what Clarke calls situational analysis. Oliver (2012) suggests grounded theory can be adapted to the critical realist paradigm, making it ideal for social work research, for example in terms of interconnectedness of practice and theory and attention to pursuit of practical, emancipatory goals.

Selecting examples for study when using grounded theory approach(es) is a key issue. How do we know where to look? In essence, choosing a set of similar research sites or individuals/cases will enable researchers to initially establish basic properties of categories which will go towards making up the theory. There may be an emphasis on choosing as many cases or examples as possible to allow this theory development. The next stage is to choose 'exceptional' or 'negative' cases so as to bring out the widest variation. When nothing new can be learnt from different cases, 'theoretical saturation' has been reached. This ultimately allows an emerging theory to be tested. A key focus in grounded theorising is thus on process. This process of choosing participants or examples, often referred to as 'theoretical sampling', means in practice that researchers taking up grounded theorising will tend to use a basically snowballing approach to sampling, rather than beginning their data collection with a fixed sample (see also Appendix D-4, Sampling).

The process of analysis using grounded theory techniques essentially consists of working with this 'constant comparative' method in a process which can produce various levels of categories which (ultimately) suggest a 'theory'. The process is intended to be systematic and rigorous. The extent to which grounded theorists can test as well as generate theories from their data has, however, been questioned by some observers (e.g. Dey, 1999)

Many researchers claim to use 'grounded theory', but in fact they focus on using it as a form of data analysis (see the section on 'Qualitative data analysis' in Chapter 5).

Project E – A 'grounded theory' study example (Fountain et al, 1999)

Fountain et al.'s (1999) paper involved poly-drug users in five selected drug marketplaces and investigated the impact of decreased availability of certain drugs. This is an example of a study which is concerned with 'process', and therefore with changing conditions in the settings under investigation. The researchers state (p. 62) that they worked with a sample of informants who are not necessarily 'characteristic of all drug users'. They analysed data from interviews and observations using a synthesis of grounded theory and analytic induction. Although these researchers produce some theories seeking to explain the events described and participants' reactions, we should note that one key problem for grounded theorising is to know when 'theoretical saturation' has been reached and when the emergent theory can be tested again in other contexts. Perhaps wisely, these researchers do not try to claim too much for any rigorous 'theory' which might have emerged from their work; they do suggest processes involved in drug markets and measures aimed at harm reduction need further in-depth exploration. In these circumstances, the 'constant comparative' method of analysis commonly associated with grounded theory seems very appropriate as the researchers try to grapple with research participants' understandings and reactions to the events described here.

Ethnography

This is (usually) a mixed methods approach to research that has been used in various disciplines, notably anthropology and sociology, and has a fairly long history in the social sciences going back to the famous Chicago school of sociologists and to work by early anthropologists such as Malinowski and Boas. More recently, **ethnography** has been used in social work research as well as in health studies or criminology, to allow researchers to immerse themselves as fully as possible in their informants' social worlds. (See below, Figure 4.2, for some basic characteristics of ethnography.)

> There is concern with observing and exploring social context, e.g. place, time, and other aspects, from the perspective(s) of those being 'researched'.

> Although seen as a 'qualitative' approach to research, ethnography may sometimes generate 'quantitative' as well as 'qualitative' data, e.g. through use of approaches such as surveys. 'Mixing methods' is often expected, and this may include using methods (techniques) such as questionnaires, interviews, observational data and/or documentary analysis.

> Ethnographic research may consist of a single case, e.g. of one hospital ward (Meyer, 1993), or include particular case studies in a wider contextual frame.

> Ethnography most often relies on observation as a method, especially participant observation, sometimes over a lengthy period of time; the researcher is not seen as an 'objective' and detached observer, but is 'part of the action'.

> Ethnography has a number of implications for generating and interpreting data, as well as raising ethical issues. For example, how exactly is the ethnographer able to 'represent' lives and experiences of the people being researched? What is the relationship between the ethnographer and 'the researched'? What would 'informed consent' from research participants look like in these circumstances?

Figure 4.2 Basic characteristics of ethnography

Project F – an example of an ethnographic study: Surviving through substance use: The role of substances in the lives of women who appear before the courts (Wincup, 2000)

In discussing her approach to researching this topic, Wincup (2000) states:

> An ethnographic approach was adopted to allow empathic understanding of the lives of women who live and work in bail hostels. The essential character-istics of ethnography include involvement in people's lives for an extended period of time, watching what happens, listening to what is said and asking questions. This takes place within their 'natural' setting. These characteristics resemble the ways in which people make sense of their everyday lives and this has been regarded as a fundamental strength of ethnography for some social scientists ... Ethnography is a methodological strategy rather than a research method. Consequently, there is potential to mix methods and contemporary ethnography tends to be multi-method research. In keeping with this tradition, the research discussed in this paper employed a range of methods, combining participant observation, semi-structured interviews and documentary analysis.

This project is also an example of taking a feminist approach to research (see below).

For other examples of ethnographic work, see:

➤ a mixed methods study involving (ethnographic) observation of social work student groups: Bell and Villadsen (2011)

➤ Bell, L (1995) 'Just a token commitment?' Women's involvement in a local babysitting circle (feminist study)

➤ Project K in this chapter

➤ using ethnographic and mobile methods to understand encounters between social workers, children and families (Ferguson, 2016).

Feminist approaches

Feminist forms of research arose largely in opposition to earlier posi-tivistic ways of employing 'the scientific method' in social research, but methodology/ies used by researchers are many and varied (see e.g. Hesse-Biber, 2014). From an epistemological perspective, they can, for example, encompass earlier, essentialist approaches to feminism such as feminist standpoint theory (Harding, 1987; Naples and Gurr, 2014), or later devel-opments in relation to hearing women's voices (Ribbens and Edwards, 1998; Bell, 1995; 1998; Project F, above). Feminist researchers have focused on research dilemmas and ethics (Miller et al., 2012; Bell, 2014), experiences that are gendered and intersectional in various contexts (Vervliet et al., 2014) and they can also explore wider political or moral issues in society such as citizenship (Sevenhuijsen, 1998). Many feminist studies make use of postmodernism, post-structuralism and critical theory, both theoretically and politically, and acknowledge the importance of addressing intersectionality (e.g. where gender, ethnicity and/or other characteristics intersect – see e.g. Nash, 2008; Krumer-Nevo and Komem, 2015; and discussion by Frost and Elichaoff, 2014).

Some may suggest that feminist researchers generally use qualitative research methods, yet many also make use of mixed methods (see also Chapter 7) or have questioned why feminists should reject **positivism** (see Oakley, 1998). **Subjectivity** is nevertheless a key issue for many feminist studies, for example when uncovering women's perspectives and voices. What remains, for most feminist researchers, is a focus on exploring gender as a key issue in society (with distinctions being made between gender and (biological) sex), including a focus on sexuality/ies (Hafford-Letchfield et al., 2010).

Social work is still dominated numerically by female practitioners, and it has been labelled a 'caring profession'; as in social work, a focus on care and carers has become increasingly evident in feminist research (see e.g. Orme, 2002; 2003; Rogers and Weller, 2013). But in academia there have been continuing moves, in the UK at least, away from a focus simply on 'women's studies' as a subject discipline; perhaps because this had seemed to privilege the perspectives of white middle-class feminists. But American feminist researchers had perhaps always taken a more pluralistic path, both methodologically and in terms of acknowledging both 'women's studies' and intersectionalities; some international researchers, including Mehrotra (2010; 2015), have called for these insights to be applied directly in social work research:

> ....feminist social work scholars need to develop and use a continuum of different theorizations of intersectionality, with various epistemological bases, that can be strategically applied, depending on the goals of a particular project or practice context. (Mehrotra, 2010, Abstract)

Recent research thus tends towards a more pluralistic view of researching gender through intersectionality/ies that is very relevant to social work research in wider contexts of social justice (see Orme, 2002). Dovetailing these kinds of evolving feminist research practices and concerns about 'caring' with approaches to social work practice are surely beneficial, although these concerns may also raise various dilemmas (see e.g. Project D; Chapters 3, 4 and 5).

As already noted, emotions can play an important part in both research and in social work; feminist researchers and social workers have long sought to uncover and highlight this aspect of their research practice(s) (see e.g. Jaggar, 1997; Mehrotra, 2015). Emotions might be seen as mainly personal and linked with a focus on 'embodiment' in some feminist research:

> Research ... is inevitably a power-laden, emotional, embodied experience (Letherby, Scott and Williams, 2013, ch 5, p. 95)

But as social workers and researchers also point out, emotions are always shared and managed through relationships with other people. For example Hubbard, Backett-Milburn and Kemmer (2001) vividly describe dealing with situations where they found themselves over-empathising, getting upset or getting angry during research encounters; this allows them to suggest ways of building support with colleagues or others during and after these encounters. However, they sometimes found it hard to come to terms with what happened; this kind of experience must surely also resonate with social work practitioners (see also Ingram, 2013; Ruch, 2012).

What is often termed a specifically feminist 'ethics of care' is relevant here. 'Ethics of care' can underpin both feminist research (see e.g. Rogers and Weller, 2013) and social work practice (Orme, 2002; 2003); this approach calls for increased reflexivity by feminists as well as awareness of wider political and moral issues (Sevenhuijsen, 1998).

In this book, several of our project examples are founded specifically on feminist ethics and principles:

➤ Project D, a project in which I have been working alongside researchers and social worker colleagues with birth mothers who had children successively removed from their care; the project includes semi-structured interviews with ten mothers

➤ Project F (above), where Emma Wincup revealed the diversity of life experiences of women residents of bail hostels in London, taking an ethnographic approach and using mixed qualitative methods

➤ Project G, focusing on lives of women refugees (Wilcke, 2002; see below – section on Phenomenology).

All of these studies share a focus on exploring and revealing the lives and voices of women, thereby taking up this well-established feminist perspective.

For wider perspectives on intersectionalities, diversity and social justice in recent social work research that are emerging from feminist perspectives, see e.g. Wahab, Anderson-Nathe and Gringeri (2015).

Further reading
Hesse-Biber, SN (ed) (2014) *Feminist Research Practice*, Thousand Oaks: Sage
Ribbens, J, and Edwards, R (1998) *Feminist Dilemmas in Qualitative Research*,
    London: Sage
Wahab, S, Anderson-Nathe, B and Gringeri, C (eds) 2015 *Feminisms in Social
    Work Research: Promise and Possibilities for Justice-Based Knowledge*, Abingdon:
    Routledge

Phenomenology

Phenomenological research approaches are perhaps closest to acknowledging the role of philosophy in research. In other words, the phenomenological researcher has often moved well beyond the straightforward
idea of 'interviewing people to see what they can tell me about X'. Depth
interviewing and participant observation will be favoured research
methods for phenomenologists, as they may be for ethnographers; but
there will also be a philosophical emphasis on **subjectivity** and on ways
in which the 'lifeworld'[1] is produced and experienced by its members.
Social systems are seen as abstractions which exist mainly as individuals interacting with each other. In research literature we can also identify different forms of phenomenological research, descriptive and
hermeneutic.

A characteristic feature of descriptive phenomenological research is to
try and 'get over' the 'taken for granted' aspects of our everyday experience. In entering others' social worlds, the researcher tries to set aside
('bracket') her/his own experience so as to view others' perspectives more
clearly; the focus should be on phenomena which are being studied. The
researcher views the 'ongoing accomplishment' of intersubjectivity, a set
of understandings sustained by participants in interaction, moment by
moment (see e.g. Gubrium and Holstein, 2000; Holstein and Gubrium,
1994).

Whilst descriptive phenomenology emphasises study of consciousness
when eliciting knowledge of the world (and thus the possibility of 'brack-
eting' off one's assumptions and experience in order to study a phenomenon 'objectively'), hermeneutic phenomenology can be seen as a 'way of
being in the world' rather than as just a methodology (see e.g. Gadamer,
2004) and suggests our assumptions cannot be so easily bracketed because
they are an integral part of our processes of understanding.

Words and accounts are seen by the phenomenologist as building blocks
of everyday conscious reality: in Schutz's terms, language is the main
means of transmitting typifications (ways of referencing and accounting
for experience: see Kim and Berard, 2009). Common-sense constructs and

categories, which are social in origin, are shared and articulated in words and accounts, taking the form of these typifications. However, we tend to overlook the ways common-sense understandings are constructed and take our subjectivity for granted, 'presuming that we intersubjectively share the same reality' (Holstein and Gubrium IN Denzin and Lincoln, 1994, p. 263).

Project G – An example of hermeneutic phenomenological research in social work

Wilcke (2002) used hermeneutic phenomenology and a feminist approach to explore the experiences of ten women who had travelled from former Yugoslavia and settled as refugees in a Canadian city. Nine women had children living with them. Wilcke explains that at that time few studies had focused specifically on the experience of women as refugees. She began by 'orienting herself to the phenomena' involved in her study, basing her thinking on Gadamer's work (who had in turn been influenced by the work of Martin Heidegger), and therefore she attempted to understand historical and cultural factors that had shaped participants' lives as well as reviewing her own background history. She then carried out two in-depth interviews with each participant, either face-to-face or by telephone. Wilcke made use of hermeneutic phenomenology because it aims:

> to elucidate lived experience and to reveal meaning through a process of understanding and interpretation. One of my reasons for choosing this method was that previous studies have been criticized for objectifying and pathologizing refugees, and ignoring the strengths of refugee women ... The choice of the hermeneutic method allowed the experiences of the respondents to be presented in a direct and evocative manner, encouraging the reader to enter imaginatively into the experiences described. In so doing, the method provided a vehicle for deepening our understanding of refugee women as people living full and complex lives. (Wilcke, 2002, p. 7)

The approach also allows the researcher to fully reflect on the meaning of her/his experiences, very relevant to social work researchers:

> [The findings] ... deepened our understanding of certain aspects of the refugee experience, and suggested directions for furthering social work knowledge, education and practice. The study made explicit the danger of objectifying and categorizing people for the purpose of research, and reminded us that peoples' lives are richer and more complex than the categories we may impose on them. (Wilcke, 2002, p. 8)

For a systematic review of phenomenological studies using interviews with people with intellectual disability, see also Corby, Taggart and Cousins (2015).

Case studies

Case studies can take various forms, including studies of communities, social groups, individuals, sets of individuals, organisations or institutions, events, roles or relationships. We would expect the primary concern is with the case per se as a theoretical example of its type (see e.g. Yin, 2014). However, a series of cases might be used to provide generalisable inferences to a wider context. Cases may also be included as part of an ethnographic study.

Some researchers have indicated that a case study approach is particularly suitable for very complex phenomena (Verschuren, 2003) – see e.g. Project J, below. Others suggest that 'case study' is merely a vague label for what is otherwise 'a small-scale, in-depth study' (Tight, 2010).

Robson's (2002) useful definition of case study is of 'a strategy for doing research which involves an empirical investigation of a particular contemporary phenomenon within its real life context using multiple sources of evidence' (p. 178). These sources of evidence may, like ethnographic sources, involve interviews or use of documents, although participant observation (which is such a feature of ethnography) is not strictly necessary for case studies. Robson (2002) also points out that when designing a case study you need to start with:

➤ a conceptual framework (theory)

➤ research question(s)

➤ a sampling strategy

➤ to decide on appropriate methods for data collection (p. 82 (diagram)).

However, the researcher's development of these elements will almost certainly continue as research begins, because the case study researcher needs to adapt to the social setting being investigated. Note that Robson emphasises the necessity for a conceptual framework (or theory) which will force you to be explicit as a researcher about what you are doing and help you to be selective (see also Rallis and Rossman, 2012, ch 5). One key problem in case study research is the tendency to want to explore anything and everything!

Case studies may involve individual case examples; we should note here the differences between interpretive/qualitative case studies (which are based on conceptual exploration and description – see Projects J and K, below) and research using 'a single case experimental design' (for example as referred to in medical or psychological texts), where the focus is on quantitative measurement and explanation of causal relationships and is based on a positivist methodology.

Two examples using case studies in social work research

Project H (see also Chapter 7)

In this **case study**, Cree, Jain and Hillen (2016) carried out an evaluation of a whole referral service relating to drugs and alcohol in Scotland. This evaluation was conducted in 2012 and had two main objectives:

1 to evaluate outputs – 'what were the outcomes of the service from the point of view of the staff, the service users and the referrers'?

2 to evaluate effectiveness – 'how well these outputs/outcomes were achieved, again from the point of view of the staff, the service users and the referrers'.

This **evaluation** used a case study approach involving mixed methods, aiming to provide 'critical, reflexive and contextual understanding' of the case and allowing the researchers to achieve **triangulation.** The methods they used included both qualitative and quantitative techniques (with perhaps more emphasis on qualitative approaches and data), such as analysis of services' reports and case records, participant **observation**, **focus groups** with staff and **interviews** with different stakeholders. The researchers comment at the end of the article:

> By scrutinising one example of evaluation research, we have shown that evaluation is always context-specific and so is inevitably political, in one way or another. Moreover, we have argued that the activity of social work, at least in the context of drug and alcohol services, may be too complex to be measured in a positivistic, scientific kind of way. This does not suggest that we abandon it altogether! On the contrary, it suggests that we need to look towards a critical, pragmatic approach to evaluation ... one that foregrounds the importance of methodological rigour as a way of achieving dependability and trustworthiness in our findings and analysis ... [so] we may yet be able to say something positive about the contribution of social work services to individuals' lives and to society as a whole.

In the next project example (Project J), the **case study** approach is represented by two individual case examples within the overall research study (which also used documentary sources extensively).

Project J

In this research paper relating to the rights of children in relation to breast-feeding in child protection cases, Gribble and Gallagher (2014) describe how:

> Two case studies are presented in which child protection authorities had interactions with a breastfeeding mother and child. In the first case, the child

protection intervention resulted in the early and permanent cessation of breast-feeding. In the second case, active advocacy allowed breastfeeding to continue. However, in both cases, the mothers' insistence that breastfeeding was important to their children and should continue was pathologised. (from Abstract)

For further details on Project J, see also Chapter 5, 'Documentary sources'.

'Practice-near' approaches

Practice-near enquiry is a useful recent approach in social work research that might be defined as:

> the use of experience-near methods for practice-based or practice relevant research. Such methods include ethnography, some forms of in-depth qualitative interviewing and observation, and the use of images and other sensory data in research. (Froggett and Briggs, 2015, p. 3)

Some researchers, including Cooper (2009), White et al. (2009), Winter et al. (2015), Ruch (2012; 2014) and Hingley-Jones (2009 – Project K, below), have developed innovative work that can:

> utilise practice approaches and interventions as research methods. This approach is characterised by a greater sense of immediacy and refers to the integration and application of new practice knowledge within the immediate research context and directly in the practice domain. (Winter et al., 2015, p.7, quote from Ruch)

Project K – A 'practice-near' example
In this study, Hingley-Jones (2009) used an adaptation of psychoanalytically informed infant observation to observe severely learning disabled young people over time in their family homes. She explains that:

> Finding ways to research young people's emotions and those of their families in difficult and complex relationships of care such as these, requires the development and adaptation of methods that have the capacity to recognize the subtleties of emotional experiences and make these available for analysis. (p. 415)

This approach 'placed the young people's experiences and feelings (their 'subjectivity) at the centre, through making use of a reflexive research methodology'. In this way the researcher 'has to attune to the subjects' non-verbal and emotional cues as well as the conscious and unconscious communications ... within the wider social field of the family. (p. 419)

Through building case studies based on observation, the study revealed two main themes:

➤ What did observing reveal about the young people as developing adolescent subjects?

➤ What kinds of coping mechanisms were the young people and their families employing to facilitate the young person's development?

Practice-near approaches can thus aim to enable practitioners to 'dig deeper' in their research to include both theory and practice, going beyond more conventional social constructionist approaches.

Key qualitative methods – interviews, observation, focus groups, vignettes/scenarios

Within the different kinds of approaches to research we have just described, researchers will need to choose and apply various techniques (methods) to gather and analyse their data. In this section we will look more closely at some of these methods in practice.

Interviews

Many qualitative researchers taking a broadly 'constructionist' approach base their attempts to 'enter the everyday understandings' of their informants mainly on **interviews** with a sample of informants. Interviewing as a method (or technique) brings its own difficulties, but it is clearly a very well used way of letting our informants 'tell it as it is'. The main issue over use of this kind of method is that some researchers seem to think that qualitative research is only about interviewing. I once witnessed a senior academic at a conference complaining about the sheer number of qualitative researchers presenting academic papers from research projects which just used this 'single' method. Interviewing as a technique is often, however, combined with other methods (as in **ethnography** or **case studies**), or it may be developed in a particular theoretical fashion, for example when using **phenomenology** or **grounded theory**. We should ask how far researchers are able to meet the intentions of a basically 'interpretive' approach by only using interviewing.

Let's go back now briefly to Project D, which we introduced in the previous chapter, as an example of interview-based work. One issue which arose when interviewing in that study is that ethical issues may be raised, as already noted, when children or adults who are perceived as 'vulnerable' form the interview sample. Choice of interview type usually relates to the research approach the researcher is taking. In Project D, where we were interviewing mothers who have had children successively and permanently removed from their care, a semi-structured approach fitted the project aims well and allowed interviewees to present their own viewpoints in a 'guided conversation' with the researcher. It also allowed for the presence of a 'supporter' to the mother in some cases.

On the other hand, a more 'formalised' approach to interviewing may allow data from interviews to be quantified more readily, and the overall emphasis in such a study would be on consistency between interviewee responses (e.g. to a question like 'How long have you been doing this job?' – recorded either in months, in years etc.), as in a survey. This implies use of a more formal interview schedule or questionnaire. I have used this type of approach during telephone interviewing, which is usually a fairly short process and may need to remain more structured, or when interviewing health professionals or social workers to gather 'demographics' as part of an overall semi-structured interview.

Where theory is expected to 'emerge from the data', as in **grounded theory** approaches, it may be that a looser interview format is useful. If the interviewer is interested in 'biographical' approaches (popular along with development of postmodern research approaches), then a more 'unstructured' approach may well be useful, although there are no 'hard and fast' rules about this. Bear in mind that although they may seem 'easier' to conduct, unstructured interviews may in fact be more time consuming and difficult to analyse than interviews using more structured formats.

Since interviewing is perhaps the commonest form of 'qualitative' research method, many people may think that 'anyone can do it'. Sometimes people attempt to carry out research interviews without being clear about:

➤ the type of interviewing they need in their particular project

➤ the sample of interviewees required

➤ the key questions (or interview guide) they need

➤ the ethical dilemmas which may occur in specific interviewing situations

➤ probably most of all, what they are going to do with the interview data once they have gathered it.

Types of interviews

Many researchers simply refer to interviews as 'qualitative', but this does not really suggest the variety of possible interview types. We summarise different possibilities in Figure 4.3 below.

Processes involved in interviewing
Sampling (See also Appendix D-4, Sampling)

There are various ways of approaching research sampling in qualitative studies. Because interviews are time consuming, qualitative researchers generally find they have to restrict the number of interviewees to those they are able to cope with (especially for student projects). A very large-scale sample, which might be required in some quantitative studies and perhaps in order to ensure statistical representativeness (probability sampling), is therefore often precluded. However, despite using 'purposive' rather than 'probability' sampling, social work researchers using qualitative methods may often aim to interview the maximum number of interviewees that they can manage. As we will see later, Rhodes and Quirk (1998 – Project L) used 'a purposive sample of 72 heroin and other opiates users' for their study of risk perception and management associated with everyday drug use. Purposive sampling involves choosing interviewees who are appropriate in terms of the research questions and objectives, so this approach to sampling needs to be tailored to the overall project context. For example, in some case studies, interviewee numbers may be restricted due to structural factors, e.g. a researcher interviewing

---

'Structured' or 'standardised' interview

A formal interview, based strictly on a 'questionnaire' type schedule with set questions, usually asked in a particular order (this may be useful, e.g. for telephone interviewing).

This may also form only part of a broader 'semi-structured' interview, e.g. for asking demographic questions ('What is your age?' 'How long have you been doing this job?').

'Semi-structured' or 'semi-standardised' interview

The interviewer uses the same major questions with each interviewee (not necessarily in the same order) but allows time for probing to gather more details and to produce a 'guided conversation'. Order of questions can vary on the day provided all topics are covered. This tends to be the most frequently used form of interviewing in qualitative research.

Unstructured interview

A monologue starting with a 'prompt' question only (e.g. 'Can you please tell us about your career history to date?') or an interview using a very basic topic guide rather than an interview schedule. However, this format may cause problems for comparison between interviewees unless obtaining individual narratives is your main aim.

Figure 4.3 Interview types

all members of one Community Mental Health team about 'dual diagnosis' issues will be restricted to the number and types of professionals employed in that team. Other researchers doing more 'personalised' interviews may choose to interview people they know and to 'snowball' out from these contacts (i.e. being introduced to new contacts via previous interviewee(s)), which can be useful but can also be a source of tension or potential bias.

For a sociological study of families which discusses interviewing personal contacts in this way, see e.g. Ribbens-McCarthy, Edwards and Gillies (2000; 2003).

Researchers taking a **grounded theory** approach may also be using a 'snowball' type of sample, or else finding other contacts who will introduce the researcher to 'negative examples' who differ in significant ways to previous interviewees (a basis for what grounded theorists would term 'theoretical sampling').

Due to the nature of their research approach, phenomenologists may restrict their number of interviewees and so carry out very few interviews but in great depth. All of these approaches contrast with much more formalised sampling techniques based on probability or 'statistically representative' sampling (see Chapter 6). For example, in some research (e.g. by Wright and Klee (1999)) there may be 'matched pairs' of interviewees; in this case, one of the pair was using a specific type of drugs intervention service and the other was not – this was done so that a formal comparison based on quantitative measures could be carried out between 'service participants' and 'controls'.

Key questions (interview guide)

As we saw in Figure 4.3, interview 'types' will vary from using a full questionnaire or structured set of questions, to a list of key questions, or a list of topics. Most researchers (apart from those using **grounded theory**) will base their questions or topics around key issues derived from literature searching and review, and perhaps also on key policy or 'practitioner'/ practice concerns in their field. In some cases, ethics committees will ask to see and approve researchers' interview questions; this is becoming more common especially where social work researchers are interviewing service users.

NOW GO TO APPENDIX B AND COMPLETE EXERCISE 4.1: PLANNING AN INTERVIEW AND PREPARING AN INTERVIEW SCHEDULE

Some further reflections on doing interviews

It is well known that how an interviewer conducts an interview will affect the results obtained. As we saw earlier (Project D), how you approach potential interviewees at the sampling stage will also affect whether or not they are persuaded to be interviewed. Remember, they are assisting you, so it pays to be respectful and to acknowledge any issues raised by the potential interviewee. For example, confidentiality is not only about informed consent (as we saw in Chapter 3). Some people will be nervous about signing anything, for example, even though you may need them to give written consent for ethics committee approval. If carrying out interviews with people in the same organisation, you would treat each interview as confidential so that, for example, I would not usually reveal to individual interviewees who else I have interviewed in the same workplace.

You will have checked in advance that interviewees are happy to be digitally/tape-recorded, and this is usually referred to on any **consent** form that interviewees will sign. If an interviewee refuses, you do, of course, have to respect this and take notes instead. Strictly speaking, you do not also have to take notes if you are digitally/tape recording, but some people find this helps later during analysis. For semi-structured or unstructured interviews in particular, it will be much easier to analyse your interviews if they are fully recorded.

In posing your questions, you should try to maintain a 'neutral' stance and be genuinely interested in what your interviewees tell you. You should never be tempted to argue with an interviewee – everyone has a right to their own opinion, after all! Many research interviewers have experienced completing an interview, turning off the digital or tape recorder, and then the interviewee makes some more really interesting and relevant comments. Sometimes the feeling is that they feel freer to say these things because they know the interview is now 'finished'. What do you do? Do you note down what they said and use it later without saying anything? This may be more difficult if you have not been making notes up to that point. Are you prepared to take these notes covertly? In my own experience, the safest plan is to ask permission to switch the recorder back on again and get the person to repeat what they just said if you can, stressing how interesting what they said was.

Suppose during the interview a topic under discussion upsets the interviewee, e.g. talking about experiences of violence. How does the interviewer react? Should you be tempted as a researcher to offer any 'therapeutic' intervention (especially if you are also a professional such as a social worker), or will you just offer relevant information? Here especially, it pays to plan ahead. Having planned your interview sample and interview or topic guide carefully, do you think it is likely that interviewees would be very sensitive to any of these questions? You may also want to 'pilot' the interview with a relevant but neutral person to see whether the interview can be managed effectively in its current form.

On the day, you should attempt to make the nature of the interview clear to interviewees before you start working with them. Show them the written information sheet, if you have one; this is usually required anyway for formal ethics purposes. As with questionnaire planning, it may be better to leave sensitive questions towards the end of the interview, when trust and rapport has had some time to build up between you and the interviewee. This process is trickier, of course, if you are not interviewing face-to-face, for example if interviewing over the telephone or via Skype. In such cases, I would send the interview schedule to the recipient in advance and arrange a specific time for the interview. A telephone interview has the disadvantage that you cannot see your respondent and there may be some awkward moments or 'overtalking'. In this case, it pays to use a fairly structured set of questions and, above all, to take your time, although shortage of time (whether your own or that of your interviewee) may be a reason why you are using this method.

In any case, be prepared for what your reaction will be if an interviewee reacts sensitively to any of your questions: if you intend to offer support by way of information, have it ready to offer at the appropriate time, e.g. addresses and phone numbers of appropriate agencies. Generally, however, remember you are conducting a 'research' interview, not necessarily a 'therapeutic' interview. For professionals like social workers, therapeutic interviews are a regular part of the work; you will have to make a choice about how to deal with this issue of 'overlap' during research interviewing, and should seek guidance from any ethical guidelines relating to your own profession/occupation. Interviewing children or vulnerable people also brings distinctive challenges. Finally, be prepared to examine your own emotional responses to difficult or stressful interview situations: how would you, as the researcher, deal with getting upset or getting angry during an interview? (See e.g. Hubbard, Backett-Milburn and Kemmer, 2001.)

For interesting research examples involving the interviewing or involvement of children in research, see e.g.:

➢ Aubrey, C and Dahl, S (2006) Children's voices: the views of vulnerable children on their service providers and the relevance of services they receive, *British Journal of Social Work*, 36: 21–39

➢ Moore, T, Noble-Carr, D and McArthur, M (2016) Changing things for the better: the use of children and young people's reference groups in social research, *International Journal of Social Research Methodology*, 19 (2): 241–256, dx.doi.org/10.1080/13645579.2014.989640

➢ Rugkåsa, J et al. (2001) Anxious adults vs cool children: Children's views on smoking and addiction, *Social Science and Medicine*, 53:

593–602 (note that permission to interview children was obtained from parents in this example)

Project L – Example of an 'interview-based' study

Rhodes and Quirk (1998) provide an example showing how qualitative, interview-based research can elucidate theories, in this case about the ways risk behaviour and drug use patterns are 'socially organised'. The paper focuses on how people's sexual relationships influence their risk and drug use: the sexual relationship is seen as a site of risk management. In this study, a purposive, fairly large sample of 72 heroin and other opiates users in London were interviewed (46 men; 26 women). Of the interviewees, 47 (67%) were current injecting drug users and 34 (47%) saw heroin as their main drug of choice. Interviews with couples also took place.

Data was collected via tape-recorded, one to two hour, in-depth, semi-structured interviews. Coding and analysis was undertaken throughout the data-collection period using inductive methods, analysis being assisted by computerised data analysis software.

Drug use and associated lifestyles were found to have a major impact on the management of sexual relationships, and types of relationships drug users have. From the interviews, the researchers discovered that drug users' perceived their sexual relationships to influence a variety of risks associated with their drug use and lifestyles. This detailed analysis enabled two types of relationships to be identified from drug users' accounts: (i) 'gear' relationships (where both partners are users) and ii) 'straight' relationships (where only one partner is a drug user). The researchers conclude that future risk reduction and drug treatment interventions need to simultaneously target individual drug users and their social relationship structures as modes of behaviour change.

We can see that in order to produce clear findings, these researchers had to be focused and systematic – something which critics of qualitative methods often overlook. In their analysis, the researchers had to examine their interview accounts in depth so as to precisely identify and then describe in detail the characteristics of different forms of relationship.

Observation

Observation as a method can be carried out in various ways (see Figure 4.4 below), depending upon the research design employed. As we already saw, observation can, for example, be adapted to include theoretical positions useful in social work, such as a psychoanalytic focus (as in Hingley-Jones, 2009 – Project K). Participant observation as used by anthropological or

> ➤ Complete participant (covert observation over a period of time)
>
> ➤ Participant as observer (overt observation over a period of time)
>
> ➤ Observer as participant (e.g. single interview visit)
>
> ➤ Complete observer (e.g. in laboratory research)

Figure 4.4 Types of observational research

sociological researchers aims to be a naturalistic form of enquiry in which researchers observe behaviour, and may also note dialogue; formal interviews may also be conducted as part of this observational work (especially during **ethnography**). Observations of this type are usually recorded in the form of researcher's field notes; these record, first of all, what is done by people (sometimes called 'process recording') as well as what people say they are doing (often gleaned from interviews). It is important that the ethnographic researcher, for whom participant observation is a key method (as we already saw), also records reflexively her/his own ideas, thoughts and reactions (including emotional reactions) to what is observed. S/he will then check these with informants (if the observation is overt).

We can see from this chart how different forms of observation compare. So, for example, the scientist in a laboratory will be observing, but is completely detached and (following the 'scientific method') and will aim to be as objective as possible. The interviewer who visits the interviewee, perhaps only once, is also an observer and may indeed record her/his impressions surrounding the interview as part of their data.

On the other hand, a researcher who aims to be a 'complete participant' would participate covertly (secretly) in the social setting(s) under investigation. This immediately raises ethical issues. Although in some disciplines, covert research may still be permissible (e.g. in the investigation of criminal activity (see Noaks and Wincup, 2004, p. 66)), most health or social care/work researchers would have a hard time getting formal ethics approval to carry out covert research. Worse still, they would probably feel this kind of observation goes against their professional principles in most cases. However, they would also surely recognise professional settings in which they might need to obtain information without letting service users know what they are doing.

'Overt' participant observation is not easy either. In order to be free to move about in the settings they are observing, to ask questions or set up interviews when necessary and write field notes, most ethnographers find that they feel as if they are moving in and out of overt and covert work. Research participants, once they have got used to what you are doing, will very often 'forget' that you are a researcher, and you may need to remind them. This is especially true when you are living or working in a specific setting for several months or even years. Meyer (1993) describes vividly how her participant observation as a nurse on a hospital ward required her to become 'everyone's friend' in order to meet the research demands. She also describes how changes of ward staff brought opposition to her research from some who had not been there when she started.

In most qualitative studies, including ethnography, the researcher still controls what happens and holds most of the power. Even when, as in feminist approaches to research, genuine attempts may be made to involve participants in research processes and to be as open as possible with them, there may still be difficulties, and this can be emotionally draining for the researcher, despite also being exciting and interesting (see e.g. Bell, 1995; 2014). Some ethnographers worry about how they will be able to adequately represent the views of their participants. When, as in Meyer's case, the research is applied to specific problems and there are political and managerial elements to the project, this makes the situation even more challenging, albeit rewarding. Even where carrying out very short-term observations, for example in a project I conducted in a prison hospital (see Foster, Bell and Serasinghe, 2013), there can be many political, ethical and managerial issues to consider; so in this example we made sure that in order to allow some staff to choose not to be observed, observation days were timed to fit in with their days off.

Some researchers will also choose to use a particular underpinning philosophy or other approach to carrying out observational work, as for example in Project K, described earlier, where Hingley-Jones used an adapted version of psychoanalytically informed observation to make observations of young people with disabilities and their families.

As anyone who has carried out participant observation will tell you, the data you manage to collect is likely to be varied and voluminous. Obviously the longer you stay in the field, the more of it there will be! Wincup (2000), whose work we considered as Project F (above), describes how after several months fieldwork she had accumulated field notes, interview transcripts, analytic memos and a variety of documents. This table below (Figure 4.5) suggests some relevant observational methods of data collection.

All these forms of data need to be organised in ways that make sense to you as the researcher. Data needs to be organised as you go along; the observational researcher's own field diary is often the pivot around which the rest collects, as this will usually be in the form of a longitudinal, time-organised narrative. You may find that you are analysing data as soon as it arrives! For more on observational data recording and analysis, see Chapter 5.

> ➤ Writing own field notes: recording what people do, what they say, and what they say they do [interviews*] in this social setting
>
> ➤ Interviewing: individual and/or focus group
>
> ➤ Use of checklists or other 'quantitative' recording methods
>
> ➤ Use of existing documents, records, publications from the social setting (see Chapter 5)
>
> ➤ Getting others to produce 'documents' specifically for the research, e.g. diaries (Bell, 2012) (See Chapter 5)
>
> ➤ Visual records, e.g. digital recording, video (See Chapter 8)
>
> ➤ Use of social media (See Chapter 9)

Figure 4.5 Methods of data collection in observational work

Focus groups

Although **focus groups** are a popular method of data generation in their own right, they are often used in conjunction with other methods, such as individual interviews (which they may precede in order to raise topics for interviews). Focus groups are essentially semi-structured interviews with small groups of people. The researcher or another designated person normally acts a facilitator, putting forward various pre-arranged questions or topics for the group to consider around a central theme. As Bowling (1997) says:

> [Focus groups] have the advantage of making use of group dynamics to stimulate discussion, gain insights and generate ideas in order to pursue a topic in greater depth. (p. 352)

Focus groups can be used to show how people think and are useful where cultural values or beliefs about health, disease or social support are being explored. For practical reasons, most focus groups are set up to contain between 6 and 12 people, which is enough to generate discussion without being too large.

Like other forms of interviewing, the focus group sample is key: selecting 'the right people' is important, and researchers will usually need to work on a purposive principle, selecting people who will bring intended perspectives to the discussion. How this is done will also depend on how many focus groups are to be held; if a series of groups is planned, it may be possible to include different kinds of interviewees in separate focus groups, e.g. in the context of drugs research, one or more groups may be held with professionals, and another series of groups with drug users. Otherwise, it may be part of your research to see how people at different levels in an organisation interact with each other, which would suggest mixed groups, e.g. of social work managers and frontline social work staff/ workforce.

Focus groups typically last between one and two hours; they are usu-ally audio-recorded, but may sometimes be videoed. I have found that it is often useful to draw a simple diagram (Figure 4.6) indicating participants by category and number (but not names) and to keep a note of the order of speakers as the group and the recording progress. This information can be collated with the recording later on. This approach can also be use-ful when undertaking observations with groups. For example, Figure 4.6 shows a diagram of a focus group discussion with three managers (M) and six social workers (S), plus notes:

```
          S1   M3   S2   S3   S4
     M2                       S5
   M1                           S6
```

Notes	Date of focus group
Researcher asks question 1	
M3 begins conversation with comment ...	
S5 responds ...	
S6 supports S5's comment ...	

Figure 4.6 Focus group diagram

Focus group research – recent social work examples:

➤ Macpherson, H, Hart, A, and Heaver, B (2016). For more on this proj-ect, see Project V, Chapter 8.

➤ Rabiee, P, Baxter, K, and Glendinning, C (2016) Supporting choice: Support planning, older people and managed personal budgets, *Journal of Social Work*

Vignettes

These may be defined as 'simulations of real events: a small illustration' (Wilson and While, 1998, p. 79). Vignettes are a less well known but very useful device, in both health and social work research (Wilks, 2004), usually presented to interviewees during a semi-structured or structured interview situation. As Wilson and While point out, in order that the illustration is realistic, researchers often draw upon their own or others' relevant experience in drawing them up. They then pilot them, e.g. with colleagues from the same occupational/professional background as those who will be interviewed, to check on their 'realism'. Each vignette is necessarily brief, but will typically describe a scenario or case, e.g. involving a patient/service user and/or professional colleagues. In Wilson and While's study, professionals interviewed were asked to identify what their own role and those of other professionals would be in each of a series of vignettes.

Although subject to some criticism (for example, that they may not be as effective as observational methods), vignettes can provide a useful way of asking people to explain what they would expect to do in specific situations, and also of getting them to think about what they do.

See also Ribbens-McCarthy, Edwards and Gillies (2000; 2003) for the use of vignettes in a study about families.

Chapter summary

> This chapter highlights the importance of relationships in both research and social work.

> We considered how to make the best use of various qualitative research methods that involve directly communicating with others in various contexts, including colleagues, users of services and different professionals.

> Using project examples, we examined a variety of underlying approaches (methodologies) in qualitative social work research: grounded theory, ethnography, feminist approaches, phenomenology, case study and 'practice-near' research.

> We identified and discussed the use of key qualitative methods (techniques): interviews, observation, focus groups and vignettes/scenarios.

Further reading

Bryman, A (2012) *Social Research Methods*, 4th edn, Oxford: Oxford University Press, chs 2, 17–21

Denzin, N and Lincoln, Y (2000) *Handbook of Qualitative Research*, 2nd edn (or later), Thousand Oaks: Sage

Elliott, J (2005) *Using Narrative in Social Research: Qualitative and Quantitative Approaches*, Thousand Oaks: Sage

McKeganey, N (1995) Quantitative and qualitative research in the addictions: An unhelpful divide, *Addiction*, 90: 749–751

Oliver, C (2012) Critical realist grounded theory: A new approach for social work research, *British Journal of Social Work*, 42 (2): 371–387

Smith, R (2009) *Doing Social Work Research*, Maidenhead: Open University Press

Wilcke, M (2002) *Hermeneutic Phenomenology as a Research Method in Social Work. Currents: New Scholarship in the Human Services*, Calgary: University of Calgary Press

Yin, R (2014) *Case Study Research: Design and Methods*, 5th edn, Thousand Oaks: Sage

5

WORKING WITH DOCUMENTARY SOURCES AND ANALYSING QUALITATIVE DATA IN SOCIAL WORK RESEARCH

Introduction

In this chapter we will first consider how to use different kinds of documents in social work or health research, and this will be followed by advice and discussion about analysis of qualitative research data.

Using documents

Many researchers, including those doing research relating to social work, and especially those carrying out ethnography or developing case studies, find they need to make use of different kinds of records or documents as part of their research project, as we have already seen in the previous chapter (see Ferguson, 2016). These documents will vary, from published or printed material produced by an organisation, to client/service user records or diaries which may be 'solicited' from research participants (see Bell, 2012) including either service users or professionals (see Weinberg et al., 2003). We can also include visual material, such as photographs (see Chapter 8) or existing statistical materials (see also Chapter 6). If you are thinking of using these kinds of documents to generate research data as part of your research design and methods, you need to consider the following questions (Figure 5.1).

So, the first issue is whether using documents is appropriate for your project? In returning to Project J, the example we introduced in Chapter 4, the researchers explain why this method was essential for their research.

> ➤ Can documents tell me what I want to know? [*evidence*]
>
> ➤ Do appropriate documents exist and how can I access them? [*evidence/access/ethics*]
>
> ➤ How should I decide which ones to use? [*sampling/ethics*]
>
> ➤ Which or whose perspectives do they represent? [*evidence/provenance*]
>
> ➤ Why were they prepared, and what were they (originally) used for? [*evidence/provenance/ethics*]
>
> ➤ Can I generate appropriate data from these documents? [*evidence/ethics*]
>
> ➤ More generally, what counts as 'data' in documents? [*evidence*]
>
> ➤ (Adapted from Mason, 1996, ch 4, pp. 74–77)

Figure 5.1 Using documents

Project J (Gribble and Gallagher, 2014)

This study relating to child protection authorities and breastfeeding used mainly documentary sources, and the two cases were chosen:

> because they illustrate salient points with regard to the *treatment of breastfeeding children in child protection assessments and interventions*. In addition, *extensive documentation was available* in these cases to assist in providing an accurate account. The cases presented here include information and quotations from court documents that were released to the families when the cases were dismissed and made available to the authors by the families involved. Maintenance of anonymity allows direct quotes from these reports and other court documents'. (Gribble and Gallagher, 2014, pp. 439–440) (my emphasis)

Returning to our initial questions (Fig 5.1), we can see that having decided to use documents, key overlapping methodological issues will concern what I have identified as how they can used to provide research knowledge or evidence, issues of sampling, access, provenance and ethics, as noted above. It is self-evident that if documents do not exist, or are inaccessible, research will have to be designed that uses other methods. For example, if an organisation produces minutes of meetings, these could be very valuable in understanding how the organisation or event operates (e.g. case conferences in mental health work). If you are unable to access these minutes despite negotiating to do so, it may be that you could ask about events taking place at meetings during interviews with those who have attended. However, you are sure to get only a partial view of what happened, from the perspective of your interviewee, and even then the person may not be able to disclose any confidential material; s/he may also simply not remember events or leave things out of their account. However, even if you did get to see the actual minutes, they would of course only be an official record of proceedings, i.e. what the organisation wanted to have recorded. Some more interesting details may therefore not have been included.

If you want to use records relating to individual clients/patients/service users, remember that these will almost certainly be confidential, and individuals may also have to give consent for them to be used for research purposes. You should not imagine that you can use confidential records for research just because you are employed as a social work or health professional; this is so even if your research would not actually involve seeing people face-to-face. In Project J, there were specific circumstances that allowed the researchers to access documents they needed. Advice to any researcher in these circumstances (whether or not you are employed as a professional practitioner) is to find out from whom you need to get permission to use such records; approval from an ethics committee will almost certainly also be needed.

Assuming you are able to gain access to appropriate records, it is important to establish next what exactly the records contain and whether or not the records are maintained consistently. For example, supposing gender is a key aspect of your study but, when you inspect them, few records you are interested in actually record any information about gender. As in the previous example of meetings, it may be that you can supplement this documentary method in other ways in order to get the information you want, or else you may have to modify your research plans.

Other existing documents you come across may include official or unofficial printed and/or published documents emanating from organisations or agencies of various kinds. 'Provenance' or origin of these documents is thus an important part of the data related to them. (As we will discuss in Chapter 9, many 'documents' are now also produced online, on the Internet, for example as part of social media). However, certainly in historical terms (even in recent history), you may also need to look for printed (hard copy) material. (See sources mentioned (including archival material[1]) in Chapter 2, pp. 17–18.)

In a project focused around an organisational **case study**, you may try to obtain as much of this printed material as you can relating to this organisation, to give you an idea of the organisation's policies etc.. In other examples, you may want a spread of documents across various organisations, so as to compare their approaches, e.g. training manuals produced by hospital trusts which I and my colleagues collected as part of the *Communicate* project (Project R) that we will introduce in Chapter 7.

The key issue for this type of material therefore really concerns the sample. Whilst with diaries or **questionnaire** responses, as we will see later on, responses received may already be clearly delineated as a research sample, when sampling any kinds of document from a wider range you will need to make choices about what to include or reject when they are being scrutinised, and so it is important to have clear selection criteria to start with, which will relate to your research questions. For service user or patient files, you would most usually sample by date (from/to) and perhaps also by type (e.g. by medical condition/clinic attended etc.) but also perhaps by team or practitioner files (e.g. all clients of an older people's team from years 19XX to 20XX).

Recording data from records

In order to use records, once you have decided on appropriate sampling criteria, for example from service user or patient files, you will need to have a consistent and rigorous means of recording data they contain. This is really the first stage in analysis, where we break down our data and reassemble it in forms that can allow us to search for meaning through our interpretation(s). One way to record consistently is to use some form of spreadsheet, with columns dedicated to particular aspects of the record (which we would identify as key 'variables') if the material lends itself to this approach. This allows you to work through a series of records (one per row) or perhaps draw out individual data row by row from a collective record (such as attendance records, as in the example below), and this method is equally useful for recording qualitative (text) or numerical (quantitative) data. However, we should be aware when doing this that our view of these records is already tending to view what we are recording as factual or fixed. (Mason, 1996; 2002 for example, asks us to decide whether our data consists of fixed variables, or is more flexible.) A different way of recording data from records such as minutes of meetings or other more narrative forms of records would be to focus on discourses embedded in the material (see below, 'Discourse analysis') and to identify these themes as you work through and analyse material. However, this approach is better suited to records that have a more narrative structure, e.g. minutes of meetings, or documents relating to serious case reviews, especially where we can identify relevant aspects of the wider context.

We need to be able to start somewhere, in a practical sense, when faced with documentary material of any kind. For example see the chart below (Figure 5.2) relating to records of a pre-school parenting group with individual members whose attendance we recorded, with some family details. The records themselves would have been kept as week-by-week lists of dates and names that we needed to work through.

Note from what we collated in this chart (Figure 5.2) that some data was missing from the original records and so they were not entirely consistent. This issue is sometimes even more problematic in service user or patient records where (different) practitioners may not always record information

Service user record number	Gender	Total number of children individual has	Children currently living with parent	Current attendance at parents' group	Began attendance at group	Number of children attending group with parent	Age(s) of children attending	Date of recording
1	F	3	1	Yes	Sept 2014	1	3 years	23.11.15
2	F	*Not known*	2	Yes	Sept 2014	1 (same?)	2 years/ 6 months	23.11.15
3	M	*Not known*	1	*Not recorded*	Sept 2014	1	3 years	23.11.15

Figure 5.2 Collating data from parenting group records – London borough of X

in a consistent way. In the above example, it is important to give each individual a number rather than a name, for confidentiality reasons (although we could have used pseudonyms). Similarly, we could have decided to record children's ages but not birthdates so they will be less identifiable. For parent 2, there seems to be two children but (presumably) we found only one child attended any single group meeting. We would need to record that detail somehow.

With hindsight, we may feel that we have missed some important data – for example do we also want to know whether the individual attends 'regularly'? What do we understand by the term 'regularly'? Do we want to record all the actual dates of attendance? (But since the purpose of our chart is to summarise what is in the records, we may also decide that this would retain too much detail.) Layout of this chart allows us to select attendance records from a specific date onwards (in this case it is from September 2014), so we have presented the first three attenders we came across in the attendance records; working through all these records to the present time (November 2015) allows us to record whether the person attends currently or not. Looking at individual 3 (a male parent), we can see he no longer appears in the current attendance register, but we may want to record when he stopped attending (as a separate variable column). If parents are also attending because they have been referred by a practitioner, this might also be a useful piece of data to record, especially if some are referred but others were voluntary attenders – so we would record data in another column for 'referred or not'.

When trying to make sense of all this data in our project, we would also need to provide more information about the group itself, who runs it etc., which will help to set everything in context and ensure the **trustworthiness** of our data. This would be particularly important in a case study or piece of ethnographic research, of which this research might be a part.

Obtaining documentary data from observational methods

This brings us back to thinking about approaches involving **observation**. In Chapter 4 we discussed both the approach of **ethnography** (often involving **mixed methods**, including documentary analysis) and specific methods involved in observation, including writing field notes, using records or other documents or production of diaries by participants (what I have called elsewhere 'solicited diaries' (Bell, 2012)).

So, for example, you may find whilst doing ethnographic work you are keeping a file for each participant which can contain both interview transcripts and copies of other field notes relating to that person; a separate file for minutes of meetings you may be attending plus any other documents about the organisation holding these meetings; and a separate chronological file containing the 'master' version of your field diary. The diary itself may also contain analytical notes, diagrams, photographs etc.. In a very real sense, the observational researcher may find s/he is analysing the data almost as it arrives, and so it will often take a while to discern the analytic 'themes' around which the data can be explained in a way that we consider is **trustworthy**.

The issue of representation is a key one in participant observation, since as a social work researcher you must continually ask yourself whose representation of the data you are presenting. When we were initially considering the interpretive paradigm, we noted that participant observers should not be under any illusions that they are simply presenting the views or words of their informants/participants 'as they really are'. Inevitably, these are filtered through the lens of the participant observer when they become written up as ethnographic 'data' (see also chapters by Birch and by Standing in Ribbens and Edwards, 1998). This issue of representation may be particularly important for social work researchers who could be used to exercising power in the lives of their clients (see Hafford-Letchfield, 2015); issues of **reflexivity** are also important here (see Cartney, 2015).

Researcher and participant diaries

In some cases you may decide to 'generate your own' documents as part of research, and one well-used method is to use diaries. We already discussed how the ethnographer will usually produce a field diary of her/his own, but you may also decide to ask informants to keep diaries for you. This may be attempted as a fairly straightforward way of 'observing' individuals' private activities or thoughts about particular issues.

Many diaries produced for research purposes have a time or activity focus which will to a large extent then determine how material they contain can be analysed. For example, Weinberg et al. (2003) did a study involving care managers working in UK local authorities, who were asked to keep diaries that included itemising 34 job related activities. With a 57% response rate, results showed, for example, that participants spent 64% of their time on direct or indirect service user and carer activities, compared to 32% of their time on administrative tasks. As I have pointed out elsewhere (Bell, 2012):

> It is clear that a written, time-focused account of everyday experiences and activities can provide expression for observation, recording and comment by the writer/ informant, and that this inevitably dovetails with unobtrusive observation by the researcher when the diary comes to be analysed. (p. 84)

Elliott (1997) also suggests that:

> The qualities in diaries which have been feted hitherto in the literature on health service research are the potential to record events, over time, as close as possible to when they occur.

Some researchers may be more interested in exploring their participants' personal or emotional responses to events. Remember, however, that in some cases keeping a diary that may require that participants 'open up' very personal aspects of their lives to the researcher needs careful handling. This may be particularly problematic if as a social work researcher you are asking service users to keep diaries. However, it may be that the researcher feels this method of diary-keeping is being used so as to benefit participants specifically by allowing them to put across their views in detail. Nevertheless, ethical dilemmas this situation poses should not be ignored. I have cautioned elsewhere against expecting those producing 'solicited' diaries to produce the kinds of revelations the researcher her/himself would not be willing to share (Bell, 2012).

Exercise 5.1 **Field diary**

Try keeping a field diary for one day. This should be based around your home/work, but should have a focus on your employment if you are employed or on your usual daily activities. Record your activities and observations, who you are in contact with and why (though you shouldn't put in 'real names') and any comments you can make about your day. Think about how to record time. Try to be reflexive: imagine that you will have to explain this day to someone else, so try to interpret what is happening. Think carefully about how much emotional content you wish to put in (although you will not need to show this diary to anyone else). However, it is important to stress that, as social workers, you should be learning how to work with feelings and emotions and that this exercise can be an opportunity for you to link this aspect of practice with research activities.

For reflection, see Appendix C, Exercises.

For more on these and other issues about diaries in family and health contexts specifically, you may want to look at:

> Bell, L (1998) Public and private meanings in diaries: Researching family and child care IN Ribbens, J and Edwards, R (eds) (1998) *Feminist Dilemmas in Qualitative Research: Public Knowledge and Private Lives*, London: Sage

> Goodwin, J (ed) (2012) *Sage Biographical Research*, London: Sage.

> Elliott, H (1997) The Use of Diaries in Sociological Research on Health Experience, *Sociological Research Online*, 2 (2), http://www.socresonline. org.uk/2/2/7.html

For an example of a study where the researcher used a combination of participant observation, documents and interviews, see also:

> Valverde, M and White-Mair, K (1999) 'One day at a time' and other slogans for everyday life: The ethical practices of Alcoholics Anonymous, *Sociology*, 33 (2): 393–410

Preparing to analyse your material – some practical issues

Interview or focus group accounts

In preparing to analyse interview or focus group accounts, you need to consider how complete an account you need, and time factors involved in preparing this account. In order to work with the tape or digitally

	Advantages	Disadvantages
Verbatim (full) transcription	Retains all data – you can develop analysis in new directions later. Makes you familiar with data – analysis really starts with transcription.	Laborious and time consuming.
Selective transcription	Saves time.	You will lose data. Without experience, difficult to know what to select; selection may waste time.

Figure 5.3 Transcription types

recorded account, you need to write it/type it up (transcribe it) so as to be able to analyse material in depth. You need to choose between complete (verbatim) and selective transcription. What are the advantages and disadvantages of each approach (Figure 5.3)?

You may decide to transcribe fully the first few **interviews** in a sequence, to get a feel for the data and how the interview accounts are organised. You will probably be surprised when listening again to interview tapes how much you have forgotten from the interview you carried out. Perhaps you were thinking ahead to the next question, and did not really hear what the interviewee was saying for some of the time. This is another reason for recording interviews wherever possible.

Generally, researchers will transcribe text clearly showing the interviewer's questions and interviewee's responses. Do not be tempted to write down only the interviewee's responses, or the account will not make sense! As you listen to the recording you might also want to make brief notes for your own analysis, although this is not necessary at this stage. Whatever you do, listen carefully. This is also where analysis starts.

When you have typed the transcript, it is conventional to add line numbering to the document, which will assist analysis. You can do this in MS Word by setting 'Add line numbers' on the Page Setup (File) menu.

Finally, if printing out your transcript, do so with wide page margins (use Page Setup again) ready for analysis. If you do not want to fully transcribe a taped interview, you should, however, listen to it carefully and make notes of key points.

For **focus groups**, there are particular issues involved in producing and analysing transcripts, for example trying to work out who is saying what (this is where using a diagram and notes, as shown in Figure 4.6, may help). You will need to transcribe using the convention of a separate identifier for each speaker (Figure 4.6).

Finally, a word about getting someone else to transcribe your material for you – in my own experience, this is fine if the transcriber is experienced with this kind of work. If you have funding for your project, you will be able to pay at professional rates and you should cost this work into your project. You may be able to reduce costs with some professionals by allowing them to take longer to do work for you if they have a sliding scale of charges. Remember, however, to keep the recordings you made until you have been able to check transcripts against the originals, especially if your interviewees are using technical language with which the transcriber may not be familiar.

Diaries

These will often have been written up in a form which emphasises the time aspects of the material. You may find it helpful, especially if you have a large amount of material, to summarise dates and perhaps the events covered by the diary or **field notes** in an initial typed sheet. If several participant diaries have been collected, you will also need to summarise some comparative relevant details about individual respondents, e.g. their genders, occupations etc.. Most researchers will regularly type up their own handwritten field notes following episodes of participant observation, using this transcription time to reflect on the material and make additional notes. Or you may record your field notes directly onto a computer or electronic tablet. It may be some time after field notes have been written up, however, that specific themes tend to emerge. Some researchers will keep an audio-recorded version of their own field diary, which they will listen to again at a later stage instead of typing up this material immediately. This is often useful in raising issues about progress of the research; it may indicate, for example, where there are still difficult areas to investigate based on problems initially raised earlier on. The researchers may have pushed these to one side and forgotten them temporarily; reminding yourself of earlier thoughts on difficult issues is uncomfortable but instructive.

Material from participant diaries can also be transcribed, and if several diaries have been collected this may be done selectively, as indicated earlier.

Dealing with 'qualitative' comments produced by respondents on questionnaires

Some open-ended questions on questionnaires produce a fair amount of qualitative data which can be drawn upon to provide useful research data. Because this material is not 'closed' and therefore not pre-coded for quantitative analysis, there is sometimes a tendency for researchers to ignore these findings whilst they concentrate on analysing their quantitative results, as they feel unable to deal effectively with this type of material. Or they may just mention one or two interesting quotes in their research report. However, it is important to try and be more systematic than this when dealing with this type of material. Usually, not all survey respondents will have completed a response, so a first step is to collect together all the questionnaires which do contain a qualitative response to the specific question. One manageable way to extract material is to type up all quotes from this question into a single (Word) document, labelling each with the key or reference number of that questionnaire. This ensures that you will be able to identify and attribute quotes to specific groups of people, e.g. comment by a female social worker, comment by a user of drug rehabilitation service. Data can then be coded and analysed (a process sometimes called 'post-coding', i.e. producing codes *after* the questionnaire is completed by respondents); a good way to do this is often by using content analysis (see below).

Analysing text taken from documents

Making use of existing documents may involve you examining them in depth to explore what perspectives (**discourse(s)**) they contain, or else you may wish to follow a more 'quantified' perspective and code/index them directly in terms of content. These are important choices involved in analysing your text-based documentary data, and so it is worth distinguishing these approaches before giving you some more general guidance on analysing and interpreting other kinds of qualitative data, including interview accounts that we discussed in Chapter 4.

   Discourse analysis is a varied approach that is particularly suited to analysis of documents or publications, although it can also be used in other types of qualitative study, e.g. those based on interviews (see e.g. Ney, Stoltz and Maloney, 2013) or visual images (see Rose, 2007). Some social work researchers have, for example, made use of Derrida's work on deconstruction, or Foucault's 'discursive' methods, including his archaeo-logical approach (e.g. Skehill, Satka and Hoikkala, 2013; Garrity, 2010). As Bryman (2012, ch 22) points out, with discourse analysis there is a focus on language and the ways in which it is used, to the extent that the discourse itself becomes the topic of study. These discourse(s) are seen as ways of constructing particular view(s) of social reality; it is not just a mat-ter of seeking to uncover what interviewees think about a topic or what documents present at 'face value'. Discourse is therefore seen as a form of action that is concerned with 'establishing one version of the world in the face of competing versions' (Gill, 2000, p. 76). In this respect, discourse analysis may be seen as associated with development of some form of narrative.

See Potter, J (2004) Discourse analysis IN Hardy, M and Bryman, A (eds) *Handbook of Data Analysis*, London: Sage.

For a methodological examination of Foucauldian discourse analysis in social work research, see Garrity (2010).

Project M – Discourse analysis

(Park (2008) Making Refugees: A Historical Discourse Analysis of the Construction of the 'Refugee' in US Social Work, 1900–1957)

The author explains that although 'no discrete sampling of materials can be proffered as the definitive representation of a discourse, as a whole, these influential publications offer a comparatively balanced glimpse into the views of the emergent profession and discipline of social work' (p. 774).

In selecting relevant articles, Park examined:

> All articles containing the terms 'refugees', 'displaced persons', 'immi-grants', 'foreign-born' or 'alien' populations, or any nationality marker (e.g. 'Armenian', 'Jugoslav', 'German') … In this earlier period, social work discourse was far more inter-disciplinary than that of the profession today, engaging not only social workers, but a larger public as active participants in its professional publications and meetings. (p. 774)

The author then employed deconstructive textual analysis methods derived from the work of Jacques Derrida as a reliable (trustworthy) way to analyse the chosen material.

Content analysis is a well-known set of methods for analysing docu-ments that takes a much more positivistic approach than discourse analy-sis because it involves coding/indexing and quantifying the content of document(s) *unit by unit* (i.e. usually word by word) in terms of categories that you have identified. In some forms of content analysis, these categories will be pre-determined, and in that case you would work through documents in relation to those pre-determined categories.

In other forms of content analysis, you may seek to build up a set of categories starting with one document and progressing through all documents in your sample, adding or combining codes until you reach a list that you consider represents a final analysis of your material. (This is reminiscent of some forms of analysis that also involve coding, e.g. grounded theory approaches, see below.) However, the intention with all these forms of content analysis is usually to remain at the level of factual understanding of your material rather than seeing it as a constructive and constitutive process, as in the case of discourse or narrative understanding. For these reasons, content analysis may be particularly suitable for analysing short pieces of text, items from newspapers or qualitative answers to open questions on questionnaires where the overall (narrative) context is less important than it would be in interviews or focus group material.

Project N – Content analysis in social work research
(Heron, G, McGoldrick, R and Wilson, R (2015) *Exploring the Influence of Feedback on Student Social Workers' Understanding of Childcare and Protection*)

The aims of this study (carried out in Scotland) were to examine: '(1) the written summative feedback students receive in relation to childcare and protection for two major practice-based assignments known as Practice Study 1 (PS1) and Practice Study 2 (PS2); (2) student perceptions of feedback about childcare and protection during the course and its usefulness for learning and practice' (p. 2320).

In addition to interviewing 21 final year(s) undergraduate students about their perceptions of feedback received from tutors, the researchers carried out a content analysis of their written tutor feedback. This analysis was done using a framework involving: 'Nicol's (2008) principles of feedback with the PS1 and PS2 ... [also] Heron (2011) separates the most relevant principles into first- and second-order principles. The first- and second-order principles are useful because their presence in written feedback gives an indication of its quality and provides a means of labelling the different instructions given to students so that any patterns and trends can be identified across a student cohort. Making the principles explicit in the learning process also provides students with a framework to help evaluate their own feedback' (p. 2320).

First-order principles of feedback are listed as:

➢ clarification: information on what good performance is (goals, criteria, standards)

➢ challenging tasks: instruction that directs students to undertake a relevant task

➢ close the gap: direction that helps students move from current to desired performance.

The second-order principles of feedback are:

➢ self-correct: information that helps students work an issue out for themselves

➢ encourage interaction: meet and have dialogue around learning with others (peers, academics)

➢ development of self-assessment and reflection in learning: direction that encourages students to think about their self and own actions

➢ encourage motivation: positive instruction that increases self-belief and self-esteem.

Thirty students agreed to their feedback being used in the study, and the content analysis used 50 feedback sheets (25 for PS1 and 25 for PS2). The researchers counted how many feedback comments related to the different principles, illustrating the 'positivistic' basis of content analysis generally, e.g.:

> Of the twenty-five students (fifty feedback sheets), twenty-two received feedback in relation to childcare and protection (fourteen students received feedback in PS1 and ten students received feedback in PS2). Only two students received feedback in both PS1 and PS2, and three students got no feedback about childcare and protection for either assignment. (p. 2323)

However, interviewing students then allowed these kinds of results to be set in a wider, more 'qualitative' context.

Selecting, organising and analysing qualitative data: Interviews and focus group material

Once you have prepared your qualitative data for analysis in a practical sense, you will need to ask yourself a number of key questions about the ways in which you can realistically categorise and analyse your material;

these will relate firstly to how you have set up your project. Your overall methodological approach will have affected the kinds of data generated, but also influenced how you view those data, as noted above in examples relating to research with documents.

To extend these kinds of approaches to interview and focus group material, and to recap:

Discussion Points

Are you interested in discourse or narrative as a focus for your analysis of interview/focus group material?

Are you trying to 'code' your data in a more 'fixed' way in order to analyse it?

Is it possible to use elements of both these approaches?

The overall intentions of your project will therefore also affect the kind of analysis you can justify (see e.g. Flick, 2014) and consider 'reliable' (trustworthy). The time you are able to spend on analysis will certainly be a factor. If you are doing an evaluative project within a very tight timescale, you may not have as much time to devote to analysis as you would like; you will certainly not have as much time as you would if you were undertaking a PhD. But even PhD students nowadays have to recognise time constraints in the research process. This is not a bad thing, as long as you recognise the need to be systematic rather than careless. Once you have transcribed your interview material, you should work through it again systematically, and by now it should be getting very familiar. This familiarity itself is an aid to selecting and organising material as well in its interpretation. There are different ways of doing this.

Grounded theory – constant comparative analysis

Processes involved in the analysis of interview or focus group transcripts using constant comparative analysis derived from grounded theory can be as suggested in Figure 5.4.

Project O – Supporting older peoples' strategies and ways of coping

In this research, Tanner (2007) focused on 12 research participants aged between 70 and 92 (seven women and five men) who were repeatedly interviewed over a four-year period. The researcher also used methods

➤ Begin analysis whilst interviews are continuing

➤ Get overview of each transcript – theoretical sensitivity

➤ Open coding (line by line analysis)

➤ Theoretical notes – 'thoughts behind the coding'

➤ Axial coding (grouping codes into categories)

➤ Analytical memos – the researcher's descriptions of her/his continuing efforts to interpret data

➤ Theoretical framework – summary diagram (at theoretical saturation)

➤ Core category/ies (unifying concept(s)) established

➤ Grounded theory

Figure 5.4 Constant comparative analysis – process

such as a network diagram and diaries with her participants. All were of White UK ethnic origin, they had varied socio-economic statuses and 11 out of the 12 lived alone.

Grounded theory was employed in this study as a form of analysis, also combined with narrative[2] analysis:

> with the identification of themes, categories, sub-categories and a core theme to which all of the themes and categories were related. The interview transcripts and diary entries were also read and analysed as whole narratives across the period of the study to allow more scope. (Tanner, 2007, p. 10)

This analysis enabled the researcher(s) to identify three themes : 'keeping going', 'staying me' and 'the slippery slope', which were interpreted in relation to other research and theoretical models of ageing and identity management.

In addition to grounded theory approach(es), there can be several ways to initially 'read' your qualitative material (such as transcripts); Mason suggests a framework of 'multiple readings' (Figure 5.5).

This cross-sectional indexing can be applied to individual interviews, but, as Mason points out, the logic of this process is that 'you devise the same set of indexing categories for use, cross-sectionally, across the whole of your dataset' (p. 128), i.e. across all of your interviews.

However, Mason also suggests you may also want to organise your data in non-cross-sectional (narrative[3]) ways; essentially this is in order to maintain a more complete and less reductionist form of indexing interview accounts. In fact, there is often a basic tension between a) wanting to understand your interviewees as individual people (thus

'LITERAL' READING: index topics of substance in the text (content analysis; variables); you could also examine 'literal' progress and style of the interview, e.g. sequence of talk in the transcript

'INTERPRETIVE' READING: 'a version of what you think the data mean or represent, or what you think you can infer from them', e.g. rules or norms expressed in the text; mismatch between perceived 'rules' and what people do/think

'REFLEXIVE' READING: 'locate you as part of the data you have generated, and will seek to explore your role in the process of generation and interpretation of data'

(adapted from Mason, 1996, p. 109)

Figure 5.5 Reading qualitative data from interviews and texts

maintaining the integrity of their individual interview accounts) and b) pulling out themes which go cross-sectionally across all of your data.

Mason suggests you may want to organise data in non-cross-sectional ways, either as a main method or in parallel with cross-sectional indexing, in order to, for example:

➢ gain a sense of the distinctiveness of different parts of your dataset, e.g. of individual experiences

➢ explore the complexity of your data, when it is not amenable to simplified categorical indexing

➢ organise your data around more idiosyncratic themes which do not appear across the whole dataset.

A 'voice-centred relational method'

There are different ways in which you can try to maintain a more holistic way of organising your interview data. For example, Mauthner and Doucet (1998) have developed a 'voice-centred relational method' (developed from the work of psychologist Carol Gilligan) as an approach to interview analysis. The overall aim of this approach is to explore the different 'voices' present in an interview text. It tries to make visible the construction of voices by the interviewer and interviewee in that transcript.

This method relies on using a series of readings of each transcript, which are:

➢ reading for the plot and our responses to the narrative

➢ reading for how the person speaks about her/himself (voice of the 'I')

➤ reading for relationships

➤ reading which places people within cultural contexts and social structures.

These multiple readings allow a close exploration of each transcript from different angles and attempts to maintain the integrity of each one, before breaking up into cross-sectional coding across different transcripts becomes necessary. In theory, coding themes across different interviews should then be closer to these different voices, as these themes:

> emerge(d) as a direct result of intensive ... work and ... (are) a way of linking ... individual respondents with the stories told by datasets as wholes. (Mauthner and Doucet, 1998, p. 135)

In practice, I have found this approach is flexible enough to allow different types of 'voice' to be emphasised in different ways in subsequent analysis, according to the overall aims of your research project. For example, 'reading for relationships' could emphasise family or personal relationships in a study around children and their families; or relationships between colleagues, service agencies or clients/service users and professionals in a study of multi-agency working. Although in theory the transcripts should be read through four times, sometimes fewer readings will still allow different voices to emerge.

As Mauthner and Doucet (1998) point out:

> If we do not take the time and trouble to listen to our respondents, data analysis risks simply confirming what we already know. (pp. 134–135)

Returning to our Project D, we can see how this method of reading and analysis was used in practice.

Project D

We used Mauthner and Doucet's approach in Project D to explore the voices of ten birth mothers who have had children successively removed from their care. It was particularly important to understand how the mothers spoke about themselves (Reading 2) and also how they spoke about relationships (Reading 3): with children, partners and professionals including social workers.

After getting the interviews fully transcribed, we analysed them, drawing on the considerable experience of two researchers, one of whom had carried out some of the interviews. This was in order to try and check for any differences in perception between the researchers and not to rely solely on the person who had carried some of them out. We tried to build up an individual (narrative) story for each woman, but the 'four readings' also allowed us to approach these interviews cross-sectionally by identifying key variables such as 'relationships with professionals', so as to make comparisons between the interviewees. In this way, we were able to use elements of both a narrative approach to analysis alongside one relying more specifically on the development of coding (e.g. as in grounded theory approaches to analysis).

For more on this project see Bell et al., 2015.

For further discussion of reflexivity in relation to this approach to data analysis, see also Mauthner and Doucet, 2003.

Chapter summary

> This chapter focused on use of documents and on qualitative data analysis.

> There are many different kinds of documentary materials available to the student social worker or practitioner. Some are in the public domain; for others, permission needs to be sought before they can be used for research. Source or 'provenance' of documentary materials is an important issue in terms of their status for research purposes.

> We looked at methods for obtaining documentary data from observational or other methods, including generation of diaries and researcher field notes.

> We discussed and introduced skills for analysing qualitative data both from documents and from other qualitative methods including interviews and focus groups. These methods include content analysis, discourse analysis, grounded theory approaches, narrative analysis and interview-based methods.

Further reading

Bryman, A (2012) *Social Research Methods*, 4th edn (or later), Oxford: Oxford University Press, chs 23 (documents), 24, 25 (data analysis)

Charmaz, K (2006) *Constructing Grounded Theory: A practical Guide Through Qualitative Methods*, London: Sage

Denzin, N and Lincoln, Y (2000) *Handbook of Qualitative Research*, 2nd edn (or later), Thousand Oaks: Sage

Mason, J (2002) *Qualitative Researching*, 2nd edn, London: Sage

6

IT'S ALL ABOUT ATTITUDE: WAYS OF CAPTURING AND UNDERSTANDING MEASURABLE DATA

Introduction

Social work students I have worked with are often unsure about how to develop research questions based around 'positivistic' research approaches and also to understand why a 'quantitative' approach might fit their project and their identified research question(s) (see e.g. Bell and Clancy, 2013). This lack of appreciation of the uses of 'quantitative' research methods is not only an issue in social work research but extends more widely across the social sciences to include students and researchers themselves: many researchers (for example Morgenshtern et al., 2011; Murtonen, 2005; Williams et al., 2008) have identified that those working in this broad 'social research' field, including social workers, may have problems with making good use of quantitative methods.

In this chapter, I will be drawing, as before, upon a few relevant project examples, so as to illustrate some ways of using quantitative methods for data collection and analysis as part of social work and social work education research projects. I use projects and original data to illustrate how to interpret and design attitudinal measures, as well as to offer advice on developing survey questionnaires. I will signpost readers to more comprehensive or specific texts covering quantitative (statistical) data collection and data analysis techniques, as well as providing some basic statistics guidance in Appendices D-1 to D-4 in case you are not familiar with this. The detailed discussions of a small number of projects in this chapter are meant to illustrate the uses of quantitative methods in social work and related research, rather than providing a definitive guide to all possible research methods and statistical procedures that could be used.

As we first saw in Chapters 1 and 2 (the section on 'positivism', Chapter 2, p. 23), research design using a broadly positivist approach involves systematic identification, gathering and recording of observed measurable data leading to explanation and theory. There is a strong tendency to quantify this data so as to produce measurable results. This approach to research can also be termed use of 'the scientific method', and it has been very influential, although it has also been criticised for numerous limitations, notably by researchers of a 'constructionist'/'interpretivist' persuasion: they point to its reductionist focus, and its emphasis on precision and what can be measured. However, such precise research data is often seen as somewhat more rigorous by policymakers, and so it is important to learn about ways in which quantitative data can be produced and best interpreted. This understanding is equally important for students doing dissertations as for practitioners who may need to draw on measurable data as 'evidence' for their social work or health practice. (See also Chapter 2 on Media and information.)

In research or evaluation terms, **surveys** are a good example of descriptive research designs that rely strongly on an understanding of quantitative data. However, other studies also relying on quantitative data can be based on experimental designs such as randomised controlled trials (RCTs) which have an explanatory goal (see e.g. Chapter 1, Question 1).

Robson (1993) compares the aims of surveys and experiments (e.g. RCTs) as follows:

> 'The typical survey is *passive* in that it seeks to describe and/or analyse, even in some cases to explore, some aspect of the world out there *as it is.*'

> 'The experiment is *active* in that it asks: What happens if this is changed?' (p. 124)

The project examples relevant to social work or health studies that I discuss in this chapter (Projects A, C and P) use quantitative data collection and analysis methods in different ways which will fit the model of either a descriptive survey; be based on a simplified 'before' and 'after' (pre- and post-) measurement (e.g. before and after an intervention or training course); or be based on the full explanatory principles of experimentation. Some studies may include more than one of these approaches. Projects A and C have already been introduced earlier in the book (for example in relation to ethical issues). Later in the chapter we will consider how researchers involved in all these projects (A, C and P) produced their results and interpreted them.

To further develop your understanding of basic statistical methods/techniques, please see Appendices D-1 to D-4 and the Glossary. The reading list of recommended texts at the end of the chapter will also enable you to expand your understanding of statistical techniques.

Descriptive survey design (methodology) and methods

The aim of a survey is usually to collect descriptive information, often by using questionnaires, which are administered 'cross-sectionally', i.e. across an appropriate sample of respondents. This sample is often selected in such a manner that those selected can be taken as statistically representative of a wider population; the aim in that case is that findings are **generalisable** to that population. This is called probability sampling. Samples not attempting to do this are termed non-probability samples and can be described in various ways, e.g. as 'convenient' or 'purposive'. Please see Appendix D-4 for more discussion of different types of sampling methods.

Please note: when we talk about 'the population' we are not necessarily talking generally about the whole geographically based population of a country – sometimes referred to as 'the general population'. We could, for example, mean the 'total population of social workers registered with the HCPC', of which we may be aiming to survey a specified percentage.

There is, however, one very familiar survey of the whole population of the UK – The National Census, which is carried out every ten years by the Office for National Statistics; this is important for policymakers and government, and legal sanctions are in place if the Census form is not completed by householders. Despite this, the national Census is inevitably incomplete, as the data it produces has to be interpreted to take account of missing people such as those who have not completed the form, who are perhaps homeless/have no registered address, or those recently arrived in the UK, whether legally or illegally.

Should I use a survey methodology for my study?

Like all research approaches and methods, surveys have their strengths and weaknesses, and you need to consider whether this is the appropriate methodology for your project:

Strengths of surveys

➤ provides data (usually quantitative) in summary form which can act as a basis for decision-making

> provides information for comparative purposes, e.g. between respondents with different characteristics

> attitudes can be explored systematically.

Weaknesses of surveys

> by reducing data down to a numerical form, complexity of human attitudes and behaviours can be underestimated

> the generalisations you make from this 'reduced' form of data may therefore turn out to be inappropriate.

Below we give an example of a survey, Project P, that was carried out with practitioners from different professional groups (occupational therapy, physiotherapy, nursing and social work) in relation to evidence-based practice. We begin by considering the aims of this survey and its sampling methods.

Project P – Preparing for professional practice: How well does professional training equip health and social care practitioners to engage in evidence-based practice (Caldwell et al., 2007)
The main stated aims of the study were to:

> ascertain the ways in which recently qualified practitioners engage in evidence-based practice

> determine how confident recently qualified practitioners are engaging in evidence-based practice

> establish the nature of educational input in relation to evidence-based practice.

As discussed by Caldwell et al. (2007), there had been several other studies involving various professional groups in relation to evidence-based practice, and the authors state that:

> We felt that the use of a **cross-sectional survey** had the greatest potential for achieving our primary research objectives, and whilst it would not have any explanatory power it would serve the purpose of *establishing patterns and trends in relation to the views and perceptions of recently qualified health and social care staff* on evidence-based practice. (p. 520)

As with all surveys, sampling was a crucial aspect of preparing for the study. In this case, the researchers aimed to sample:

> UK based graduates in nursing, occupational therapy, physiotherapy, and social work who had completed their undergraduate training between December 2001 and June 2003 (therefore qualified for no more than 2 years) at three London universities. A total of 50 graduates from each professional category were sampled to give an overall sample of 200. (Caldwell et al., 2007, p. 520)

In order to ensure that this sample was randomly generated,[1] we needed to have access to a complete list of the population under scrutiny (i.e. all these graduates), and the authors tell us that 'the sample was randomly generated from the universities' graduate databases by university data managers not otherwise involved in the study' (p. 520). However, as the researchers point out, it may also be a limitation of the study that these managers from different universities might have used different methods to generate their samples.

The researchers involved in Project P, like many researchers planning a single cross-sectional survey, decided to design their own questionnaire because reviewing literature did not suggest any existing questionnaire or other measure that could be used appropriately. This need to design their own questionnaire was also partly due to the 'local' nature of this study (the focus on three London-based universities) and due to the chosen combination of professional groups involved (i.e. specific interests of the researchers).

When designing a questionnaire yourself, you will first need to pay attention to the following:

1) Which areas/subjects will the questionnaire cover (Oppenheim (1992) calls these 'modules')?
2) Which specific 'variables' should be covered within each module?
3) Which types of question should be included?
4) Wording of questions
(Adapted from Oppenheim, 1992)

Figure 6.1 Process for design of a questionnaire

Note that you should consider **variables** in advance of actual questions. This is because a variable when used on a questionnaire needs to be 'operationalised' to become a (measurable) indicator of that variable; some identified variables may need to be covered by more than one question. For example, how would you measure whether or not someone has 'good health'? What would be a suitable indicator? You might think that you could use something like 'number of times you have visited your GP in the last six months' as an indicator of 'good' or 'poor' health. However, applied to pregnant women, for example, this assumption could be completely wrong. You may need to ask more than one question to operationalise your chosen variable adequately. You will certainly need to read relevant research literature in your field to establish which kinds of 'variables' should be covered in your questionnaire, then work out appropriate questions and how they should be worded. 'Demographic characteristics' is an important section on any questionnaire, as this will allow you to make comparisons within your resulting data based on these characteristics (e.g. age, gender, length of time since obtaining professional qualification etc.). Some people recommend putting this demographic section first on the questionnaire, and others put it last; as with all survey questions, respondents should be instructed to complete as many questions as possible but told they are free not to respond to any questions they find sensitive/unacceptable (from experience, this can apply to questions about personal income, age, ethnicity or religion in some cases).

In Project P, the authors explain that following scrutiny of relevant literature, the following sections and questions were included in their questionnaire:

Project P – Questionnaire Design – Sections Covered

> ➤ demographic characteristics, including: profession; length of time qualified; where qualified; academic level at which qualified; sector where currently employed
>
> ➤ pre-qualifying educational preparation for evidence-based practice, including specific research methods training; experience of undertaking a research project
>
> ➤ skills training for evidence-based practice, including literature searching; critical appraisal
>
> ➤ access to bibliographic databases frequency and location
>
> ➤ experience of research changing practice
>
> (Caldwell et al., p. 521)

The questionnaire used in Project P included a series of attitude statements where respondents were asked to indicate their answer on a five-point Likert scale covering the responses, 'strongly agree; agree; unsure; disagree; strongly disagree'. Topics covered by these attitude scales were:

➢ views on the relevance of research to practice

➢ views on key aspects of evidence-based practice including employer encouragement; importance of evidence to practice for own and other professional groups; time available for own/other professional groups to implement evidence-based practice

➢ demands of evidence-based practice

➢ confidence to engage in evidence-based practice. (Caldwell et al., 2007, p. 521)

Likert scales are frequently used on questionnaires as a more specific way of addressing a respondent's attitudes in terms of how much they agree or disagree with something based on their own (self) report. See Project C, below, for more on Likert scales.

Wording of questions on questionnaires

Students and other researchers may agonise over the actual wording of questions but still forget to follow a few simple rules that will ensure as far as possible that questions will produce consistent answers from all respondents. It is usually very important to try out (pilot) the question-naire with a few respondents who are not part of the main survey so that necessary adjustments can then be made to questions, questionnaire layout and instructions. Here are some examples of problematic ques-tions relating to work with children and families that break some of these rules. No matter how experienced the researcher, some of these prob-lems do not become apparent until a pilot study is conducted, and if not amended they could lead to partial completion or non-completion of the questionnaire.

Ambiguous question

> *Is the child's behaviour 'normal'?*

What does 'normal' mean? It is best to ask about the way(s) in which the child has behaved more specifically, or to define what would be consid-ered appropriate in context.

a) Imprecise question

> *At what age did the child develop X behaviour?*

Age 2 – 3

Age 3 – 4

Which box relates to a child aged 3? Make sure categories for response are mutually exclusive.

b) Making an assumption

Which type of school does your child attend?

Nursery	
Primary	
Comprehensive	
Other	

This question may assume the respondent only has one child, and, indeed, that the child attends a school. Some explanation should be inserted into the question allowing for more than one box to be ticked if required, or a number might be inserted if more than one child is included.

c) Assuming memory

What services were you using in 1998?

Will people remember that far back?

d) Assuming knowledge

Asking a social care worker whether they feel the document 'Modernising Social Services' informs their practice.

Although this may be a legitimate question to ask if your focus is on this document, this question also assumes that the worker is familiar with the document.

f) Double questions

Do you use services X and Y?

What if the respondent uses only X or only Y, how does s/he complete the questionnaire? It would be better to ask two separate questions and a third asking whether X and Y are used in combination.

g) Leading questions
A question asked to a worker such as, *'Do you agree that service users should have a say in service provision?'* This is a rather leading or loaded question – it is very difficult for the respondent to say no.

h) Presuming questions

Do you think this service offers enough counselling sessions?

There are two presumptions present here:

1 Counselling is necessary and a good thing.
2 There are not enough counselling sessions.

It would be better to ask first how many counselling sessions the person received over a given period (if any). This could then be compared with data from other services. Attitudes towards counselling that is offered could be addressed by a separate question, perhaps using an attitude measure (e.g. Likert scale).

i) Hypothetical questions

If you had no family responsibilities, what would you do about ...?

What is the point of this information? There is a strong likelihood it will be ignored.

j) Offensive/sensitive questions

You should of course try to avoid asking any question which is obviously offensive or disrespectful, but some questions may still appear unacceptable to some people, e.g. questions about personal income, age, ethnicity or religion in some cases. You have to decide whether you need to ask such questions in your survey. Sensitive questions would be of particular concern to an ethics committee, and piloting will certainly help to gauge the response you may get from potential respondents.

For more on question wording, see Oppenheim (1992) or Bryman (2012, ch 11).

Questionnaires – reliability, validity and responsiveness to change

If you are designing your own questionnaire, you will need to consider these issues:

> If a questionnaire or measure is to be 'valid', it should measure what it is intending to measure.

> If a questionnaire is to be 'reliable', it should produce similar results when re-administered to the same respondents, or to different respondents in similar contexts or circumstances.

> ➤ If you are intending to use your questionnaire/measure again as a fol-
low-up in a longitudinal study (repeat measures), it should be capable
of being responsive to change.

For more details on these points, see Project C, below, and Appendix D-2.

In some projects it is possible to identify an existing questionnaire or
measure that has been tested out before; this may be particularly important, for example, if you are trying to develop a longitudinal study and
you need something that is already validated without needing to take time
to design your own. Or this may be essential if you want to use more than
one measure for different purposes in your study and similarly do not
have time or the need to design all these measures yourself.

We now return to a previously mentioned project (Project C), as an
example illustrating the development and use of measures; this will also
allow us to provide more guidance about how to develop survey and
experimental research designs and work with the resulting quantitative
data.

Developing and using a questionnaire/attitude measure on 'attitudes to research'

You will remember that in Project C, I and a colleague used a pre-existing questionnaire relating to 'Attitudes to Research' (ATR), reported in
Papanastasiou (2005). We then approached the author of this paper for
her permission to use her questionnaire with our own students. The questionnaire was developed at the University of Cyprus for use with students
there and was designed in two parts: demographic questions (e.g. student's
course or their age) and a series of 32 positively or negatively* worded
attitude statements[2], with responses being recorded at an ordinal level of
measurement using a seven-point Likert scale:

		Strongly Disagree						Strongly Agree
1	Research makes me anxious *	1	2	3	4	5	6	7
2	Research should be taught to all students	1	2	3	4	5	6	7

Figure 6.2 Likert scale examples (Taken from ATR questionnaire,
Papanastasiou, 2005)

You should note first of all that on any Likert-based attitude scales such as these, we are trying to measure something uni-dimensionally (only on one dimension). Individual statements need to be carefully worded so that it is clear what exactly is being measured. In addition, because this type of scale records only at an ordinal (scale) level of measurement, we are relying on the respondent to indicate subjectively on the scale 'how much' or 'how little' s/he agrees or disagrees with the statement. This means that we record this subjective meaning and we cannot get a precise or accurate measure of the distance between e.g. 1 and 2, or 2 and 5 on an ordinal level scale.[3]

Typically, on a questionnaire such as this, containing uni-dimensional Likert scales, several different statements may be contributing to one concept (such as anxiety). Papanastasiou realised that overall 'attitude(s) to research' is in fact a multi-dimensional concept that needs to be accounted by different variables. The statements are thus designed to allow a further sub-set of explanations contributing to respondents' overall attitudes to research; these will be based on different dimensions or factors, such as 'research anxiety'. This questionnaire allows you to record not only the respondent's answer to each individual statement but also to work out a 'total score' for each person (indicating how positively they regard 'research'[4]) as well as their scores for each key dimension (subscale) – see below).

In a discussion of how the questionnaire was developed, Papanastasiou (2005) explains that she started out by testing an original questionnaire with 56 statements firstly for **validity** and **reliability**, measuring internal consistency of questionnaire items using the statistical test Cronbach's alpha coefficient. This produced a very satisfactory reliability coefficient of 0.947.

Following this process, the author wanted to explore the multi-dimensional nature of the scale further and to understand, as noted above, which factors might account statistically for answers her respondents were giving to all the statements. She explains the factor analysis process she undertook as follows:

> Eleven factors were originally extracted, accounting for 66.4% of the variance. However, ... several of the items of the original version of the questionnaire were removed because they were considered as inappropriate. Once the inappropriate items were removed, 32 items remained in the scale. Once the factor analysis was re-run with those items, a five-factor solution remained, which included a robust set of constructs that were relatively easily interpreted. (p. 19)

This exploratory factor analysis using results from University of Cyprus students indicated in other words that there were five meaningful factors (subscales) embedded within the 32 items (statements) on the questionnaire, and these were:

1 the usefulness of research in the student's professional life (nine items)

2 research anxiety (eight items)

3 positive attitudes towards research (eight items)

4 relevance or usefulness of research to the student's life (four items)

5 difficulty of research (three items)

Further statistical testing of these factors for reliability and validity using Cronbach's alpha coefficient showed that, like the overall questionnaire, reliabilities for responses to each of these five subscales were also relatively high.

This rigorous testing of the ATR questionnaire/measure meant we were confident that it was reliable and valid for use with the kinds of respondents it was aimed at (students). We felt it could be used in our own study without further testing for validity, and it was also useful for the educational/pedagogic purposes we needed (although we were working with postgraduate social work and health students and not undergraduates like Papanastasiou). Our students commented favourably about using the ATR in their course, although they also commented on the somewhat ambiguous use of the term 'research' within this questionnaire. This ambiguity did, however, also give our students a useful opportunity to reflect on what they think the term 'research' means. (See Bell and Clancy, 2013, and the next section in this chapter for more on this project.)

Note: for further information about different kinds of measures and those commonly used in health or social care research and/or practice, e.g. outcomes in mental health, see Appendix D-2.

For another research example using an existing quantitative measure to explore social work students' attitudes towards professional stereotypes and interprofessional work, see Bell and Allain (2011).

Building explanations from quantitative data

In the next section, we consider the generation of quantitative data from our measures/questionnaires, then analysing and interpreting this data. First we look at how, in Project C, we tested two hypotheses using our data and found out whether or not our results were 'statistically significant'.

Project C – pre-intervention (survey) statistical results and interpretation

In Project C we collected quantitative data using the ATR questionnaire from a series of annual student cohorts comprising social work and some health postgraduate/master's students taking a research methods course. This survey data was recorded onto an SPSS[5] data file for students to use as part of their assessed work. In Bell and Clancy (2013), we explain that we were able to work out a pre-course 'total research attitude' (TRA) score for each student based on the overall score from the 32-item questionnaire (each item having a seven-point Likert scale), then we could calculate the mean for the cohort by adding up all the scores for each person and dividing this figure by the number of students.

In the first student cohort for 2007/2008 (n = 43 social work students), we showed that the mean TRA score across the whole cohort was 4.37 (standard deviation SD 0.662). Interpretation: on a scale of 1–7, a mean score of 4.37 falls just over the midpoint in a positive direction; in other words, prior to taking the course these students tended on average to have an overall positive attitude towards research.

Were there any significant differences between our respondents at baseline (pre-course survey)?

We also wanted to know whether gender or having previous research experience might affect the student's TRA score prior to taking the course, so we proposed two **null hypotheses** for our students to test using a 't' test. (For more detailed information on statistics, see also Appendix D-1.)

Hypothesis 1

There will be no statistically significant difference between female and male students' scores for 'total research attitude'.

Hypothesis 2

There will be no statistically significant difference between 'total research attitude' scores for students having previous research experience[6] and those without previous research experience.

These hypotheses were both tested using the SPSS cohort data file by the students, using an independent samples t-test.[7]

The t-test requires you to use data from two variables:

➢ one categorical, independent variable (i.e. in this case – gender (hypothesis 1) and previous research experience (hypothesis 2))

➢ one continuous (scale), dependent variable (in both cases, the total research attitude score (TRA))

Results for our first cohort of 43 social work students showed firstly that:

> there was no statistically significant difference between female and male students on the TRA scores, and so the null hypothesis was upheld – results were presented as: t = –.693, df 40, p = 0.49

Interpretation: the t-test result reported here shows the t value, followed by degrees of freedom of the table (df), followed by the p value. The p (alpha) value being considerably above the 0.05 level indicates that there is no statistically significant difference between the TRA scores of male and female students.

For the second hypothesis, however, we did show a statistically significant result between TRA scores for students having previous research experience and those without experience. In this case, the null hypothesis was not upheld:

t= 2.58, df = 40 , p = 0.01

Interpretation: the t-test result reported here shows the t value, followed by degrees of freedom of the table (df), followed by the p value. The p (alpha) value being considerably below the 0.05 level indicates that there is a statistically significant difference between the TRA scores of students with and without previous research experience.

Checking our results

There are further statistical checks that researchers need to be aware of when considering their results from hypothesis testing (for example when using the t-test procedure). The p (alpha) value only tells part of the story, and as Pallant (2013) points out, there is always the possibility of coming to the wrong conclusion when testing for statistical significance.

We need to consider whether we have rejected the null hypothesis when it is in fact true (called making a Type 1 error). Alternatively, we need to consider whether we have accepted the null hypothesis when it is in fact not true (called making a Type 2 error). These two errors are unfortunately inversely related – if we try to control for a Type 2 error, this can make it more likely that we will make a Type 1 error!

One important consideration is sample size – if you have a small sample and your results suggest there is no statistical significance between your groups, e.g. male and female students (above), it could simply be that your study is 'underpowered' and that with a larger sample you might have shown significance and not ended up making a Type 2 error. In order to address this issue in Project C, we continued to add to our dataset year by year to improve our chances of avoiding these errors by obtaining a larger overall sample.

Another way to check our results is to consider effect size (the strength of the difference between groups, or the influence of the independent variable) (see Appendix D-1 for more information).

Finally, we need to consider what alpha level (p value) we are using. The convention in many studies is to use the 0.05 level, but this can be adjusted to different levels to compensate e.g. for small sample sizes (see Appendix D-1, Statistical significance).

'Pre' and 'Post' test design – showing whether or not there are changes before and after an intervention

It is often important in social work research to show whether there have been any measurable changes in respondents' scores, in order to try establish whether the intervention they have experienced has played any part in these changes.

To recap:

Project C was a survey of students PLUS a before/after experimental design using the ATR questionnaire in which the researchers aimed to 1) provide our students with experience in using 'quantitative methods' which could be assessed as part of their research methods course and 2) to provide ourselves with the opportunity to research how master's students were learning about research in this particular course. (See, again, Chapter 3 for discussion of ethical aspects of the project.)

In Project C, we asked all students to establish the characteristics of their student cohort at baseline (before the course started) as part of their assessed work, and we also asked for student volunteers (following the ethics committee's advice) to complete follow-up questionnaires which were virtually identical to the pre-questionnaire and contained the same 32 attitudinal items. This simple pre-post research design is often used in 'quasi' experimental[8] work where other aspects of clinical trials are not feasible. (See Appendix D-3.)

We intended to see whether or not taking the course had made any difference to students' TRA scores, and also whether their attitudes as measured on any of the five subscales had shifted. We discovered, in similar vein to Papanastasiou (2005), that pre-course the respondents tended to have lower, more negative scores on the 'research anxiety' subscale. On the other hand, the subscale related to the usefulness of research in the student's professional life (career) tended to produce more positive results in both Papanastiou's and in our own study.

Some further discussion of this pre-post design is given in Bell and Clancy (2013), although, unfortunately, in the first student cohort only 19 students volunteered to complete the follow-up questionnaire (out of 43 in total), making our sample very likely to be unreliable in terms of Type 1/Type 2 errors. If it was possible to subsequently compare pre- (Time 1) and post- (Time 2) results for the same student cohort, we would use a paired samples t-test (for parametric data) or a Wilcoxon Signed-Rank test (for non-parametric data) to see whether there was any change in scores over time.

Gathering and analysing data from randomised controlled trials (RCTs) – a form of experimental design

Controlled trials are becoming increasingly useful in social work research, covering a variety of topics. They may incorporate a combination of research methods e.g. pairing of participants and/or **randomisation**. For example, in relation to work with families, Kratochwill et al. (2009) describe data from a trial which sought results from the international FAST (Families And Schools Together) parenting programme. This programme engages parents and their children in multi-family groups to address behavioural issues and parent-child bonding, and has been shown to have low dropout rates. In this study, children in eight urban schools in an American community were initially paired on the basis of five relevant matching variables, including teacher assessment of behavioural problems. They were then randomly assigned to either usual school services (control) or to the FAST programme. Parents and teachers completed various pre-, post-, and 1-year follow-up measures and assessments such as the Strengths and Difficulties Questionnaire (SDQ) (see Appendix D-2). Data were analysed for 67 pairs of children and showed, amongst other results, that 'FAST' parents reported statistically significant reductions in children's aggressive behaviours.

Returning to Project A (MacDonald and Turner, 2005), first introduced in Chapter 3 in relation to ethical issues, this is an example of an experimental study which the authors identify as an RCT. It uses a pre-/post-design, and (as with FAST study above) it also includes randomisation; it uses a wide range of measures, compared to the single questionnaire we used in Project C. The researchers divided their foster carer participants into two groups, those receiving the intervention (cognitive-behavioural training) and those in a control group (on a waiting list for the training). Data was gathered using a series of measures/questionnaires. As noted earlier, participants in Project A were randomly allocated either to a cognitive-behavioural training group or a waiting list control group. The researchers tell us that:

> Those in the control group continued to receive standard services and were assured that should the training prove helpful, it would be made available to them in the future. (p. 1270)

As we already saw in Chapter 3, the study was done in six local authority areas in England, with randomisation of the final sample of 117 foster carers into two groups being done separately within each of the six areas (67 'training group' participants and 50 'controls'). The study was conducted using three different measures and by making a record of the number of unplanned breakdowns of placements (this 'breakdown' data was obtained from interviews). Measures used were:

> ➤ a measure of participants' Knowledge of Behavioural Principles as Applied to Children (KBPAC)

> ➤ the Child Behavioural Checklist (CBCL)

> ➤ a Foster Carer Satisfaction Questionnaire

> (see Appendix D-2 for further details)

As we would expect, the same measures were given to both the participants and the controls at specific points in the research design, (which is always important in an experiment, so as to make comparisons between the groups and test for possible changes in their scores). Whereas in Project C we used a simple pre-post design administering the ATR questionnaire, in this example several measures are used in combination alongside qualitative interviews (see also Chapter 7). The researchers explain that in the research process:

> Participants were interviewed before and after training, and at six months follow-up. ... At the end of the first and second interviews, participants in both groups were asked to fill in the KBPAC. At the first and final interviews, they were asked to complete [the CBCL]. (pp. 1271–1272)

This combination of measures and interviews provided a set of 'pre' and 'post' intervention data whilst allowing the researchers to compare results from their 'control' and 'training' groups. The researchers discuss their analysis and group their results in the paper according to the following headings based on their research questions:

➤ knowledge of behavioural problems and how to manage them

➤ skills in the management of behaviour problems

➤ frequency and/or severity of behavioural problems

➤ foster-carers would feel more confident in their abilities to manage difficult behaviour (hypothesis[9])

➤ placement stability

It is important to note how the researchers used their results from the three
different measures plus the record they kept of the number of unplanned
placement breakdowns. It is very important in any project to plan out in
advance how you will use different measures to gather data and then interpret various parts of it to address your questions of interest, especially with
this type of experimental research design. However, it would also not be
truthful to say that all researchers always follow exactly what is needed by
planning in advance! This research paper presents a very good example of
the need for flexibility in research whilst still using measures appropriately,
especially when things do not turn out as you have predicted.

The researchers found that to answer their questions about 'knowledge', issue (1), they could make use of the mean KBPAC scores for control
and training participant groups; pre-training (at baseline) scores were not
different enough to show any statistical significance, indicating that they
were starting with groups that were comparable (as should be the case[10]).
However, each time the KBPAC measure was used subsequently to compare controls and training group participants, we are told that:

> participants in the control group scored significantly lower than those in the
> training group (as measured by mean scores). (p. 1272)[11]

Interpreting this, the authors tell us that this means that the training
group participants:

> showed a small but significant increase in their knowledge of behavioural prin-
> ciples as applied to children ... those in the control condition ... as expected,
> did not show any increase in knowledge in this area. (p. 1273)

For the second issue, (2) skills in the management of behaviour problems,
it is clear from the research paper that much of this data was derived
from interviews, then quantified by the researchers so that any differences between groups could be measured (see also Chapter 7). Simply put,
such quantification may be done by counting up participants who gave

particular kinds of answers in interviews (and then subjecting these percentage figures to further testing for statistical significance). This measurement process enabled the researchers to show, for example, that by the six-month follow-up project stage (Time 3), training group participants were more likely to be actually using the skills they had learnt for analysing behaviour (in this example, those commonly referred to as the 'ABC of behaviour'[12]) compared to control participants.[13]

As the researchers point out, other results they obtained in relation to this topic were not as they had predicted, and in one case, 'controls' (compared to training participants) were more rather than less likely to behave as predicted. The authors discuss possible reasons for this in their paper. In addition, they had hoped the CBCL data might show whether these cognitive-behavioural methods were successful to the extent that children's behaviour improved; but once again they were not able to demonstrate this, as results of their statistical analyses did not reveal any statistically significant results between training group and control group participants. No significant differences between groups were found in relation to issue (3), 'frequency and/or severity of behavioural problems', but in terms of their hypothesis (4), the researchers did discover that, as predicted, those who had received training were more confident in dealing with behavioural problems, especially using the 'ABC' method. Results for placement breakdown (5) were, however, not as predicted:

> [foster] carers in the training group showed a slight increase in the number of unplanned terminations of placement from post-training to follow-up. Over the same period, those in the control group reported a slight decrease in unplanned terminations of placement in which behaviour problems were implicated. (p. 1275)

Project A is valuable for the light it sheds on some of the exact processes involved in gathering and analysing quantitative data during an RCT. Importantly, it shows exactly how you can use a combination of measures and also qualitative methods with accepted statistical tests such as ANOVA alongside the researchers' own methods of quantification etc.. We should note the researchers' useful interpretation of their findings depends in part on addressing and accounting for results where hypotheses may not have been supported by data. We should not expect all our hypotheses to be supported, but in too many cases, if they are not, researchers just 'leave it at that' rather than trying to explore possible explanations.

In this particular project, the CBT-based training involved did not appear to work very well, which was clearly a disappointment to these researchers, and so it was important to them to explore and demonstrate why this happened, for policy reasons as much as in terms of research.

This approach offered the chance for training as well as research processes to be improved in future (MacDonald and Turner, 2005).

Exercise 6.1 **Clinical trials/errors**

There are usually four ways that errors could be introduced into experimental studies/trials. These are due to issues of:

➤ Sampling

➤ Assignment

➤ Conditions

➤ Measurement

Provide an example for each of these issues suggesting how such errors could occur.

See Appendix C for solutions/suggestions for exercises.
See Appendix D-3 for more information on the design of clinical trials.

Chapter summary

➤ This chapter used relevant research examples to offer suggestions for using quantitative methods for data collection and analysis. My intention is to clarify these processes for those who may not be experts in statistical analysis, but who need to understand the importance of rigorous use of quantitative data collection and analytical techniques.

➤ We introduced some methods and advice on developing survey questionnaires using a project example.

➤ The chapter draws on some original data from a research project carried out with social work and health students, to illustrate how to interpret and design attitudinal measures.

➤ Using a published social work case example (Project A), we examined the use and interpretation of statistical data in a randomised controlled trial (experiment).

➤ Finally, I have signposted readers to more specific texts on quantitative (statistical) data and data analysis.

Further reading

Bryman, A (2012) *Social Research Methods*, 4th edn, Oxford: Oxford University Press, chs 15 and 16

Harris, M and Taylor, G (2014) *Medical statistics Made Easy*, 3rd edn, Banbury: Scion Publishing

Oppenheim, AN (1992 or later edn) *Questionnaire Design, Interviewing and Attitude Measurement*, London: Pinter

Pallant, J (2013) *SPSS Survival Manual*, 5th edn (or later), London: Allen and Unwin

Rosenthal, JA (2012) *Statistics and Data Interpretation for Social Work*, New York: Springer

7

MIXING IT UP: HOW TO COMBINE RESEARCH APPROACHES WITHOUT GETTING INTO A MUDDLE

Introduction

It should already be clear from earlier chapters in this book that many researchers, especially those involved in professional practice such as social workers, are often using 'mixed' methods in their projects. This often seems to be for pragmatic reasons, with researchers being driven more by 'getting research done', albeit appropriately, rather than by adherence to a particular methodological line (such as closely following the 'scientific method' in order to do research that is considered rigorous). Despite the continuing presence of discussions about 'qualitative' and 'quantitative' research (including it has to be said, in this book), there is also a lot of methodological and other research-based literature suggesting that having a rigid divide between 'qualitative' and 'quantitative' methods and/or approaches is unhelpful; this is especially so in applied or practice-based research, including that carried out by social workers or health professionals (see e.g. McKeganey, 1995, on research on addictions).

You will also remember in Chapter 1, when discussing the role of research questions, we considered Bryman's study (2007) in which he interviewed a number of researchers who were already using mixed methods. There he argued that researchers may use 'mixed methods' for tactical reasons, such as increasing their ability to get funding, and this could be useful in evaluative projects and/or those that are relevant to policy makers where a more pragmatic approach can be useful.

In this chapter, I will outline some of the various approaches to mixing methods, discussing relevant underlying issues such as what is meant by **triangulation**. I am not, however, taking the position that mixed approaches are automatically better than single methodological approaches, nor that a divide between 'qualitative' and 'quantitative' methods (or data) is necessarily unhelpful. I will be using some research examples to illustrate, for example, where a combination of specific techniques has been tried, or where mixed approaches, including work on larger projects, may include several different strands of methodological endeavour. Although this chapter will focus, like most methodological guidance, on thinking about mixing methods in primary studies, we should not forget that mixed approaches or methods can also be an issue in secondary research such as systematic reviews (for more specific advice, see Harden and Thomas, 2005). Secondary research may also be of particular relevance to student projects in social work. I would also encourage students to consider whether working on a primary research project with mixed methods requires a much larger scope than necessary, and to establish whether or not this is feasible for their purposes (e.g. what is suitable for a research degree would be beyond the scope of an undergraduate project). These kinds of initial decisions are important to avoid getting into a muddle!

Some key theoretical issues in relation to 'mixing methods'

The first question is, what exactly do we mean by 'mixed methods'? Most researchers think they know; but as Bryman (2007) found out, when you actually ask people about this they give different answers. At what level is the mixing being done? I have emphasised in this book that I think it is important to distinguish between research design (what I would call **methodology**), which depends in part on the philosophical issues of **ontology** and **epistemology**, and methods which are actual techniques researchers use to gather and/or analyse their data, such as interviews or questionnaires.

In terms of mixing, then, what exactly are we mixing? Is it possible to 'mix' at the level of **methodology**? (Some authors, such as Blaikie (2007), have tended to be doubtful about this.) Would you get confused if you tried to work with different sorts of epistemological positions in one project? On the other hand, if you simply try to use different techniques (methods) in combination in your project, especially for practical reasons, can you safely and always forget about their underlying epistemological bases? Personally, I think this is too risky; and this tends to be what lays researchers, including students, open to charges that their research methodology is 'weak' and hasn't been thought through. As Brannen (2005) comments:

> Data collected from different methods cannot simply be added together to produce a unitary or rounded reality. (p. 176)

She further advises that when we have produced those data:

> they need to be analysed and interpreted in relation to those methods and according to the assumptions by which they are generated. (p. 183)

My own position on research in general is that it is important to at least know and understand the 'rules' before you can break them (successfully). So what are the 'rules' here?

It is probably most helpful to start with why you, as a social work or health researcher, would want to use mixed methods in the first place, what would be the possible research outcome(s) for you in taking this sort of approach? Brannen (2005, p. 176) again helpfully sets out these possibilities as a typology of mixing 'qualitative' and 'quantitative' methods:

➤ corroboration – the 'same results' are derived from both qualitative and quantitative methods

➤ elaboration – the qualitative data analysis exemplifies how the quantitative findings apply in particular cases

➤ complementarity – the qualitative and quantitative results differ but together they generate insights

➤ contradiction – where the qualitative and quantitative findings conflict

In addition to these useful ideas, we may add a possible advantage of using multiple methods may be that this can help to reduce inappropriate certainty that might result from obtaining apparently clear-cut results through using only one method (but this is also a key justification for triangulation – see below). Conversely, we should not assume mixed methods will always produce 'better' research, especially if we take account of the different potential outcomes of this 'mixing', suggested by Brannen (above).

We need to look more closely at how we are doing our research in practice, and only then to see whether this may suggest considering the use of mixed methods. It is also useful to think about these different possibilities by considering the often-used concept of **triangulation**. Some researchers may think obtaining data from different 'perspectives' will somehow automatically give them a more realistic picture of something that is being investigated. This idea of triangulating has been promoted within the tradition of 'postpositivism' and seems to be popular in health research where (as with the development of grounded theory) attempts have been made to make research (and especially qualitative research) somehow more scientific or rigorous. However, triangulation is actually a complex idea, and first we need to recognise that it has been defined as having different forms (Figure 7.1):

DATA triangulation – to be collected at a variety of times (TIME), in different localities (SPACE) and from a range of people (PERSON)

INVESTIGATOR triangulation – multiple rather than single observers of the same object

THEORY triangulation** – particularly using more than one kind of approach to generate categories of analysis (see Ma and Norwich, 2007 below)

METHODOLOGICAL triangulation – 'within-method' (e.g. using different types of questioning in a questionnaire – open/closed/scales etc.); or 'between-method' (e.g. interviews plus measures in an experimental/empirical study)

Figure 7.1 Forms of triangulation

These definitions of different forms of triangulation also suggest we may need to use them as justification in different parts of the research process. For example Ma and Norwich (2007) examine more recent understandings of triangulation in relation to theory**, asking what determines our choice of theory when we are attempting to apply theory triangulation in research. In the research example they give (relating to special educational needs), they demonstrate the relevance of connecting several fields or disciplines when using explanation-based knowledge for prediction/control alongside intervention-based knowledge that seeks to influence professional practice. This type of approach would also be very relevant to evaluative studies in social work – for example in Project A, as previously discussed, which used data from interviews plus data from quantitative measures, although those researchers did not emphasise the project's 'mixed' nature.

Discussion Point

Triangulation – do you think this is an important justification for using 'mixed methods'? If so, why?

Mixing methods during the research process

Brannen (2005) helpfully guides us to think about how we can embed 'mixing' of research methods within the research process itself. Returning to our list of outcome possibilities, she illustrates achieving appropriate use of different research methods in practice in the key project stages of:

➤ research design

➤ fieldwork (data gathering + analysis)

➤ interpretation and contextualisation

In the research design stage, you may be planning to draw upon different research questions and these may require different (qualitative and quantitative) methods which may aim to 'elaborate' or 'complement' (but hopefully not 'contradict') each other. For example you may want to know whether a particular intervention is effective in reducing specific behaviour (focus one). At the same time, you need to know about the reactions of those receiving this intervention: what did they think of it, and how would they describe their experiences of it (focus two)? In this example, we might try to develop a 'positivist'/empirical approach to investigating the first question (perhaps by trying to measure reductions in certain behaviours amongst a cohort of people going through the intervention). Then we could interview some of these participants, thereby using a qualitative ('interpretive') approach in parallel with the first approach. Depending on your overall research design, you might decide more 'weight' needs to be given to one approach or the other, with the other approach taking a supporting position. On the other hand, some people would argue that there is no reason why you should not try to operate both approaches in parallel (i.e. to 'mix methodologies'), although some authors are sceptical about this (for example Blaikie, 2007).

In the 'fieldwork' stage, conceptual or other changes in your project may lead you to incorporate a mixture of methods that had not necessarily been planned in the research design stage. (As Brannen points out, taking such a developmental approach to your project may be useful but will have implications for your resources.)

In the final interpretation and contextualisation project stage, Brannen warns us to pay particular attention to contextualisation, for example in cross-national studies; social concepts may be viewed differently in different places, and there may be risks of 'insider bias' if issues of 'translation' are not considered when interpreting data in relation to differing concepts and theories. This contextualisation project stage is often not considered in much detail, and (in agreement with Brannen) I feel it ought to be given more attention. Situating this idea within social work research, we can see the relevance of context(s) to data interpretation in relation to various settings such as place (Hatton, 2001), institutions or 'spaces' such as student groups (see Bell and Villadsen,

2011). In these kinds of examples, **reflexivity** is essential to ensure limitations of insider bias are avoided as far as possible. (See the Project H example in this chapter.)

Examples of research using 'mixed' methods in different ways

Project Q – Using quantitative measures and qualitative interviews to address the same areas of enquiry (McAuley et al., 2006)

In this study, researchers used mixed methods to assess maternal and child well-being in families that were under stress. The authors tell us that data presented in their paper from 162 respondents were produced 'as part of a wider study of outcomes and costs of Home-Start support in the UK' (McAuley et al., 2006, p. 43). Comparisons were made between families receiving Home Start support and similar families living in areas where this support was not available (controls).

The researchers describe the overall study design as 'quasi-experimental' and explain that the methods used were mixed, and included:

> gathering quantitative data from validated measures[1] alongside qualitative data generated from interviews with the mothers. The measures were completed during the same visits as the interviews were carried out. Interviews were conducted according to a semi-structured interview schedule which addressed *precisely the same areas ... as the measures*. This method was used during baseline and follow-up interviews with all 162 respondents. The subsequent data analyses explored *convergence and contradictions in the results* as well as the emergence of new perspectives. (McAuley et al., 2006, p. 45) (my emphasis)

In presenting their findings, the authors give extensive results by topic from the quantitative (statistical) results, interspersed with interview quotes from their qualitative data. Taking this approach to their research design and processes, with results presented side by side, the authors state:

> A combined approach was adopted to ensure that we drew upon the strengths of both [quantitative and qualitative] methodologies in assessing the needs of the mothers at outset as well as the outcomes over time. Overall, *we found a large amount of convergence between the qualitative and quantitative results on maternal and child well-being at baseline* and, we would argue, some fresh perspectives on the needs of stressed mothers in young families. (McAuley et al., 2006, p. 53) (my emphasis)

However, whilst both qualitative and quantitative data showed most mothers interviewed were under considerable stress, it was the interviews with mothers:

> which conveyed that their sense of stress was usually caused by multiple, inter-related factors, and it was here also that we gained some insight into the factors causing the stress (McAuley et al., 2006, p. 53).

Qualitative data were also able to bring out more clearly the nature and depth of mothers' mental health issues and depression compared to what was derived from the quantitative data.

Project R – The *Communicate* project – a mixed methods approach using quantitative measures and techniques 'in parallel' with qualitative methods to answer different research questions (see Bryan et al., 2002; Jordan et al., 1998; Maxim et al., 2001).

In this NHS-funded *Communicate* project, researchers, including myself, were engaged in evaluation of a training package called *Communicate*, developed by a voluntary sector organisation, that aimed to provide care workers and professionals including social workers with training in specific communication skills. The focus of this training was on skills required by care staff where service users have communication impairments such as aphasia, e.g. following experience of a stroke, many of whom are older adults. Working within a social model of disability framework, we aimed to see if care environments could be changed through use of a specific one-day training course aiming to enable care staff and other professionals (including social workers, nurses, managers in residential care and administrators) to communicate in better ways with these older adults.

As a research design, this project fell into two parallel methodological strands. One aspect of our evaluation was to answer the research question – whether or not the training was effective in achieving its precise aims – and so this required us to use questionnaires before and after the training for participants (and at the same intervals for control participants, who were on a waiting list for training); these questionnaires were intended to produce rigorous quantitative data (see Bryan et al., 2002). To check on effectiveness of the *Communicate* training, we also developed a video technique that was used to observe selected interactions between care worker participants and older adults, plus visual analog scales for the older service users, so as to obtain their perspectives on the care they received (these data were also recorded quantitatively). The videos were viewed by speech and language therapist members of the project team who assessed these interactions using a validated quantified checklist.

The second parallel aspect of the study was to pay attention, using separate research questions, to contextual aspects of the project (as indicated previously, Brannen, 2005). These research questions concerned issues such as why the training had been developed; how the training was used within organisations; who was receiving it, and how useful/not useful did managers and others think it was for their staff. This aspect of the project mainly generated various kinds of qualitative data. Methods used included a documentary analysis relating to materials underpinning the development and delivery of *Communicate*, followed by interviews with key stakeholders (e.g. voluntary organisation staff, *Communicate* trainers) and with managers whose staff were being included or considered for training in partner organisations. This was to establish how and why people were being considered for inclusion and also to examine wider issues concerned with the place of training and workforce development in the organisation(s).[2]

During 1998/99, we therefore set up our research processes and worked with four partner agencies in South East England (two local authority social services departments and two NHS Health trusts) to provide 12 *Communicate* workshops, facilitated by specially trained speech and language therapists. Different members of our team worked on the two parallel 'strands' of the project, but it was important that we held regular project meetings including everyone. During the experimental phase of the project, some team members were instead responsible for documentary analysis and subsequently for interviewing various stakeholders and staff managers.

Staff managers in the agencies involved were responsible for identifying staff whom they felt would benefit from the training (because this training was not in the category of statutory (required) for all staff.) We divided our participants into 'training (intervention) groups' and 'control groups' (the latter being those who were put on the waiting list for training). This sampling was done in a similar 'quasi-experimental' way to the participants in Project Q (where they were either living in a Home-Start area, or were not). Unlike Project A (discussed above) **randomisation** into these training/control groups was not possible, since we were dependent on staff managers to act as 'gatekeepers' and to allocate their staff for immediate or delayed *Communicate* training depending on local workforce conditions.

This also led to an important ethical issue: we worked closely with managers in the four partner agencies to the extent that on more than one occasion, front-line staff found themselves being 'volunteered' by their manager for participation; on the day when researchers arrived in their workplace, some front-line staff who did not realise they were being volunteered refused to take part in the project work. The researchers then had to re-group to discuss the issue with all parties and return on another occasion to conduct the work with those who had freely chosen to take part.

In terms of data analysis, it was important that various kinds of project data, once gathered, were, as Brannen (2005) advises, analysed in their own terms. We therefore analysed the quantitative data from measures according to conventional forms of statistical analysis, whilst the qualitative data from interviews or documentary sources was analysed using thematic analysis or content analysis, respectively, as appropriate.

The two methodological strands of this project were designed to complement each other and to produce a rounded picture of all aspects of effectiveness, delivery and use of *Communicate* training in the example partner organisations. Whilst seeking to address different, parallel research questions initially, we intended that organisational context should strongly connect with outcomes relating to effectiveness of training, when project data was interpreted. This project demonstrated significant gains for those taking part in the training (compared to controls): for example their increased confidence when working with people who were living with communication impairments, as well as care workers' increased ability to develop appropriate strategies to help interaction between carer and the older person. The wider organisational study helped us to understand more clearly how *Communicate* training had been developed and to explore the ways organisations were able to use this resource with their workforce.

Project H – Using mixed methods as part of a 'case study' approach (Cree, Jain and Hillen, 2016)

Revisiting this project first introduced in Chapter 4, we already saw that the researchers in Project H carried out an evaluation of a drug and alcohol referral service in Scotland using a case study approach. Mixed methods that were used seem to be mainly qualitative, though quantitative data was also obtained from examination of agency reports and case records. The authors explain that following a literature review they carried out:

> the examination, coding and analysis of agency reports and case records, seeking to identify, first, how initial problems were recorded by staff and, second, changes in behaviour or outcomes for service users over the course of the sixteen-week intervention programme. We hoped that, by doing so, we *might be able to replicate what might be regarded as a 'pre' and 'post' test in evaluation.* (Cree, Jain and Hillen, 2016, p. 4) (my emphasis)

This project stage was then followed by:

> ➤ **participant observation**, which (rather than being identified by the researchers as an 'ethnography') consisted of 'spending time with

social workers [that] would give us a better "feel" for what it was they were actually doing with clients both in the office and on client visits' (Cree, Jain and Hillen, 2016, p. 5)

- ➤ **focus groups with social work staff**, which were held to 'allow for an open exploration of the social workers' views on recovery and social work' (Cree, Jain and Hillen, 2016, p. 5) and to facilitate the overall evaluation

- ➤ **interviews with different stakeholders (including clients)**, which took up the largest amount of time on the project; interviews made use of standardised 'questionnaires'

Qualitative forms of evaluation can be very useful in social work research (see e.g. Shaw, 1999), and these researchers point out that client/service user recovery in this project was 'too individual' to be measured by outcome targets or scales, and in any case tended to happen within the context of a 'trusting relationship'. At the same time, they point out that their work:

> shed light on the importance of having monitoring and recording systems that support, not hamper, social work activity. (Cree, Jain and Hillen, 2016, p.12)

In Project R (*Communicate*), we also saw the need to examine organisational aspects of our research context carefully and, like the researchers in Project H, we paid attention to being reflexive throughout the research process (two members of our team were professional speech and language therapists). Cree, Jain and Hillen, who were social worker researchers with their own professional perspectives, also considered both the different perspectives involved in their evaluation (including those of service users/ clients) and explored the overall context in which this drug and alcohol referral service is set. This 'layered' approach to evaluation is especially important where the researchers know that this is largely an internal evaluation which could be seen as open to insider bias if context and researcher reflexivity were to be neglected.

One further important element to add to this kind of health or social care research evaluation is where stakeholders in the project include users of services who may take a leading role as partners in the co-production of projects. There can be many forms of user involvement (see e.g. Carr, 2007; Needham and Carr, 2009; Boxall and Beresford, 2013), but co-production offers the possibility of a shared positive experience for all stakeholders, as in health Project S (below). This example also hinges on creative use of mixed methods. Equally, it relates to the broader field of disability research (for other relevant research examples, see Shakespeare, 2015). Boxall and Beresford (2013) also usefully discuss the potential for further links between disability studies and social work research, including the use of social model approaches.

Project S – Research on the experience of staff with disabilities within the NHS workforce (Ryan et al., 2016)

In this very recent project (2015/2016), staff from Middlesex University and University of Bedfordshire and members of service user groups came together to work on an NHS-commissioned project. Elements of the project included comparison of quantitative data from two NHS national staff datasets and a literature review drawing upon publications using various kinds of research methods; these data were then reviewed and discussed in project workshops with all parties. Video-based feedback from participants was also included in project data. This overall research and evaluation process enabled the experiences of service user group researchers and university staff to be shared, and to fully inform the co-production of a report and planned further publications and seminars/presentations. Recommendations are being developed to inform good workforce practice.

Key issues mirrored in the project data and in the experiences of team members included:

➤ definitions of 'disability' and issues raised by these definitions

➤ prevalence and range of disabilities in the NHS workforce

➤ issues of (self-)disclosure

➤ support and 'reasonable adjustment' for staff with disabilities, including those who become disabled during the course of their employment

➤ issues related to appraisal, remuneration and reasons for leaving NHS employment

➤ difficulties encountered, including bullying, harassment and lack of support

Practical considerations when deciding whether or not to mix methods in a project

These project examples are intended to demonstrate the kinds of decisions – about research design, research processes (fieldwork) and contextualisation – facing researchers who need to consider mixing methods. It should be clear that these mixed projects are often complex studies, even if they have been carried out in a limited context, which means researchers may feel they have needed to use mixed methods in order to pick up various aspects of their project adequately. This complexity has serious implications for project organisation as well as for funding or other resources, although these can often be mitigated, for example by carrying out the project over a longer period or in different stages. For these reasons, I also ask my undergraduate or postgraduate students (though not doctoral students) to think very carefully before attempting even the simplest forms of 'mixed' projects (e.g. a survey followed by interviews or a focus group).

If you intend to use the same research questions or areas of interest, but address them through different methodologies (perhaps in order to provide some basis for **triangulation**), you need to consider the various outcomes that could potentially arise. What will you do if your resulting data might turn out to be contradictory? McAuley et al. (Project Q) discuss this issue in their paper, showing how a deeper level of understanding was generated by their qualitative data (what Brannen's typology refers to as 'elaboration'), but without rejecting the quantitative findings which were useful in providing a broader scope for their study.

In some mixed studies there still seems to be an over-riding dominance of one methodology (as, for example, in Project A which the researchers label as an 'RCT' though it includes interviews as a technique). This often results in most data being 'translated' into the dominant mode. (In the Project A example, interview data had been quantified when the study was published.) In contrast, researchers in Project H, as we saw, tended to emphasise their 'qualitative' credentials although we know they also gathered useful quantitative data. (See also Plewis and Mason, 2005.)

In Project S, much of the project data was quantitative, but the reflexivity generated by discussion within the co-production team allowed this material to be more meaningfully contextualised in terms of lived experience, which was in turn enabling to participants and supported by the NHS commissioners.

Where different research questions are being used in parallel (e.g. in Project R), it is particularly important to pay attention to different epistemological underpinnings within the project. This is a useful strategy to consider if you want your data to be complementary and consider different forms of data to be of equal value within the overall project. It can also be useful in order to play to different strengths and skills of your research team. In a practical sense, especially if you see these different 'sets' of data as separate but equal at least initially, each should be analysed on its own terms and in relation to its own underlying methodology. Interesting joint work can (always with goodwill!) then result at the stage of contextualisation overall when everything is brought together. Unfortunately, in these situations, funders/commissioners may not share researchers' methodological concerns and may give more credence to some aspects of the project's results (often the quantitative findings, in my experience).

Exercise 7.1 **Project ideas: 'mixed methods'**

Can you think of some ideas for a research project in your subject/field (or perhaps something which you may have read about) which would require you to combine different research approaches/methods?

Write down the basic aims or questions for your proposed project, and see if you can suggest some of the advantages or disadvantages which may result from combining:

1) more than one research approach in the overall design

2) several methods /techniques during the research process

Chapter summary

> ➤ This chapter has tried to illustrate that there is not one 'right way' to use mixed methods (techniques) or methodologies.

> ➤ We have presented some key theoretical issues in relation to 'mixing methods', including questions of corroboration, elaboration, complementarity and contradiction. We have considered significance and practical implications of 'mixing' at different stages in the research process.

> ➤ Using project examples, I have outlined various approaches to 'mixing', such as combining specific techniques in one project, as well as working on larger projects that may include several different 'strands' of methodological endeavour.

> ➤ Students are encouraged to consider whether a project with a larger scope, implied by the use of various methods, is feasible for their purposes (e.g. what is suitable for a research degree would be beyond the scope of an undergraduate project).

> ➤ The significance of developing appropriate analytical techniques for different kinds of data is discussed and advocated, particularly to avoid 'getting into a muddle'.

Further reading

Brannen, J (1992) *Mixing Methods: Qualitative and Quantitative Research*, London: Avebury

Brannen, J (2005) Mixing methods: The entry of qualitative and quantitative approaches into the research process, *International Journal of Social Research Methodology*, 8 (3) (Special Issue: Combining Qualitative and Quantitative Methods in Educational and Social Research): 173–184

Bryman, A (2012) *Social Research Methods*, 4th edn, Oxford: Oxford University Press, ch 27

Mertens, D (2003) Mixed methods and the politics of human research IN Tashakkori, A and Teddlie, C (eds) (2003) and reproduced in Plano Clark, V and Creswell, J (2008)

Plano Clark, V and Creswell, J (2008) *The Mixed Methods Reader*, Thousand Oaks: Sage

Plewis, I and Mason, P (2005) What works and why: combining quantitative and qualitative approaches in large-scale evaluations, *International Journal of Social Research Methodology*, 8 (3) (Special Issue: Combining Qualitative and Quantitative Methods in Educational and Social Research): 185–194

Tashakkori, A and Teddlie, C (2003) *Handbook of Mixed Methods in Social and Behavioural Research*, Thousand Oaks: Sage

8

CAN YOU INNOVATE? DEVELOPING ARTS-BASED AND VISUAL METHODS FOR SOCIAL WORK RESEARCH

Introduction

Arts-based and visual methods are undergoing a renaissance in research methods generally, and social work research is no exception (see e.g. Bryant, 2015). This chapter will suggest examples of research and illustrate research techniques that can be used in these innovative contexts, including how they can be used in terms of co-production with colleagues and/or service users (as previously discussed in relation to Project S in Chapter 7). I will be drawing in this chapter upon some recent research and knowledge transfer examples relevant to social work or health. Firstly, we need to briefly outline some key underlying aspects of visual and arts-based research and research methods, and I will suggest further reading that will introduce you to these fields as developed within the social sciences and also cultural studies.

Searching relevant research methods literature shows that researchers such as Sarah Pink (2012), an anthropologist, and Gillian Rose (2007) have done extensive work on the varied possibilities of using visual research methods in the social sciences. In discussing visual anthropology, Pink (2003) suggests visual researchers coming from different disciplines can:

> have common interests in reflexivity, collaboration, ethics and the relationship between content, context and the materiality of images. (p. 191)

However, she also suggests that their different disciplinary aims make it harder to critique such methods across all these disciplines. Added to this, we can see from current research examples that visual methods include use of such varied forms as photography, video/film or drawing. From a methodological perspective, many visual and arts-based researchers have tended to use broadly qualitative methodologies (see e.g. Bryman (2012, ch 19) on visual ethnography) and to link analysis of arts-based data to existing methods of qualitative data analysis, e.g. Banks (2009), Prosser (1998) and Rose (2007). In some contexts there is a focus (as in cultural studies) on issues of images and representation (see Stanczak, 2007) which is also relevant to study of identities for social work researchers.

Meanwhile, Leavy's recent text (2015) suggests an even wider range of approaches and techniques that can be used when incorporating other forms of creative arts with social research: these include (in addition to visual methods) narrative and fiction-based research, poetry, theatre/drama, music and dance/movement. Leavy (2015) talks about arts-based researchers 'shaping' and 'sculpting' new research techniques leading to possibilities of more holistic or integrated perspectives 'where passion and rigor boldly intersect' (p. 3).

We should also note that there have been key overlaps for many years between therapeutic use of visual and arts-based methods in social care or health and their more recent use as research methods. In social work or health contexts, we should expect that these two aspects may often be linked. Some researchers have pointed out that until recently it was the therapeutic use of arts-based methods that was most prevalent in health contexts (see Fraser and Al Sayah, 2011). In their systematic view of arts-based methods in health research, these authors identified 30 relevant studies, these most commonly being based around visual arts, followed by performance arts, and then literary arts. They suggest that in their view, within health research:

> Artistic methods are a useful technique for both knowledge production and translation purposes, albeit to a limited degree. (Fraser and Al Sayah, 2011, Abstract)

In social work contexts, writers including Mazza (2009) have indicated what he terms:

> a place for the arts as a *poetic approach* to family social work practice, research, and education. (p. 3) (my emphasis)

He states that this kind of social work approach would allow family social workers in particular to recognise that what they do is already an 'art', in which they need to be able to:

> recognize a family's unique history, strengths, and context … [and that this] … comes about largely through language, symbols, and stories. (p. 4)

Such 'narrative' approaches to social work practice are already used in a number of contexts and in relation to ethics (see e.g. Wilks, 2005) and clearly lead us into thinking about the value of other arts-based approaches. But, in contrast, when we examine the kinds of health or social care research that is sometimes done mainly into the therapeutic effects of arts-based initiatives, we may find that this kind of research or evaluation is often quite 'traditional' in terms of its reliance on more positivistic research approaches. So, for example, in studies coming from art or music therapy (which may also be of interest to social work researchers), we find studies that measure the benefits or otherwise of particular therapies that are in the main 'done to' and well as 'with' participants. Examples here would be Ho's (2015) study of dance/movement therapy for survivors of child sexual abuse or Cooke et al.'s (2010) research on music therapy for older people with dementia, studies where the emphasis remains firmly on clinical work for the benefit of participants/patients.

Further strands of arts-based research may come closer to social workers' research perspectives where the focus is more directly on development of social justice, empowerment or identities, whether for individuals or communities. Some researchers (e.g. MacPherson, Hart and Heaver, 2016) found a considerable evidence base (across diverse fields including social work, community health and art therapy) connecting visual arts practice with individual and community resilience (see Project V, below). We can find examples of this kind of research in relation to work with people at all stages of life, from young people through to those who are older, including studies such as those by Wright et al. (2010) on the use of participatory photography to empower socially excluded young people; Allen's (2008) research relating to young people's agency in relation to sexuality research; Huss et al. (2015) on community intervention in international social work; Hafford-Letchfield et al. (2010) on a drama project about older people's intimacy and sexuality; or Pilcher, Martin and Williams (2015) writing about participant-led visual diaries for older people. In addition, there are a number of studies relating to participative arts in relation to working with people living with dementia(s); a useful review of this literature is provided by Zeilig, Killick and Fox (2014). This 'arts-based practice' may often cross boundaries between research, evaluation and therapeutic practice, and as such this would be an interesting model to explore and develop further within social work research: in fact, it may turn out to become one of the most valuable reasons for pursuing arts-based or visual research methods within social work / social care. For more detailed examples of three such studies, see Projects T, U and V, below.

Researching and using arts-based methods in social work education

Social work education is another more specifically delineated field in which arts-based methods are being used to bring together these various strands of reflexivity, creativity, research/evaluation, empowerment and co-production. Research and reflection in this educational field also connects with the participatory focus of interest to social work researchers, as noted above. In the cultural studies field, the main focus may sometimes be on visual objects (artefacts) such as photographs or videos in their own right; however, this focus can also be directly relevant to purposes in social work education, for example if these artefacts are discussed in relation to relationships and/or personal experiences. Phillips and Bellinger (2011), for example, use analysis of 21 photographs and accompanying text on the subject of asylum seeking to suggest how they can use such visual methods in their own teaching about relationality and difference within social work education. This can help to raise questions for social workers/students such as:

➤ 'What sorts of images do we have of ourselves in relation to this person/family/group?'

➤ 'How do I "allow" service users and carers to bring themselves into our interaction? Can I see their individuality? Can I see their everyday life? Can I see my own?' (Phillips and Bellinger, 2011, p. 101)

As these authors usefully point out, the link can be made in this kind of social work research between:

> photographs, like acts of social work practice, [that] become productive only as they can be 'experienced' and felt by the viewers and service users (Phillips and Bellinger, 2011, p. 91)

In a special issue of the journal *Social Work Education* focused on arts-based approaches, the co-editors consider that:

> employing techniques in social work education that mobilise imagination and creativity through artistic expression has transformative potential for learning and intercultural dialogue. (Hafford-Letchfield et al., 2012, p. 684)

The international research examples in this journal issue are very varied and range from:

➤ a paper covering three American projects linking social work, the arts and humanities – Arts in Recovery (AIR); the Leaving Homelessness Intervention Research Project (LHIRP); and Interdisciplinary Research on Environmental Design (IRED) (Moxley, Feen-Calligan and Washington, 2012)

➤ poetry used to promote social justice (Foster, 2012a)

➤ using play-based methods to support social work students learn communication skills with children and young people (Ayling, 2012)

> visual methods (Huss, 2012; Walton, 2012)

> using narrative (Phillips, Macgiollari and Callaghan, 2012)

As the co-editors also discuss in their editorial:

> crossing boundaries between the social sciences with the arts and humanities can help to communicate service users' and carers' experiences more power-fully. (Hafford-Letchfield et al., 2012, Abstract)

Using arts-based methods can also contribute to more transformative discussions of social problems during learning/teaching. Learning about leadership is another relevant area for social work and health education (see Leonard, Hafford-Letchfield and Couchman, 2013); evaluation of this kind of arts-based approach has identified emotional engagement in learning, with participants acquiring a sense of achievement as well as understanding the significance of co-production when learning a new skill.

Examples of arts-based social work research/evaluation

In this section, we will look at three examples where arts-based approaches have been used in relevant projects, to illustrate how these researchers/practitioners have developed newer and more creative ways to carry out research and to cross boundaries between research, evaluation and therapeutic practice.

Project T – Evaluating a Sure Start[1] programme in England using arts-based methods (Foster, 2012b)

In this project, a local Sure Start programme was aimed, as expected, at improving the health and well-being of families with young children and also at developing parenting skills. A range of methods including poetry, visual arts and video were used when undertaking an evaluation of this programme. These methods were used to collect and analyse data as well as to disseminate the evaluation's findings, with participatory methods involving local mothers and artists/practitioners crucially involved in both stages. Methods included the development of two plays at the dissemination stage; one was a realistic 'ethnodrama' developed from the project's interview data:

> the words of this short, two-act play come straight from the mouths of local parents and carers and reflect a range of attitudes towards the Sure Start programme. (Foster, 2012b, p. 539)

The other play is described as a 'pantomime', and the researchers explain that these plays were performed and produced by mothers of children attending the local Sure Start programme:

> in order to re-tell the stories told to us during the course of the research. (p. 534)

Whilst some local mothers were recruited and trained to use more 'conventional' research methods in the early part of the project (interviews and a survey), the researchers found that in addition, using arts-based methods:

> that did not privilege the written word were successful in engaging 'hard-to-reach' groups in telling their stories (video proved particularly useful here). (Foster, 2012b, p. 537)

A range of arts-based classes for local parents focusing on visual art, film-making and poetry had been set up with the collaboration of local artists. This allowed collection of rich data taken from participants' own experiences, to enhance the research material gathered through more conventional research methods. Whilst a full project report was produced by the researcher (Foster), the plays allowed project data to be co-produced and then disseminated to a much wider range of people than those who would read the report. The researcher makes an interesting connection between scriptwriting for the plays and data analysis:

> The scriptwriting process can also be understood as *a form of data analysis,* since it involves careful thinking about which stories need to be told, and how best to represent them. (Foster, 2012b, p. 539) (my emphasis)

Foster (2012b) suggests that using arts-based approaches in social work research offers the chance to:

> address *power relations* in the research process, not least by reducing the focus on the written word and looking at other means of communication. Furthermore, they allow participants to engage their imaginations and creativity; they facilitate empathy and challenge misconceptions by giving insight to their audience into aspects of their lives, revealing what their lives are like and the potential for how they could be. (p. 533) (my emphasis)

This evaluative project illustrates how processes of building empathy and understanding can be successfully constructed through using arts-based methods, which were described as 'fun' by participants. However, Foster also suggests how developing the potential for audience response could have been enhanced in this project (as also suggested by Leavy, 2015):

> On reflection, asking for brief, written responses to the plays, although it did provide some useful data which added a dimension of validity to the work, was not the ideal method to use within an approach to research that sought alternatives to the written word. Had we built in a critical discussion following the performance, this might have strengthened the ability of the research to confront stereotypes and challenge people's ways of thinking and working. (Foster, 2012b, p. 542)

Project U – Comedy activities in day services for older people living with dementia(s) (Hafford-Letchfield, 2013)

This was a partnership-based community project for older people living with dementia(s) involving a day centre in London, a specialist comedy provider and a university. The project sought to actively engage older people attending the centre ('Grangers') in activities that would enable them to reflect on aspects of their care environment:

> As an experiential project, we were not prescriptive about any outcomes, but had a broad aim of capturing some of the content from the project in the form of digital learning materials that could be subsequently used in the delivery of professional education. (Hafford-Letchfield, 2013, p. 843)

The connection to professional education in this example is important in terms of the eventual outputs. The partnership team began by engaging older people through improvisatory work at the centre and after various discussions it was decided to use a 'mockumentary' style of filmmaking using improvised and unscripted acting in which:

> fictitious events are presented in documentary format and are commonly used to analyse or comment on current issues. (Hafford-Letchfield, 2013, p. 843)

It was important to choose a meaningful theme that would build on Grangers' strengths (e.g. existence of longer term memories), and enable them and family carers to enjoy creative activities. A planned visit of 'Her Majesty the Queen' to the day centre thus became the project's focus. This idea was developed through a series of four workshops, held weekly, where the event was planned through various creative preparations, singing and dancing as entertainment, culminating in the visit of the 'Queen' (played by a carer) at the final workshop:

> The workshops did not work to an exact script but allowed scenarios to develop based on the main theme. Experiential drama techniques were used to work with the issues that Grangers came up with themselves. All of the workshops were continuously filmed and photographed. Footage from the former was edited to make the ... 30 minute mockumentary. (Hafford-Letchfield, 2013, p. 844)

This project was not considered to be 'research' by the partnership team, with the main focus being on providing direct activities for older people and subsequent production of the digital learning tool for professionals (mockumentary). The mockumentary was also presented at an event for participants and local dignitaries. Nevertheless, as a project it raises many similar issues to those that underlie research projects, including questions of ethics, and understanding how to assess what the project achieved for all the participants.

These points are all usefully discussed by Hafford-Letchfield, who used all the materials contributing to the 'mockumentary', consultations and debriefings of participants as well as her own involvement to evaluate the project; she drew together a broad thematic analysis into three key themes: 'being in the moment', 'how comedy allowed us to "challenge" stereotypes' and 'building relationships within the day centre'. Careful consideration was paid throughout to issues of consent to participation by the Grangers, whilst their enjoyment of the whole process was also noted by carers and staff.

Project V – Building resilience through group visual arts activities with young people who experience mental health complexities and/or learning difficulties (Macpherson, Hart and Heaver, 2016)

These authors undertook a wide-ranging cross-disciplinary scoping review and carried out a small-scale case study that aimed to identify and evaluate the possible benefits of visual arts interventions for young people with complex needs. They identify existing literature that suggests building resilience[2] is particularly important for:

> disabled young people and young people with mental health challenges ... Resilience-based practice offers a strengths-based approach to evaluating and addressing the needs of young people. (Macpherson, Hart and Heaver, 2016, p.2).

The case study involved a series of weekly arts-based workshops for ten young people. Learning a specific skill set and helping others have been shown to be important issues in building resilience. However, the scoping study part of this project also shows that there can sometimes be risks in arts-based activities, if for example these open up difficult feelings that cannot necessarily be dealt with effectively by those facilitating the activities.

In terms of evaluative methodology, this research used mixed methods including the development of a resilience scale (to be used pre and post the intervention), focus group and interviews. The resilience scale results revealed limited improvement post-intervention, but as the researchers point out:

> The accessible resilience scale we constructed was only trialled on 10 participants and some of these participants with moderate learning difficulty still needed help reading the questions. The scale was useful for helping us talk about resilience in the focus group and interviews, however it needs to be trialled further and potentially revised in order to prove whether it is a valid measure of resilience in young people with complex needs. (Macpherson, Hart and Heaver, 2016, p. 15)

One key lesson learnt by the researchers was that:

> Visual arts strategies for achieving resilience need to be tailored effectively to the setting and objectives of a community or individual. (Macpherson, Hart and Heaver, 2016, p. 16)

This research is now connected to an ongoing programme and website related to resilience, including an 'arts for resilience' practice guide. See www.boingboing.org.uk.

Discussion Points

You have the opportunity to work with a small group of social work students who are volunteering at a community group concerned with developing parenting skills. Some of the parents have already had more than one child taken into care, but most have a child still residing with them. One student suggests developing a group project that will draw upon her experience as a photographer. Suggest some means by which you, as the social work tutor, could address:

➤ ethical issues concerning:

  ➤ confidentiality

  ➤ ownership of any identifiable project 'outputs'.

➤ issues of co-production with parents and students all taking part in the project

Methods of data collection, analysis and interpretation in art-based research: discussion

These three examples illustrate some issues involved in doing social work research using innovative, arts-based approaches. There are a number of strengths to these approaches, especially for social workers, which could be outlined here as:

➢ possibilities for crossing boundaries between research, evaluation and arts-based + therapeutic practice

➢ possibilities for 'involving' users of social work and health related services in more active ways, including use of co-production techniques (see also Project S, Chapter 7)

➢ being able to make use of existing and more familiar research approaches and methods such as interviews, or surveys, alongside newer approaches linked more directly to arts-based practices, e.g. photography or digital-storytelling

➢ many methods of data analysis (particularly qualitative) can be adapted for use with arts-based research methods, e.g. drama (see e.g. 'script-writing' as a form of data analysis (Project T)); Rose (2007) suggests a number methods for analysing visual data including discourse analysis[3]** or content analysis (see also Chapter 5) as well as those focusing more specifically on deconstruction of language (e.g. semiology) or on more directly 'visual' methods such as compositional interpretation or photo-documentation

➢ there are varied possibilities for project 'outcomes' using arts-based approaches to social work research, in addition to the more traditional 'project report' or academic and professional publications; as we have seen, these can include videos/digital media (including digital story-telling), exhibitions or dramatic performances/other role playing, some of which can also be utilised for professional education (see also Villadsen et al., 2012)

Our discussions of **discourse analysis and content analysis in Chapter 5 suggest how these methods of analysis could be adapted to use with visual or other arts-based material.

Discussion Points

Are you interested in discourse or narrative (story-telling) as a focus for your analysis of visual or arts-based material, e.g. poetry, video?

Are you trying to 'code' your data in a more 'fixed' way order to analyse it?

Is it possible to use elements of both these approaches in your analysis?

Some further aspects of research methods to reflect on when using 'arts-based' approaches:

➤ Researchers sometimes need to work out how to display greater transparency over their methodological choices (as they would with more conventional methods, both qualitative and quantitative).

Some of the examples we have given are clearer than others in delineating exactly how data was analysed and project results were arrived at; 'creativity' may sometimes seem to take precedence over specificity (though this may also be true in some other forms of qualitative research methods where subjectivity is to the fore). This issue of 'what are the outcomes of the project?' needs to be balanced against seeing creativity as a strength of the approach.

➤ Ethical issues can sometimes be more complex when using arts-based approaches (as noted by Hafford-Letchfield, Project U). This complexity can also be a feature of Internet-based research (see Chapter 9).

Careful attention is therefore needed when considering issues such as confidentiality, especially when working with those who may be deemed 'vulnerable'. However, such research does not always have to be 'anonymous', especially if participants themselves want the opportunity to be identified as having taken part or as co-producers (as in Projects T and U, for example).

➤ Arts-based methods should not ignore the potential for using quantitative methods (such as measures), especially in their evaluation processes (e.g. Villadsen et al., 2012).

Although qualitative methods may seem to have a better 'fit' with arts-based approaches, there is sometimes the opportunity to develop measureable outcomes, although these may sometimes need to be carefully refined; more 'traditional' approaches, for example, to sampling may sometimes be needed in order to achieve such outcomes (as noted by Macpherson, Hart, and Heaver in Project V).

Exercise 8.1 **Photographs/concept of 'family'**

Select ten photographs or poems that you decide relate to the concept of 'family' in some way.

Having made your selection, try to analyse each one in terms of the (sub)themes it contains.

What is it that links the photographs in terms of your original 'family' concept? Do they make a 'story'/narrative, or do you think they are 'discrete' objects? What possibilities does this raise for your analysis?

What does engaging with this exercise reveal about your own attitudes towards the concept of 'family'?

Chapter summary

> In this chapter we have examined use of arts-based and visual methods in social work and health related settings. We distinguished between their use in therapeutic and research contexts, and suggested where these can overlap.

> We considered examples of researching and using arts-based methods in social work education.

> Using recent examples, we discussed recent arts-based social work research and evaluation projects and suggested issues arising from these approaches including:
>   > working with service users in participatory ways
>   > displaying greater transparency over methodological choices
>   > addressing relevant ethical issues
>   > potential for using different kinds of research methods of data collection and analysis

Further reading

Banks, M (2009) *Using Visual Data in Qualitative Research*, London: Sage

Bryant, L (ed) (2015) *Critical and Creative Research Methodologies in Social Work*, London: Ashgate

Hafford-Letchfield, T, Leonard, K and Couchman, W (2012) Editorial: Arts and extremely dangerous: Critical commentary on the Arts in social work education, *Social Work Education: The International Journal*, 31 (6): 683–690

Leavy, P (2015) *Method Meets Art: Arts-Based Research Practice*, 2nd edn, New York: Guilford Press

Pink, S (2012) *Advances in Visual Methodology*, London: Sage

Prosser, J (1998) *Image-Based Research: A Resource for Qualitative Researchers*, London: Routledge

Rose, G (2007) *Visual Methodologies: An Introduction to the Interpretation of Visual Materials*, 2nd edn, London: Sage

Stanczak, G (ed) (2007) *Visual Research Methods: Image, Society and Representation*, London: Sage

Thomson, P (2008) *Doing Visual Research with Children and Young People*, London: Routledge

9

WHAT'S OUT THERE? USING THE INTERNET AND SOCIAL MEDIA FOR RESEARCH

Introduction

Throughout this book we have been drawing upon Internet sources; such is the ubiquitous nature of our current relationships with 'the Web'. We can hardly remember, no doubt, what it was like to have to rely only on paper sources for all our information and for our methods of carrying out various forms of enquiry. Increasingly however, new(er) technology has been catching up with us and suggesting ever more complex ways of conducting those enquiries. As we noted in Chapter 1, increasing use of social media means that in some circumstances our data and communication in general is becoming much more about instant response, sometimes through short, decontextualised comments which are challenging to analyse (e.g. Twitter/tweets). This in turn can generate many methodological as well as ethical issues when trying to be 'research minded' in these shifting contexts.

In this chapter, I will discuss and try to demonstrate ways in which online techniques can be useful for social work research, for example for survey work or other interviewing purposes; or for drawing upon visual or written materials such as e-mails or online forums. We will once again illustrate these points through using relevant project examples (Project W and Project X). Although some guidance on relevant websites may be also included here, any website addresses signposted in this book do risk becoming outdated, so I will also try, as before, to reference these to their relevant organisation(s), as appropriate. We will also need to take into account the sometimes ambiguous status of online sources for research purposes, as we already discussed in Chapter 2. Ethical issues relating to 'online' research are also particularly relevant, and these will be discussed in this chapter and linked to what was already discussed in Chapter 3.

Using online methods in social work research

Searching for recent social work research literature reveals examples where researchers have used directly 'online' methods for example to carry out surveys, as well as studies of people's Internet usage or computer-mediated communication (CMC) (e.g. by young people using chat rooms, May-Chahal et al., 2014); via online forums (Leece and Leece, 2011); student e-mails relating to interprofessional discourse (Reynolds, 2007) or blogs. Some of these studies have, however, also continued to use 'traditional' research methods such as paper questionnaires (e.g. Best, Manktelow and Taylor, 2016); studies of young people's use of digital media including mobile phones or the Internet may have also used conventional quali- tative methods such as interviews (e.g. Sen, 2015). It is clear from these examples, as already pointed out by Hine (2015), that there many crosso- vers in research methods between 'online' and 'offline' approaches:

> In order to understand mediated communications one is also often led to study face-to-face settings in which they are produced and consumed and to compre- hend the settings in which they become embedded. (pp. 6–7)

Not only this, but as Hine also usefully points out, one reason for study- ing these new developments (especially for social work research) is that despite their apparently ubiquitous spread, not everyone's experience(s) of the Internet, CMC or other digital technologies (nor indeed access to them) are the same (see e.g. Murthy, 2008). As we will see, exploring individuals' experiences of digital or online contexts may be particularly useful for social work research, especially where we could be concerned by issues of inequality or social justice. Some of these issues will be high- lighted in our project examples below (Projects W and X).

Furthermore, researchers' involvement in these digital or online con- texts may vary considerably depending on the kinds of approaches and methods they choose to work with and through. Ethnographic work, for example, in any context requires a much more 'embodied' sense of involvement for the researcher than other types of research approach, bringing particular challenges as well as strengths. This means that certain techniques such as field notes are likely to remain very important to eth- nographers using and embedding themselves in digital sources and con- texts (Hine, 2015, p. 184; see again Chapters 4 and 5).

Survey researchers (some of whom are also carrying out ethnographies or case studies) may to some extent be simply 'extending' their reach with questionnaires or other forms of cross-sectional study by using online contexts. These kinds of studies can be valuable for researching both the attitudes of professionals and/or users of services. They can also explore uptake of various digital or online information or other services (see Project W, below). Many of my social work students now expect to be able to use online questionnaires to reach a larger number of potential survey respondents, and whilst this is encouraging in some ways, it is also disappointing if, in the process, important issues relevant to more conventional survey methodology such as piloting the questionnaire or testing of attitude scales for validity are neglected in digital contexts. Innovative projects making use of various digital media (from e-mail to blogs or online forums) are nevertheless surely to be welcomed.

At the other end of the scale from the immersion required by ethnography, some researchers may set out mainly to observe much more 'at a distance' how we are all making use of digital technologies. An example of this more 'distant' social research is that being developed around Twitter.[1] A recent DEMOS scoping exercise (Bartlett and Norrie, 2015) examined conversations taking place on Twitter about the topic of immigration. (Megele (2014), for example, defines tweets as continuous 'multilogues' – 'many to many' conversations.) DEMOS researchers met policy specialists initially to identify areas to study in depth; they produced data for specifically identified periods of time in relation to key topics (which had been identified by keywords), subsequently showing results for thousands of tweets based on: trend analysis (frequency and type of conversations), content analysis (what was discussed) and profile analysis (types of people who 'tweeted' about these topics). These authors identify several issues in relation to methodological and ethical implications of such a Twitter scoping exercise, some of which are also identified by Megele (2014). These include the value of being able to obtain and analyse a very large dataset of 'real time' conversations, which are likely to be more naturalistic than data obtained by other methods such as surveys. The immediacy of responses observed is thus a strength in this type of analysis. However, they also suggest that this very immediacy has limitations in terms of interpretation; coupled with the 'self-selecting' nature of many of those involved in these multilogues[2] (for example, a few individuals may 'tweet' repeatedly about a particular topic, whilst many people will do so only once or twice), it is clear that such exercises may have limited, if useful, relevance to social research.

Ethical issues in online/digital contexts

A recurring theme in this book has been to consider how researchers themselves need to take responsibility for their own ethical practice during research processes (see also Iphofen, 2009). This issue goes much wider than simply getting ethics approval to do your study from a relevant authority. This is no more, nor less, true for online/digital contexts. Despite attention being paid to issues such as consent (with Twitter being considered a public platform in many ways – see Megele, 2014; Bartlett and Norrie, 2015), the sometimes ambiguous public/private nature of online conversations in various contexts should be an ethical concern for most social researchers. Back in 2004, this issue was already being picked up by a number of social researchers (see Buchanan, 2004).

For example Bober (2004), writing in Buchanan's edited volume, discusses ethical issues involved in doing 'virtual' research with young people. There are a number of useful suggestions here that can assist social work researchers who are also working with young people or with adults we might consider to be vulnerable. Firstly, whilst it might be wrong (and unethical) simply to exclude such people from participation in research or evaluation merely because we consider them to be vulnerable, researchers using online/digital contexts also need to be aware of ambiguous private/public spaces that these contexts can throw up, as mentioned above. Young people in particular may simply not be fully aware that involvement in digital/social media can be very 'public', sometimes with quite devastating consequences for them. I would concur with Bober that in these situations it is the researcher's responsibility to ensure that steps are taken to protect their participants as far as possible by ensuring they can rely on confidentiality and anonymity where appropriate. It may be more difficult in some digital studies to obtain parental consent to young people's participation, as you might expect to do in face-to-face environments, but again the researcher needs to consider this issue carefully (perhaps with advice from the relevant ethics committee).

May-Chahal et al.'s (2014) very interesting and carefully set up exploratory research is about young people's use of chat rooms in relation to safeguarding issues in social work. This research suggests that whilst the role of parents may be emphasised in keeping children safe 'online' (especially for younger children), there are certainly a number of ethical issues relevant to social work practice in this context, not least that:

> routine aspects of practical reasoning in childhood can become less reliable when applied into mediated settings [CMCs etc.]. (May-Chahal et al., 2014, p. 610)

These authors therefore recommend that children's CMC should be thoroughly appraised in social work assessments, with computer literacy education also offered to parents. The implication is that CMC/social media and online issues need to be seen as of central relevance to social work (and by implication therefore to social work research as well), so we can develop greater understanding of the deeper issues involved.

See also Hafford-Letchfield (2013) and Project U (Chapter 8) on ethical issues around involvement of older people with dementia in research/evaluation.

Discussion Points

Can you list up to five differences you think may exist between ethical concerns in digital/online research contexts compared to face-to-face or paper-based (survey) research?

Examples of online/digital social work research

We will now examine in more detail processes involved in two social work–based studies relevant to digital/online contexts. As before, these examples draw together methodological, subject-based and ethical concerns in order to illustrate some issues arising from these projects.

Project W – Internet technology: An empowering or alienating tool for communication between foster-carers and social workers? (Dodsworth et al., 2013)

This project represents an independent evaluation, commissioned by government in 2009, of a commercial Internet service that had been acquired by a number of English local authorities. The evaluation focused on three of these purchasers (a London borough, a city outside London and a rural authority) who had set up Internet services (ICT) for foster carers. The researchers conducting the evaluation wanted to find out whether or not this service had improved communications between foster carers and social workers (if so, the implication being that this would also improve outcomes for the young people who were fostered). (There had already been earlier calls for ICT to be used more widely in social work, especially to empower service users – see e.g. Parrott and Madoc-Jones, 2008.)

Dodsworth et al. (2013, p. 778) explain that they aimed to evaluate the following five areas. Had the internet service:

➤ altered, and potentially improved, the way in which social workers and foster-carers communicate with each other and work together?

➤ facilitated access by foster-carers to training resources and enabled them to efficiently book training courses online?

➤ provided secure file transfer between foster-carers and social workers?

➤ given carers greater access to support materials and an extensive online knowledge base that could be expected to improve child outcomes and placement stability?

➤ created an 'online community' of carers who use the social networking aspects of the site to message each other, share ideas and provide mutual support?

Due to the nature of this evaluation, a mixture of research methods was required, both online and offline, in order to provide an all-round evaluative process. An important initial step was for the researchers to be given access to the Internet site, so that they could monitor its use by foster carers and social workers. The site itself had been set up to record demographic data such as the number of site (or specific page) visitors, and when and how much time a visitor had spent on the site; there were also open areas giving information about events, training etc..

Research methods used for the evaluation were interviews with key staff in each of the three local authorities concerning implementation of the Internet service; a paper-based survey using questionnaires that was sent to all foster carers in the three areas; and separate focus groups for social workers and foster carers. The authors state that they were not able to provide an online survey option due to issues about confidentiality. They tell us that the questionnaire covered the following areas:

> Carers' current computer use and their confidence in using e-mails and the internet; their views and expectations of the fostering internet service; their training requirements and booking preferences; the degree of contact they had with other foster-carers and through what medium; and their patterns of communication with their own supervising social worker and their foster child's social worker. (Dodsworth et al., 2013, p. 780)

An incentive was also provided to foster carers taking part in the survey in the form of entry into a prize draw (the winner's number being generated randomly). The response rates to the survey in each area were, however, fairly low: 20% in the London borough, 27% in the rural authority and 38% in the city authority.

Results of this small-scale evaluation suggest that lessons can be learnt in terms of the issues that were raised about the following topics, already highlighted in other literature in some cases:

➤ access to computers and/or broadband services

➤ access to ICT training and developing competence

➤ confidentiality in digital/online settings

➤ promotion of the Internet service (which was used more extensively in the local authority which promoted its use more effectively)

➤ accessing knowledge passively instead of sharing knowledge within a developing 'community'

➤ some social workers' concerns about power issues between themselves and carers

Project X – Personalisation: Perceptions of the role of social workers in a world of brokers and budgets (Leece and Leece, 2011)

In this project, the authors (one of whom is an experienced social worker) aimed to research an important recent issue in adult care by using computer-mediated communication directly. A key aim was to be able to access 'hard-to-reach' participants who were affected by issues involved in personalisation – in particular, to examine their attitudes towards social workers becoming more like 'brokers' to support service users in a future context where self-directed assessment is likely to become more significant. Issues such as adult safeguarding, aspects of risk and social workers returning to a more therapeutic role are all considered in this paper.

The researchers tell us they aimed to use a **grounded theory** approach and that in order to do so they first identified 18 online forums, 3 forums relating to older people, 3 carers' forums and 12 forums relating to disability groups. A thread concerning the future role of social workers was then posted onto these 18 online forums. The researchers tell us that due to the nature of online forums, any thread that is posted needs to be 'concise and easily understood by a wide range of people' (Leece and Leece, 2011, p. 212).

Responses from these forums varied considerably depending in part on the number of participants in each; no responses at all were obtained from one of older people's forums, nor from five of the disability forums. The researchers describe how some of their interactions with individual participants became more like 'in-depth interviews', whilst where a larger group of participants took part in a conversation, the strategy was that the researchers would also participate from time to time. In total they obtained 153 responses from 66 separate participants over a four-week period in 2009. In keeping with their grounded theory approach, the researchers decided after four weeks that no new, relevant data was being posted and so 'theoretical saturation' had by that time been reached and data collection stopped.

Ethical issues have already been mentioned as being of concern in digital/online projects, and in this case Leece and Leece mention that in this CMC context it was problematic for them to obtain full consent from their participants; demographic details such as ethnicity or other personal data were also unobtainable (unless participants volunteered these details). However, the researchers did try to address issues of confidentiality by withholding details of the forums they used and also by use of pseudonyms. They tried to address issues of informed consent to participate in the study by reassuring their participants through full disclosure of their own details and institutional affiliations.

Whilst enabling the researchers to obtain views of hard-to-reach populations (and to allow those, for example, with mobility issues to participate), the researchers also acknowledge that because they were able to find more Internet forums relating to people with disabilities, the sample was skewed in that direction. Also, we do not know how many of those in one forum category ('older people') were also people with disabilities or carers. (It is not clear whether there was any actual overlap between the forums.)

Discussion

Leece and Leece acknowledge that their Project X must have been affected by issues such as participants' access to computers, broadband and computer literacy more generally (as in Project W); but in their case the researchers cannot know exactly how or how much this may have restricted participation in their study. Paper-based questionnaires used in Project W revealed these issues to some extent, although the reported survey response rates were also quite low. In social work more widely there still seem to be issues about uses made of ICT for the benefit and inclusion of users of services, compared to ICT's adoption by managers or policy makers (see Parrott and Madoc-Jones, 2008), and I suggest that these attitudes need challenging. More research using such methods can only encourage social workers and those who research with them to explore these issues more fully.

Examining online and digital research methods in this chapter does suggest that many of the same methodological issues, including ethical concerns, still recur whether researchers are working in 'traditional' or ICT research methods contexts. However, some newer concerns are raised for both social work research and social work practice by the very ambiguous nature or form of these new technologies themselves. How easy is it to obtain informed consent from people in 'virtual' contexts? Is everyone participating in these contexts really who they say they are? What implications does this have especially for young people or for vulnerable adults? (See again May-Chahal et al., 2014.) What are the ethical as well as the methodological challenges involved in trying to analyse short, decontextualised communications? However, do people always tell the truth when completing paper-based questionnaires? It is very unlikely! (Although risks if they do not are perhaps less significant than in virtual contexts.)

Exercise 9.1 How are digital/online methods being used within your own organisation?

Explore how digital/online methods are being used within your own organisation (or university/college):

➢ Plan out how you would research this and decide on an overall research question.

➢ Will you use only 'traditional'/non-CMC research methods, some CMC and some traditional methods or all CMC research methods (such as use of e-mails, blogs or digital forums)?

➢ What scope is there to work collaboratively with/for the benefit of users of social work services on this project?

Chapter summary

➢ This chapter discussed and suggested ways in which online techniques can be useful, e.g. for survey work or other 'interviewing' purposes; for drawing upon visual or written materials; for examining actual usage of websites or digital information sources by service users and professionals (e.g. Project W).

➢ Examining online and digital research methods does suggest that many of the same methodological issues still recur whether researchers are working in 'traditional' or in ICT research methods contexts.

➢ However, some newer concerns are raised for both social work research and social work practice by the very ambiguous nature or form of these new technologies themselves.

➢ Using project examples, we showed how researchers as well as users of digital technologies (including children) may 'overlap' their use of CMC and face-to-face or paper techniques.

➢ We discussed ethical issues relating to 'online'/digital research and some specific concerns raised, such as obtaining 'informed consent' from people in 'virtual' contexts. Is everyone participating in these contexts really who they say they are? What implications does this have especially for young people or for vulnerable adults? What are the ethical as well as the methodological challenges involved in trying to analyse short, decontextualised communications?

Further reading

Bryman, A (2004) *Social Research Methods*, 4th edn, Oxford: Oxford University Press, ch 28

Buchanan, EA (ed) (2004) *Readings in Virtual Research Ethics: Issues and Controversies*, Hershey: Information Science Publishing

Cantijoch, M, Gibson, R and Ward, S (eds) (2014) *Analysing Social Media Data and Web Networks*, Basingstoke: Palgrave

Hine, C (2015) *Ethnography for the Internet: Embedded, Embodied and Everyday*, London: Bloomsbury Academic

10

BECOMING A SOCIAL WORK RESEARCHER: BUILDING CONFIDENCE AS WELL AS SKILLS

Introduction/Summary

In this final chapter, I want to encourage you to develop your research skills to the 'next level' and to consolidate what you have learnt from this book and from the projects and other research and evaluative examples we have discussed. This is intended to help you to think about developing your own project work and also to enable you to appreciate the value of existing research and evaluation: we can and should all learn from each other when conducting research relevant to social work. I will make some suggestions in this chapter about how to produce an effective research proposal (or protocol) that you can use to develop towards a master's level or doctoral dissertation, or if you are applying to do funded practitioner research.

As we have seen throughout this book, research mindedness depends upon many things. You need to consider how you access and evaluate media, information, publications and all the other varied sources we considered in Chapter 2. You really need to reflect on how use of these sources can impact on your own professional practice before you begin to consider doing your own project.

Also in Chapter 2 we introduced the idea that doing research and evaluation is not just about techniques, the process is also grounded in theories and ideas about what underlies research; you need to be able to design your project in a way that has integrity, especially in terms of its **epistemology** (or 'way of knowing'). What does this mean? The following quote from Gringeri, Barusch and Cambron (2013), who are speaking particularly about qualitative social work research, gives a flavour of what I understand by taking this approach to research:

> *Epistemological integrity* means that researchers hold themselves to high standards of accountability in their published work with regard to open and clear discussion of their research paradigm, application of theory, reflexivity, and

understanding of power in their relationship with participants. Building our work on a solid epistemological foundation requires anchoring the work in theory, consciously interweaving reflexive accounts throughout the process, and deliberately linking each aspect of the work within the paradigm. (p. 62) (my emphasis)

I would argue that this way of thinking about research integrity should equally well apply to quantitative research approaches; it is and should be possible to reflect on and justify the quantitative methods you have chosen and used whilst carrying out projects that are grounded in more 'postivistic' epistemologies. These kinds of projects are designed to answer questions about effectiveness and statistical evidence, and so they have an important role to play in supporting the idea of 'evidence-based practice' even though (as we have also seen) this concept can sometimes be slippery or contested (see, for example, the discussion in Smith, 2009). In Chapter 6 we saw how, in some research examples, researchers had not only used 'quantitative' methods but had done so in a way that was reflexive and which acknowledged weaknesses as well as strengths of these ways of doing research.

Underpinning all of this from the perspective of supporting social work values is the attention all researchers need to pay to research ethics. We saw that whether you are a student or qualified practitioner, you must also pay careful attention to your own professional ethics and values and examine how these may cross-cut ethical concerns that all researchers face from time to time. Some of these issues were discussed in the project examples we presented in Chapter 3 and in later chapters, including Chapter 9 where we discussed ethics in relation to online/digital contexts. We also made a link here between research ethics and ethics underpinning social work practices.

For many social workers, relationship-based work lies at the heart of their professional endeavours. In Chapter 4 I tried to demonstrate that, whilst not always being exactly the same, there are many connections between the talking and listening skills researchers use when gathering or analysing qualitative data and those that are involved in relationship-based approaches used by social workers during their professional practice. **Reflexivity** is also a key aspect of such processes: as discussed at the end of the first chapter, reflexivity can involve not only considered decision-making in specific contexts, but also taking a critical approach to knowledge generation, towards power and towards working with emotions.

In order to develop all your research skills fully within your own projects, you also need to be aware of the more technical aspects of working with and generating documents (such as diaries) and then analysing qualitative data from both documentary or face-to-face methods. These areas of knowledge and skills were tackled in Chapter 5 and should encourage you to build upon these kinds of techniques in your own work. Throughout this book I have also provided discussion points and exercises to enable you to practice and test out ideas involved. In parallel with these analytical skills, Chapter 6 provided you with some examples of how measurable statistical data can be gathered and analysed. Such numeracy-based skills can again be useful to underpin everyday practice for social work and health students and in professional social work. Once again, I should emphasise that there are different ideas about what constitutes rigorous methodology, and as Gringeri, Barusch and Cambron (2013) pointed out, we are aiming at integrity grounded in transparency about our methods, rather than at simplistically 'correct' techniques, and certainly not at 'perfection' in an abstract sense!

To your developing relationship based skills, we should add 'seeing' or even 'performing', as these are also part of the arts-based methods we discussed in Chapter 8; these skills and methods are becoming particularly useful as social workers and other researchers aim to develop more innovative and participatory forms of research and evaluation. We also noted here the possibilities for crossing boundaries between research, evaluation and arts-based and therapeutic practice. More crossovers and overlaps are evident between online/digital and face-to-face processes and links, and in Chapter 9 we examined how in some projects, researchers have made use of both 'traditional' research methods and digital forms; this again raises issues around ethics, which also connect with ethical professional practice in relation to topics such as safeguarding.

Now I am going to make some suggestions about producing a research proposal for your own student or practitioner project. You will need to go back to Chapter 1 to review what we said there about developing research questions and researchable topics. Remember, 'where does your shoe pinch?'

Exercise 10.1 **Design Your Own Research**

Design your own research proposal for a project related to social work practice, approximately 3000 words.

Producing a research proposal

A research proposal (also called a protocol in some types of research) is a plan or blueprint that the researcher prepares before carrying out the research. It may need to be scrutinised so that ethics approval can be given, and/or peer reviewed (especially where research funding is sought). Some kinds of research are easier to plan in detail in advance; for other studies, the research needs to develop during the research process. However, planning ahead to some degree is always necessary.

First you need to consider who the proposal is aimed at and whether there are any requirements in terms of word length, contents or formatting. Some applications (bids) for funding actually supply you with a form to complete, covering all necessary sections. If so, the trick is often to be able to say the same or very similar things in the different sections, but without looking as if you are repeating yourself. Invariably you will need to present not only your own methods but also a review of background literature or other material that justifies the importance of your topic and shows why you are choosing to research it in the way that you are. For some evaluative work nowadays there will also be a heavy steer towards what funders expect you to be doing. Again, a necessary trick is to try and show what you (and your team) can bring to this project that no one else can. This is not only demonstrated by your project description and curriculum vitae (CVs/resumés) but also in terms of saying what you think the key issues are and why.

If you are applying to an ethics committee or for a research degree, you may be told to produce a short research proposal of, for example, 'about four pages'. It is quite a good discipline to have to restrict yourself in this way, contrary to what you might think. You have to explain yourself succinctly to other people and cut out any 'waffle'! On the other hand, if you are a student preparing a research proposal for assessment as part of your course, you will typically be asked to write a piece which may be of up to 3000 or 4000 words. Whatever the required length of your proposal, it needs to have the characteristics discussed below.

Written in a straightforward and accessible style, that communicates well to the reader

Your proposal should state what you intend to do and why, giving enough detail for the person reading it to be able to evaluate how well you are justifying your research approach and your choice and planned use of research methods. Not explaining directly what you are planning to do can be a problem, as can using obscure reasoning to things that the reader may not know anything about (unexplained acronyms are a case in point – SSI? What's that? – Answer: it used to be the 'Social Services Inspectorate'). This approach is especially problematic if you are also trying to propose a complicated project that uses a number of different methods (techniques). Why do you need so many methods anyway? (See again Chapter 7.) A simple project proposal, explained clearly but with sufficient background justification (to include discussion of research literature, policy and, if relevant, practice ideas) is often most successful. If you are going to use terms such as **phenomenology** to explain why you are doing the project in the way that you are, be sure to let the reader know what you understand by this term and why it is relevant to your project. If you are a student writing an academic proposal, you will need to reference relevant research methods literature in order to justify your choices of methods.

The proposal needs to be coherent and consistent

By this I mean that you should pay attention to detail and make sure that you have not, for instance, said you will interview ten people on page 1 and then 25 people from three different teams on page 6. Similarly, if you state at the outset that this is a qualitative project involving semi-structured interviews and then later on you suddenly mention focus groups or survey questionnaires, whoever is reading this will become confused and probably give you a lower course grade than you would otherwise have achieved.

The proposal needs to be well organised

The structure of your proposal is important, for you as the writer to be sure that you have covered all the main points, and for the reader to ensure that you have done this. A set of clear headings within the proposal will usually help, even if the proposal is very restricted in length. (See below.)

Take good account of the methodological and/or subject focus of your study when designing the proposal

Despite what I have already said, not all proposals can be exactly the same; this is why proposals that are written down by 'filling in a (standardised) form' are not always easy to do and can result in repetitiveness, depending on your project's focus. For example how do you write a proposal when you know that the design and perhaps the theoretical/conceptual framework(s) for the study are going to emerge during the study, rather than be clearly defined at the outset? (A study involving grounded theory or some other kinds of qualitative research are possible examples here.) You need to grapple with these issues and justify what you are telling the reader, without simply saying something like 'I don't know how many people I am going to interview.' Estimate the size/scope of your study at least (is it going to involve 8–10 people or up to 100+ people?) – these differences will have implications for resourcing including timetabling. Again, justify your choices by referencing methodological texts or perhaps other research literature where the approach may be similar to your own.

Outline of headings for a research proposal

The following headings may prove useful and are typically what I have asked my (postgraduate) students to write for me:

Introduction and statement of the problem

In this section you outline why your chosen issue or topic is relevant and can potentially be researched. In social work contexts, this may relate to a topical or significant practice issue. Set out your aims and objectives for the study. ('Aims' are usually broader issues relating to the purpose of the project, whilst 'objectives' are more specific, perhaps focused on particular outcomes.) Try not to make over-ambitious claims for your project when setting out your objectives (such as 'This masters project is going to change social work practice nationally'), however enthusiastic you are about your topic. Your tutor may not be so convinced. It may be better to simply speak about the possibility of influencing practice as well as contributing to academic research on the topic. State your research questions (or hypothesis to be tested in relevant studies) here, or else place these after the literature review section.

Literature review and background

Start with a brief outline of your literature search, key words you used etc., and indicate how many research papers you identified from the search. Also include legislation and relevant policy material here as appropriate. (Generally the literature review takes up no more than one third of the proposal, to allow room for methods proposed.)

Depending on the required length of your proposal, critically examine your material briefly or in more depth (depending on word length), comparing results and methodologies from different studies (see Hart, 1998; Aveyard, 2007). Identify any gaps in literature and any inconclusive evidence that have led you to want to develop your research in a particular direction. At the end of the section, restate your research questions, which should follow from the existing literature review material (or gaps in this) that you have identified.

Methodology

State your overall study design – e.g. is it an RCT, survey, qualitative (including a specific label if appropriate, e.g. grounded theory) study? – explaining why you have chosen this design and critically discussing it with reference to appropriate subject-based and research methods references/literature.

Methods proposed (in detail)

Explain what these are and why they have been chosen to fit your study design, with critical justification(s) (again using research methods references). This section should include details of your sampling approach, sample composition and estimated sample size; and data collection methods, data analysis methods, including discussion of issues of reliability, validity or trustworthiness. If you are proposing to use an existing measure or questionnaire, describe the measure and its potential strengths or weaknesses in relation to your project. (Note: sometimes measures are copyrighted, and so they may not be reproduced directly in your proposal.)

Ethics

Discuss both the necessary requirements you have been told about for obtaining formal ethics approval, as well as the anticipated ethical issues that may arise during the research process itself that you may have to address. Explain how and why you will need to address these issues.

Potential limitations of the study

This section may include discussion of the proposed scope or parameters of the project, for example with implications for its generalisability. ('I have never done a research project before' is sometimes written here, which is honest but not really relevant; be confident!)

Timetable and budget

The timetable is often best shown as a diagram or Gantt chart. You will need to check whether you need to present a budget (especially if you are a student).

Conclusions and proposed relevance to professional practice

This section may be required for an academic research proposal and will help you to justify and pull together the whole document.

Reference list

Don't forget to include both subject-based and research methods references here.

Any relevant appendices

For example indicative lists of interview questions, measures to be used etc.

Understanding all these methodological topics and how they link, drawn together in the above outline for a research proposal, is intended to provide you with a foundation for developing your own skills in this exciting and extensive field of social work related research and evaluation. What I also hope comes across to you from this book is the dedication and enthusiasm shown by researchers in all the projects we have drawn upon. I am sometimes disappointed when I hear people say 'Oh, research methods is such a *dry* subject.' For me, other people's research and how they have carried it out (as well as doing my own research) is endlessly fascinating, and I have learnt a great deal from all the students I have worked with as well as from colleagues. To others, research may seem interesting but daunting: how can you deal with these research processes all at once? The answer to that is that research is inevitably a process and there will be quiet times and busy times during any project. Research or evaluation requires attention to detail and a great deal of patience; it usually takes longer than you thought it would! But most people do not carry out projects entirely alone (and if you are a student you will have supervisors to support you), so partnership and willingness to collaborate are also key skills to be recommended and encouraged. And, of course, these are important skills in social work practice too. It is often the good collaboration that sticks in your mind once a project is completed and written up.

I hope you have enjoyed this book and found it useful, and I am going to leave you with some final suggestions as you get going (I hope) on your own research or evaluative project:

My final suggestions

> Being research minded means first of all starting from where you are. What are your interests, concerns and values as a practitioner or social work student?

> What are you trying to do and find out? Fit your methods to your question(s), and not the other way round.

> Be prepared to choose from a range of existing methodological approaches, both quantitative and qualitative, especially to provide good evidence to underpin your social work practice.

> Mixing methods may be useful for an appropriate project, but it does not necessarily make 'better' research.

> Pay attention to the dual responsibilities you hold towards your professional ethics and research ethics, both with strong connections to social work values.

> Remember that in many projects, 'political issues' (including issues of power and authority in organisations) may affect your research processes and you need to be aware of these in order to keep steering things 'in the right direction'. Sponsorship or a helpful steering group may be useful, although these can also raise tensions in some cases. The involvement of service users can be crucial, but always consider what is intended and meant by 'involvement'.

> Don't forget the importance of theory (both subject-based and methodological) alongside reflexivity and partnership when trying to produce credible research/evaluative studies that have integrity.

> Look beyond narrow definitions of 'social work' or 'social work research' to include wider multi-disciplinary approaches, including those from disciplines such as psychology, social policy or sociology;

this is particularly useful where these connect with social workers' practice concerns and values embracing social justice, partnership or participatory approaches. Our project examples illustrate this.

➤ Don't be afraid to embrace and develop newer forms of research practice such as visual, digital, social media or arts-based methods that, as we have seen, are increasingly helping social workers and other practitioners to cross boundaries between research, evaluation, therapeutic and participatory practice.

➤ Good luck!

GLOSSARY OF KEY TERMS

analysis of data   In simple terms, this means breaking down your findings in order to reassemble them in ways that can provide understanding and interpretation, for example in relation to theory/ies and/or practice.

ANOVA (analysis of variance)   These are *parametric* tests that are used to establish whether or not there are significant differences between two or more groups. Different forms include: one-way ANOVA (where you have one independent variable); two-way ANOVA (where you have two independent variables); and multivariate MANOVA (where you have more than one dependent variable).

auditing   A cyclical process in which professional actions are checked against expectations, for example clinical audit that is often used in health settings.

bias   Bias generally means prejudice or unfair influence, perhaps stemming from our personal convictions. In research, bias may emerge when the researcher thinks s/he already knows the answer(s) to research questions before carrying out an enquiry and only looks for 'proof' to support her/his own view, instead of keeping an open mind. Techniques exist for eliminating specific forms of bias systematically (but somewhat differently) within both qualitative and quantitative research processes, for example in sampling, data collection and data analysis.

bibliographic (online) databases   These contain references (and abstracts) to publications, including journal articles. You can search for publications by keyword, author, date etc. There may also be useful indexes listing which journals are covered by that database and a thesaurus or glossary of keywords/terms used in it.

case study   A research example studied intensively, and usually based on a particular setting (e.g. a local authority staff team), an individual person/persons or focused on a particular event. In qualitative research, a case study is used to explore theoretical issues/the research question through use of the chosen example(s). Some experimental (quantitative) research may include case examples (e.g. patients) who are sampled individually and sequentially (rather than in group(s)) in order to test the study's hypotheses.

Chi square test A test using contingency table(s) to explore the relationship between two categorical variables, having two or more categories in each.

Cochrane Library and Campbell Collaboration Two established online databases of systematic reviews in various subject areas relevant to health and social care.

conceptual framework The guiding framework for a project, structuring key theoretical ideas, other research findings and/or policy statements in order to provide a basis for enquiry.

consent It is important for research participants to agree to taking part in research; most ethics committees require that someone's consent is both written and recorded (though it can sometimes be verbal), and that is informed – that the person understands what they are being asked to do. Ethical issues are raised where an individual could find it difficult either to consent on her/his own behalf and/or understand information explaining what their participation would involve. (See also Chapter 3.)

Consequentialism A general (philosophical) theory underpinned by the principle that morally right actions are those that produce the best consequences. It is associated with the philosophies of JS Mill and Bentham (Utilitarianism), which seek to maximise happiness, and is one of two dominant Western ethics philosophies. (See also **Deontology.**)

constructionism A constructionist approach suggests that researching social issues needs an understanding of social worlds derived from the ways people construct and maintain everyday social reality in different contexts. For example, this means that researchers will expect that social 'reality' will be pre-interpreted; a constructionist researcher will need to identify whose perspective(s) are being considered when investigating social behaviour.

criteria, inclusion or exclusion Establishing who or what is to be included or excluded from a study is important and depends on the study's purpose and the specific research question(s) or hypothesis/es:

literature search – it may be important to include or exclude material written in a particular language, published during a particular time period (include publications in years 2000–2015) or with particular methodological characteristics (e.g. to include RCTs only).

primary qualitative or quantitative studies – study participants may need to be included or excluded according to some identified characteristics (or variables) relevant to the project, for example their gender, age, occupation etc..

experimental or quasi-experimental research – usually requires very precise inclusion/exclusion criteria, for example in health research a participant may be excluded if they already have certain health condition(s) or are receiving particular treatments that would either confuse (confound) data resulting from the study, or especially if having these characteristics indicates taking part would be risky and could result in harm to the participant.

Cronbach's alpha coefficient   One of the most commonly used indicators of the internal consistency of a scale (or measure) (ideally the result should be above 0.7, but can be lower in short scales of less than ten items).

deduction   See Hypothetico-deductive approach.

Deontology   A philosophical approach stating that actions are considered morally right or wrong in themselves; this does not depend on consequences or outcomes (also associated with Kant's philosophy). This is one of two dominant Western philosophies of ethics (with **Consequentialism**).

discourse analysis   There are different forms, but they are generally based on constructionism relating to 'versions' of the world and to an extent anti-realist. See Gill, 2000, p. 76; Chapter 5.

epistemology   An epistemology is a theory of knowledge, presenting a view and justification for what can be known, for example if working with a feminist epistemology, we may research women's voices in order to know about women's experiences.

ethics of care/care ethics   An approach focusing on care as a relationship and how we understand the (virtuous) carer or caring practitioner; it has particular links to some aspects of feminist research and practice.

ethnography   The ethnographic researcher participates in everyday life with people who are the focus of the study (participant observation). There is concern with observing and exploring social context, for example place, time, activity, from participants' perspective(s). This approach may provide opportunities for co-production and/or community development work depending on context.

evaluation   This involves rigorously and systematically collecting data in order to assess whether services, interventions or organisations are effective in achieving predefined objectives, with different forms of evaluation depending on their aims. See Chapter 1

experiment   An 'active' research design, testing and comparing what happens when participants are assigned to different conditions/

interventions; a true experiment relies on ideas about causal effects and randomisation of participants into different conditions.

field notes   Notes or a diary (written or audio) kept by the researcher whilst research is carried out – essential in ethnographic or other observational research (where it forms a key part of study data), but may also be used, for example, to accompany interviews or focus groups.

focus group   A form of group interview in which a topic or theme is explored in depth with between about 4 to 12 participants who are chosen purposively. It is usual to use an interview/topic guide and have a facilitator.

gate keeper   Someone who acts as an intermediary and provides access to research participants.

generalisability   See **validity**.

'grey' literature   Includes 'documents that may not have been published through conventional routes, and which may therefore be trickier to find and access' (Kiteley and Stogden, 2014, p. 7). For these reasons they may also be more up to date/cutting edge.

grounded theory   An approach first developed by Glaser and Strauss, it was intended to focus on the development of theory from data. More recent developments by other researchers suggest this is an adaptable approach, particularly useful as a means of data analysis (using a constant comparative method, and structured forms of coding).

hypothesis   A prediction about the possible relationship between two or more variables; a null hypothesis will predict there is no relationship between two variables.

hypothetico-deductive approach   A 'falsificationist' method of hypothesis testing, starting with tentative hypothesis/es which are tested ('top down') against evidence (data).

induction   Gathering data and then developing hypotheses and broader theories from this, ('bottom up') instead of using pre-determined hypothesis/es.

interpretivism   An approach depending upon the researcher being able to grasp and interpret the everyday, subjective meanings of participants' social action.

interview guide or schedule   A list of questions or topics to be used in an interview or focus group. The format will depend on the type of interview.– See **interviews**; **focus group**.

interviews   See Figure 4.3, Interview types, Chapter 4.

➤ structured

➤ semi-structured

➤ unstructured

Keyword(s)   Term/s used for carrying out a literature search, for example child safeguarding: Signs of Safety.

Likert scale   A frequently used way of measuring a participant's attitudes towards specific statement(s) on a questionnaire. Typically s/he will be asked to tick or circle on a 4 to 7 point scale indicating for each statement how strongly s/he agrees with it or finds it useful (with e.g. 'strongly agree/find very useful' and 'strongly disagree/do not find at all useful') marking the two end points of the scale. An even number of scale points will force a choice between agree/disagree, whilst including a midpoint allows for a neutral or 'don't know' response. This type of scale records quantitative data at an 'ordinal' level of measurement since absolute distance between each of the points cannot be determined.

measurement, levels of

➤ categorical or nominal

➤ ordinal

➤ ratio

➤ interval – see Appendix D-1

meta-analysis   Usually involves direct statistical comparison of data from different selected studies that use the same concepts.

methodology   A theory of how research is carried out – more pragmatically, an identified research design, for example, a survey, an RCT, a phenomenological study.

methods   Actual techniques carried out by researchers within the chosen research design (methodology). For example, interviews (in a grounded theory study); use of questionnaires (in a survey).

'mixed'/multi- methods   This term is often used simply for a combination of qualitative and quantitative techniques, for example using a structured (mainly quantitative) questionnaire and interviews in the same project. However, underlying issues around 'mixing' are more complex: multi-method strategies can involve all stages of the research process, including design, data collection and analysis, data interpretation and contextualisation.

non-parametric tests Statistical tests that do not make certain assumptions, for example about the shape of the population distribution. They are useful for data measured on categorical/nominative or ordinal levels, or for small samples. But they are less sensitive than parametric tests and may fail to detect certain results. Example tests include Chi square, Mann-Whitney, Wilcoxon Signed-Rank, Friedman. (See also **parametric tests**.)

null hypothesis See **hypothesis**.

objectivity Conventionally, when researchers aim to be objective they try to be transparent about using rules or pre-determined categories that will aim to eliminate personal bias, for example when making observations, gathering or analysing data. This usually involves adherence to the 'scientific method' in social research, though total objectivity is virtually impossible and in practice there are 'trade-offs' to negotiate in research processes. Objectivity is sometimes seen as being in direct opposition to subjectivity, although this has been disputed by some researchers (see e.g. Letherby, Scott and Williams, 2013) who debate, for example, the nature and contributions of more value-laden 'situated objectivity' as well as 'theorised subjectivity'. (See also **subjectivity**.)

observation Used if researchers want to see first-hand how people behave; some (particularly ethnographers) immerse themselves in their participants' social settings in order to gather and interpret data in its relevant context(s) (participant observation). Observations need to be recorded in order to capture data: techniques depend on the project's aims and design, for example structured observation using a measure or checklist will produce quantifiable data, whilst some researchers record their observations qualitatively in a field diary or by visual or audio methods. Researchers will often interview participants or share findings in order to check their own observational impressions.

ontology Ontological theories and assumptions relate to perceptions about the nature of social reality/ies.

paradigm A term relating to clusters of beliefs in subject disciplines, influencing how research is carried out; paradigm shifts may be said to accompany changes in research practices.

parametric tests Statistical tests assuming that data conforms to certain 'parameters', for example that it is 'normally' distributed (see

Appendix D-1, Figure D.1). More powerful than non-parametric tests, they should be used in preference to them, provided you have appropriate data. Example parametric tests include the t-test (independent samples or paired samples) and ANOVA. (See also **non-parametric tests**.)

participant Someone who takes part in a research project or evaluation.

participant information Information provided to explain, in lay language, how a project is going to take place and what the participant's rights, responsibilities and expectations should be if they agree to take part.

participant observation See **observation**.

peer review Assessment of publications, research applications for funding or for ethics approval by peers (who have relevant expertise). This form of review is increasingly important as an aspect of quality assurance processes in research.

phenomenology An approach relating mainly to how people perceive the world around them. Social systems are thus seen as abstractions existing mainly as individuals interacting with each other. Descriptive and hermeneutic phenomenology are different forms of this philosophy.

positivism An epistemological position advocating use of the 'scientific method' in social research. Positivist research emphasises objectivity (reduction or elimination of bias) by trying to keep facts and values separate.

power calculation Using the calculation, the researcher establishes the requisite sample size to potentially show a statistically significant difference in results. Studies with smaller sample sizes than can achieve this are said to be 'underpowered'.

'practice-near' research This approach aims to use practice approaches and interventions (e. g. from social work, psychology or psychoanalysis) as research methods. An example would be psychoanalytically informed child observation techniques. (See also **observation**.)

primary research Research which involves direct collection and analysis of original data.

questionnaire A document or online set of questions, usually for self-completion. The questionnaire may be entirely or partially composed of standardised measure(s) which may already be validated for use in particular contexts. See Appendix D-2.

randomisation Where inclusion of someone as a participant is entirely by chance (random sampling), or where their allocation to either a control group or an intervention group is done randomly (random assignment). Randomisation is the basis for 'true' experimentation.

reflectivity/reflexivity Different terms with various meanings encompassing aspects of practice, research, emotional involvement, ethics and values as well as epistemology. There is a concern with considered reflection and use of self in both research and social work practice. See Chapter 1.

reliability The degree to which an instrument (e.g. a questionnaire) can produce acceptable and consistent results over time or with different participants. See **validity** and **trustworthiness**. (See also Appendix D-2.)

research question A research question forms the basis for an enquiry; it should be framed so as to be answerable by using appropriate research design and method(s). It can be exploratory and/or predictive; if predictive, it relates to relevant hypothesis/es. (A 'research question' is not the same thing as the questions researchers ask interviewees during an interview.)

Sampling See Appendix D-4.

secondary analysis Data analysis or a review in which the analyst/reviewer was not involved in the original research. Secondary research can sometimes mean simply 'a (published) literature review', but it can also include use of other pre-existing documentary sources, in studies which do not directly involve human participants. (See also Chapter 5.)

'scoping' study This generally aims to establish the scope of a particular research and/or practice field by making use of a wide range of material, also looking ahead to future research possibilities.

semiotics The study of signs, relating to the deconstruction of language so that deeper meanings can be sought, for example when analysing documents.

subjectivity Subjectivity/ies can refer to perspectives held by different research participants and to how the researcher is (or considers s/he is) positioned within research processes. Expressions of subjectivity/ies are thus worth studying in their own right (being theorised) and should not only be considered as something researchers have to eliminate in order to be 'objective'. Subjectivity is sometimes seen as being in direct opposition to objectivity, although this has been disputed by some researchers (see e.g. Letherby, Scott and Williams, 2013).

survey A cross-sectional research design involving collecting data from different respondents over a specific time period, using self-completion (or otherwise administered) questionnaires or structured interviews. A survey is often a 'passive', descriptive design, not aiming to provide causal explanations (compared, for example, to an experiment).

systematic review Usually a very focused and comprehensive review of research-based literature, requiring adherence to a strict protocol. It may be intended for a specific database (e.g. the Cochrane Library); this kind of review may also be updated regularly, and is a cornerstone of evidence-based practice (EBP).

triangulation Use of more than one method, researcher or source of data in a project, usually with the intention of being able to cross-check findings (although this will not necessarily increase potential for 'objectivity').

trustworthiness Criteria sometimes used in qualitative research projects to assess their quality in providing results that can be relied on. (See also **reliability** and **validity**.)

validity In relation to quantitative measurement, does the instrument measure what it is intended to measure? Or, has a causal relationship between two variables been demonstrated? (This is internal validity.) Can results from this study be generalised to different settings? (This is external validity or generalisability.) (See also **reliability** and **trustworthiness**.)

variable An attribute or entity which varies by case, for example gender. Variables are usually considered to be discrete (separate) and fixed in the context of quantitative research, so as to aid measurement processes. (Qualitative researchers may consider attributes as flexible or overlapping rather than being labelled and fixed as 'variables'.)

variable, dependent A variable that is predicted to be affected by independent variable(s), and which is therefore being explored by the research.

variable, independent A variable that is predicted to have a causal effect on other variable(s).

visual analog scale A scale that intends to measure a characteristic or attitude that cannot be easily measured directly, across a continuum (line) between two extremes; usually the participant is asked to mark a point on the line corresponding to their experience (e.g. of pain intensity – continuum from 'worst' to 'least').

virtue ethics Relates to what the virtuous person or practitioner would do in certain circumstances, rather than deciding according to fixed ethical principles.

APPENDIX A

	List of Project Examples	**Used in chapter(s)**
PROJECT A	MacDonald and Turner (2005)	3, 6, 7
PROJECT B	Bell (2003)	3
PROJECT C	Bell and Clancy (2013)	3, 6
PROJECT D	Bell et al. (2015)	3, 4, 5
PROJECT E	Fountain et al. (1999)	4, 5
PROJECT F	Wincup (2000)	4
PROJECT G	Wilcke (2002)	4
PROJECT H	Cree et al. (2016)	4, 7
PROJECT J	Gribble and Gallagher (2014)	4, 5
PROJECT K	Hingley-Jones (2009)	4
PROJECT L	Rhodes and Quirk (1998)	4
PROJECT M	Park (2008)	5
PROJECT N	Heron, McGoldrick and Wilson (2015)	5
PROJECT O	Tanner (2007)	5
PROJECT P	Caldwell et al. (2007)	6
PROJECT Q	McAuley et al. (2006)	7
PROJECT R	Bryan et al. (2002)	7
PROJECT S	Ryan et al. (2016)	7
PROJECT T	Foster (2012b)	8
PROJECT U	Hafford-Letchfield (2013)	8
PROJECT V	Macpherson, Hart and Heaver (2016)	4, 8
PROJECT W	Dodsworth et al. (2013)	9
PROJECT X	Leece and Leece (2011)	9

APPENDIX B

Exercise 4.1: Planning an interview and preparing an interview schedule

The idea is that you are planning to interview several people about their role in the same organisation. We have chosen this topic because it is likely to be based on your own employment or other experiences and will therefore not require you to conduct an extensive literature search. Remember, this is a hypothetical (imaginary) situation – you would usually need to obtain ethics approval to carry out real interviews.

You should select a setting with which you are familiar, and imagine that your interviewees both have some connection with the chosen organisation.

1) Planning the interviews

You need first to take account of the following:

➤ What is your sample going to be – number of participants and type of sample (purposive, snowball, representative etc.)?

➤ How will you access participants and publicise your study?

➤ What type of interview will you carry out (structured, semi-structured or unstructured)?

➤ How long is the interview going to take? Where is it going to take place?

➤ Any other issues to consider, e.g. ethics.

Interview guide or schedule

You will need to decide on your list of questions about the person's role in the organisation, depending on the type of interview you have chosen:

For example you may begin with: How long have you worked for the organisation? OR What is your attitude to your current role – positive, negative, mixed feelings?

Remember that the first example question (How long have you worked for the organisation?) may be a key demographic point of comparison between your interviewees when you come to analyse your material. Otherwise you may decide the interview will be much more unstructured, hinging around the key topic, 'Can you tell me about your role in this organisation?', followed by probes as the conversation progresses.

Beginning the interview with a question about 'attitude' may turn out to be too abrupt or contentious – think about how you would feel if this was asked of you, without any preliminary 'warm up' questions. Now design your interview schedule.

See Appendix C, Exercises, below, for reflections/suggestions for this exercise.

APPENDIX C EXERCISES: SOLUTIONS AND SUGGESTIONS

Chapter 1

Possible methods appropriate for project titles

Some suggestions

1 *Is dementia care mapping a useful tool for social workers?*
   Interview-based study with social workers; OR
   Using the tool in practice and setting up a focus group discussion afterwards

2 *Using outcome measures in child protection social work*
   Detailed review of the use of measures in the context of 'managerialism'
   Focus groups with staff to discuss findings

3 *Social workers' experiences of working with young people who are leaving the care system*
   Interview-based study with social workers OR Questionnaire-based survey
   Participatory approaches to involve young people in social work education initiatives

4 *How do social workers manage 'endings' when working with young people in care?*
   Interview-based study OR focus groups with social workers and/or young people

5 *Working with 'recovery' models in mental health social work practice*
   Interview-based study with social workers and mental health staff

6 *Challenges and opportunities for social workers when working in partnership*
   Interviews or focus groups with social workers and foster carers/health professionals

7 *Working collaboratively with black and minority ethnic communities in social work*
   Arts-based approaches or focus group discussions
   Participatory approaches involving service users

8 *Advocacy in child protection safeguarding*
Interviews with advocates, children's social workers and managers
9 *Using 'mindfulness' approaches in social work*
Telephone interviewing with practitioners OR survey using online questionnaires
10 *Female involvement in gangs: Challenges for social work*
Interviews with children's social workers and managers

Exercise 1.1 **(See feedback p. 8.)**

Discussion point – p. 10: I have sometimes heard students say they are going to include hypothesis testing in their own projects, but then they suggest something like, 'I predict that the Care Act (2014) is going to make a big difference to social work practice.'
Do you think this is a credible hypothesis that could be tested?
If so, how? If not, why not?

No, this is not a credible hypothesis, it is not precise enough to 'test' as a prediction. However, it could be used as the basis for future exploratory work in interviews or focus groups, though it is a fairly 'speculative' issue at present.

Chapter 2 Exercise 2.1

Ways to 'focus' your list of potential publications (and reduce too many 'hits')
Have you reduced your list by date of publication? (e.g. only those published since 2010)

Have you made sure your keywords are sufficiently precise?

Look at the content of the papers (by reviewing their abstracts) and only select those that meet strict criteria, depending on your area of interest. (This is better than cutting out publications that use certain methodologies which may weaken your overall research coverage.)

Chapter 3 Ethics scenarios – possible solutions

Scenario 1

Ideally, the lecturer would have 'sounded out' her colleagues before going through ethics approval processes, so as to find out whether any of them would be willing to take part in the project. She is under no obligation to include them in her proposal, but she ought to have found it helpful to gauge possible reactions in advance. Some ethics committees may also ask for evidence that access to participants will be forthcoming. If the lecturer has not prepared the ground in this way, she may have to be very persuasive to obtain participants' agreement. In any case, she cannot assume that colleagues will take part in her project, still less try to set up focus groups or interviews and then expect colleagues to comply with her wishes. Confidentiality is also important here, and I would not be prepared personally to reveal to interviewees who else is being interviewed, especially if they all know each other. Focus groups will, in addition, require a degree of mutual planning to suit everyone's timetables, with confidentiality 'shared' within the participating group.

Scenario 2

Openness and transparency are very important in these kinds of situations. It may be that one organisation is formally taking the lead in the project and so they would usually expect to deal with matters of ethics approval across the whole project within their country/ jurisdiction. However, it is also usual to have 'local' ethics approval agreed in other participating organisations or countries where interviews or other data collection methods are taking place. This would also mean going to separate ethics committee(s) in those locations. Often, once these different processes are agreed between the group members, then it becomes a matter of sorting out the timescale and the order in which these ethics processes need to happen. It may be helpful to have two project members (one for each country) working together on behalf of the group so as to ensure that all ethics requirements are dealt with effectively. If the project has a steering group, they might also have a useful role to play.

Scenario 3

As with Scenario 2 above, openness and transparency are key. If initial discussion reveals different ideas, as I have indicated, it may be useful to do a structured exercise with all parties to determine some of the following points:

1 What could be some of the key ethical principles involved relating to 'giving voice' to service user participants within and also outside the project itself?

2 How would service users/patients' representatives be selected/invited to participate, and on what basis?

3 What role would they be asked to play – as research participants (limited)? As consultants? As co-producers? (These points may need to wait to be discussed once service users are already part of the team.)

Increasingly, health and social care researchers do expect at the very least to 'consult' service users/patients when carrying out projects, especially those that directly affect them (the NHS usually requires this). But it depends on what 'consult' (or 'participate') actually means; it is often the way this issue is approached or (conflicting) use of language that causes stumbling blocks in research teams. Sorting out who the principal investigator is to be may sometimes help to diffuse power issues, especially if a funded bid is being prepared, although this may also become a source of tension if people feel ignored or resentful. Paying attention to power relations within the team can pay dividends in these kinds of situations, especially where newer members are being invited to join in. (See e.g. Mauthner and Bell, 2007.)

See also Project S, in Chapter 7.

Chapter 4 (Exercise 4.1 found in Appendix B)

Exercise 4.1 Reflection A

➤ How did you decide on the characteristics of your sample?

➤ Why did you choose this type of interview?

➤ How did you decide about questions of access, publicity and ethics?

Exercise 4.1 Reflection B – when you have completed your interview guide

➤ How exactly did you decide upon:

   ➤ The number of topics to cover?

   ➤ The overall shape of the interview (especially beginnings and endings)?

➤ How did you address these issues when designing the guide?

➤ How can you demonstrate that your methods are reliable, trustworthy and accurate?

➤ What kind of generalisations or wider claims do you intend to make on the basis of this data?

Chapter 5   Exercise 5.1 Your field diary

Reflection

Think about how you recorded the material. Was it in the form of a checklist? Did you put in specific items about particular activities?

How did your diary reflect issues about time and timing – did you aim to produce 'quantitative' evidence about amounts of time spent on different activities? What happened when several things were happening at the same time – how did you try to record that?

Thinking about any emotional content you recorded – did you feel this was relevant or irrelevant to the research process? Did you feel uncomfortable about recording emotional details? How can this link to your professional practice as related to working with feelings and emotions?

Supposing that you were recording a diary for somebody else's research project – would you have been more guarded about what you were prepared to put into it?

Would you expect a researcher to ask for the diary to be produced in a more 'standardised' form, to aid comparison with diaries from other people?

Chapter 6   Exercise 6.1 Errors in clinical trials: suggestions

Sampling: In an RCT we might introduce a sampling error if we did not ensure that participants were randomly selected. This would not apply in quasi-experiments, where we knew randomisation was not possible. (However, we would still need to ensure in a quasi-experiment that participants were selected appropriately in a purposive sense.)
(See also Appendix D-4.)
Assignment: By 'assignment', we mean how the participants are selected for each group, e.g. the control group, the experimental group. If the control or experimental group contained more participants who might

have a better prognosis following an intervention (e.g. such as no drug users in one group), in a study of drug use, an error would be introduced. Randomisation of participants is again a good method for avoiding this kind of error.

Conditions: This refers to how the experiment is applied. An error could be introduced if for example a service user discovers whether they are receiving the active treatment or the placebo. In order to avoid this issue, you should, where possible, keep apart those on the active treatment or intervention and those on the placebo/waiting list. If those administering treatments are 'blinded' to which participants are receiving the active treatment/intervention, this may help to avoid such an error. However, this kind of issue is arguably more difficult in social work research where participants will often know whether they are 'controls' or are receiving a 'usual' intervention compared with a new one. (See also Project A, in Chapter 3.)

Measurement: An error can be introduced by using questionnaires or measures that have not had their psychometric properties fully tested and established. It is usually better, where possible, to use existing measures rather than design new measures. (See Project C, in Chapter 6.)

Chapter 7   Exercise 7.1 mixed methods project(s)

Reflection

Did you find it as useful to try and combine methodologies in the overall research design as you did to aim to combine methods/techniques?

What implications would your answer to this question have for your attitudes towards epistemological integrity? (See Chapter 10 and Gringeri, Barusch and Cambron, 2013.)

Chapter 8   Exercise 8.1 Photographs/concept of 'family'

Reflection

Having considered your own attitudes towards the concept of 'family' after doing this exercise, what implications may this raise for a) your future research interests/activities? b) your own social work or health practice?

Chapter 9   Exercise 9.1 Digital/online methods in the organisation

Reflection

After deciding on your research question, how did you decide whether to use 'traditional' and/or CMC methods or a combination? (Try listing advantages/disadvantages for each method you identified.)

If wanting to work collaboratively with service users, what training needs might have been raised (for yourself/for the service users)? Were any issues of leadership likely to emerge?

APPENDIX D-1

Information about statistical (quantitative) methods

Definitions of 'statistics'

Statistics can be termed **descriptive** or **inferential**.

Usually when **descriptive statistics** are presented, only one group or sample is being described. Resulting data may be presented descriptively in terms of frequencies (how many) and/or percentages, e.g. in tables, bar or pie charts showing characteristics of that sample, such as showing how many survey respondents belong to particular ages/age groups.

Inferential statistics compare two or more groups and make use of a wide range of statistical tests, depending on the type of data and its level(s) of measurement.

Levels of measurement

When data are recorded as variables in our dataset, they will fall into the following levels of measurement, going from the simplest to highest level:

Categorical or nominal   The data is simply recorded numerically in discrete categories, e.g. gender; occupation (social worker, nurse); ethnicity.

Ordinal   The data is ranked on a scale, but the distance between the ranks is not measurable, e.g. a Likert scale with indicative points 1 to 7 used for measuring attitudes to statements.

Interval   Data is recorded on a scale in which the intervals between ranks are equal and are thus measureable, e.g. temperature as measured on a thermometer.

Ratio The highest level of measurement incorporates the interval level but also starts at absolute zero, so that the ratio between points is measureable, e.g. age, if recorded in years: someone aged 40 years is twice as old as someone aged 20.

Describing our data

Measures of central tendency

a) Mean: this is the 'average' value in our data set calculated as:

Sum of individual values
─────────────────────────
          Sample size

The mean can be influenced by extreme values known as outliers.
b) Median: this is the midpoint of the data, calculated by listing the values in order and then finding the midpoint. It can be a more useful statistic than the mean as not so susceptible to outliers.
c) Mode: this is the most common (prevalent) value in the data.

Measures of Dispersion

i. The Range: this shows the minimum and maximum data values (for example 25 – 100).
ii. Quartiles (or 'perecentiles'): the lowest quartile is the point where 25% of all values fall. The upper quartile is the point where 75% of all values fall. The quartile range is the difference between these two values. Both quartiles and range values are usually presented where the data is abnormally distributed.
iii. The Variance:
The formula for calculating the variance is:

Sum of all squared differences from the Mean
───
              Sample size – 1

The variance is a stepping stone to calculating the standard deviation (below).
iv. Standard deviation: this is the most common index of dispersion. It represents the average distance of all individual observations from the mean value and is calculated as the $\sqrt{}$ (square root) of the variance.

Distribution of data – is it 'parametric' or 'non-parametric'?

In order to decide which statistical tests to use with our data, we have to decide whether our data is 'normally' or 'abnormally' distributed. On that basis we can decide whether to use
parametric tests (e.g. t-test, factor analysis)

or

non-parametric tests (e.g. chi square, Mann-Whitney U test).
Figure D.1, below, shows age data from a survey of college students in the form of a histogram which shows our data is 'normally' distributed. This normal distribution is reflected in the accompanying curve (known as a bell-shaped curve). We can see from the histogram

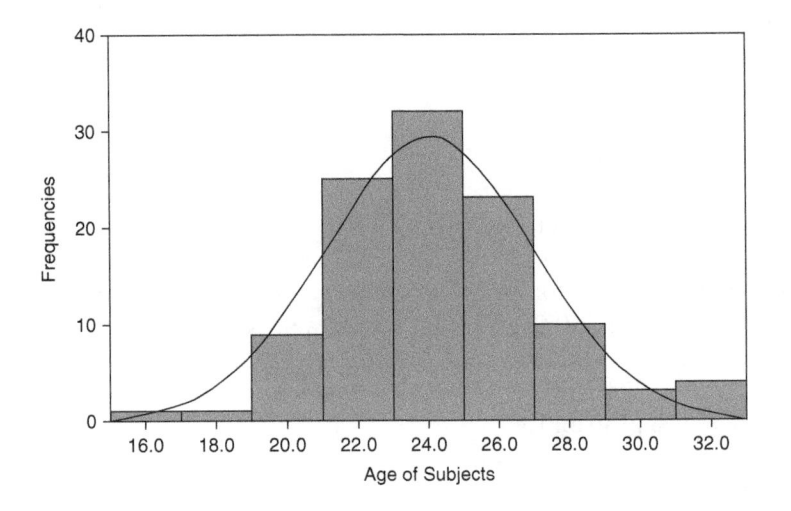

Figure D.1 Illustration of 'Normal' data distibution (parametic)

that the youngest respondents are 16 and 18, the oldest are aged 32 and the 'mean' age of our sample is 24.

Variables such as weight and height are usually normally distributed, since in any sample 'most' people will be of 'average' height and there may be a few very short or very tall people at either side of the distribution. When a distribution of data is 'normal', **parametric testing** is appropriate.

If data is not 'normally' distributed, the data in the graph above would be 'skewed' towards either of the sides and the bell curve will not therefore 'fit' the data so well. In that case, we would need to use statistical tests that are **non-parametric** to analyse our data.

When presenting data that is 'normally distributed' (parametric) it is usual to make use of the Mean and Standard Deviation statistics; when data is not 'normally distributed' (non-parametric), the median and range values would be used.

The Null Hypothesis

The Null Hypothesis (NH) states that there is not a statistically significant difference or relationship/association between the two comparison groups. Statistical significance is then tested on the (probability) basis that the NH is true. When there is statistical significance, it is usually shown as a small p value (see later), and the NH is rejected.

Statistical significance

When we conclude that something is statistically significant, we mean that the result could not have been arrived at by mere chance.

The cut-off point for statistical significance is usually considered by statisticians to be $p \leq 0.05$. This equates to a 95% probability that findings were not arrived at by chance. However, we could decide to use a stricter level of probability instead – $p < 0.01$ means a 99% probability, $p < 0.001$ means a 99.9% probability.

The smaller the p value (above), the greater level of statistical significance.

Effect size ('strength of association')

Showing 'statistical significance' (above) does not tell you the degree to which variables are associated with each other. There are several different effect size statistics that will indicate the relative size or magnitude of differences between means: these will allow us to predict the amount of total variance in the dependent variable from our knowledge of the independent variable. These statistics are eta squared, Cohen's d and Cohen's f.

Eta squared values can range from 0 to 1, and as a guide to their strength we can interpret these as follows:

Small effect   e.g.   .01

Moderate effect   e.g.   .06

Large effect   e.g.   .14

APPENDIX D-2

Questionnaires / Measures

a) **Validity**

Validity concerns whether the instrument (questionnaire) is measuring what it is intended to measure. It has several forms, including:

Face/Content Validity. This establishes that the instrument reflects items that are important to the group being assessed and can be tested statistically.

Construct Validity. A test of both method and theory. If the intention is, for example, to design a quality of life measure for alcohol dependent subjects, we might theorise that having a greater number of problems will result in diminished quality of life. The measure will then be designed to take account of this before being subjected to psychometric testing.

b) **Reliability**

Does the instrument produce acceptable and consistent results over time? The most common way of establishing this is by carrying out a test/re-test methodology. In a wider context, we would expect a measure to be 'reliable' if it produces the same or similar results if given to different groups of respondents in broadly similar contexts. When using this approach, a new questionnaire would be given to respondents at baseline (start of the study) and then soon after, within a few weeks. The intention is to establish that there is an acceptable consistency in the results if the questionnaire is re-administered within a short period. However, it is important to ensure that the circumstances of the participants have not changed significantly in that interim period.

c) **Responsiveness to change**

If designing an instrument such as a quality of life measure for drug dependent subjects, it would have to be shown that quality of life scores changed significantly from baseline to a later date (e.g. at 12 months) for subjects who have relapsed to heavy drinking within the study period. If a measure is to be used repeatedly to measure changes, we should consider its:

➤ length

➤ specificity

➤ sensitivity to small changes

➤ whether it is self-administered or based on observer rating

d) Rating Scales/measures and outcome measurement

Questionnaires may be termed 'rating scales' or 'instruments', and as such are frequently used in experimental research designs where they are intended to produce quantitative data which is both reliable and valid for the purpose intended, e.g. measurement of specified outcomes.

In research terms, this converted quantitative data derived from rating scales are regarded as 'soft'; the data may be based on self-report, involving the recording of an individual's attitudes/opinions, and as such the researcher knows that there may be no way of checking its absolute accuracy or validity.

1 **Rating scales used to screen people into groups,** for example into psychiatric cases and non-cases (e.g. using a measure such as the General Health Questionnaire), although these scales do not in themselves offer a diagnosis (which would be established subsequently). The GHQ is frequently used in research where grouping of individuals is important, e.g. where one group is being 'screened out' for research purposes.

2 **'Generic' health instruments** or scales which measure people's health status on a number of dimensions, including mental health. Such scales are commonly used in many kinds of health research and are useful as they link measures of one aspect, e.g. mental health to other aspects of health. A good example is the *Medical Outcomes Study 36-Item Short Form Health Survey* (known as the SF36 – and its briefer version, SF12) which has been extensively used in health research.

3 **Rating scales used mainly for diagnostic purposes** (e.g. *Brief Psychiatric Rating scale*) which can also be used to provide data for evaluations or research projects.

4 **Rating scales used to measure changes** in levels of particular symptoms or for specified population groups, e.g.:

➤ the Beck Depression Inventory (BDI), which measures depth of depression, and so can also be used as a measure of treatment outcome.

➤   the Child Behavioural Checklist (CBCL), a frequently used and psychometrically rigorous but extensive measure of behavioural problems, for use with children aged 4 to 16 (see Achenbach, 1993).

➤   Knowledge of Behavioural Principles as Applied to Children (KBPAC), useful for research and educational assessment (see O'Dell et al., 1979).

➤   the Strengths and Difficulties Questionnaire (SDQ): a brief behavioural screening questionnaire covering 25 items that can be completed quickly by parents or teachers for children aged 4 to 16 (with a self-report version for children aged 11 to 16) (see Goodman and Scott, 1999).

➤   Parenting Stress Index (PSI), Short form (SF), 36-item self-report measure used to assess sources and levels of stress in parents with children aged up to 10 years (see Abidin, 1995).

➤   Brief Infant–Toddler Social and Emotional Assessment Scale (BITSEA) recently developed 60-item scale with ongoing validation, based on parental self-report (see Briggs-Gowan and Carter, 2001).

APPENDIX D-3

Research designs – clinical trials including RCTs

Most clinical trials have a pre-test/post-test design. This means that the measures of outcome are taken both before and after the (clinical) intervention. The 'between-subjects' design is the most common: two groups that have been randomly selected are compared (see Appendix D-4, Sampling): we need an experimental group and a control group. This is illustrated diagrammatically in Figure D.2.

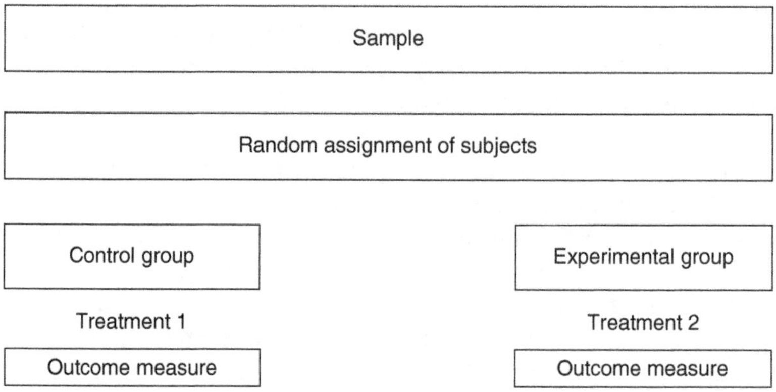

Figure D.2. Clinical trials: Between-subjects design

Another more precise but complex experimental design also using randomisation is the Solomon four-group design, which aims to minimise any problems with pre-testing by administering both conditions (1, 2) to both groups (A, B) in sequence, as, for example A1, B2, + A2, B1.

Sample

Baseline measurement

Intervention 1

Outcome measure

Intervention 2

Outcome measure

Figure D.3. Clinical trials: Within-subjects design

Another common design is the 'within-subjects' design. This is used, for example, for the evaluation of short periods of treatment. Two or more treatments are given over a short period of time and both are evaluated with all participants; this is shown in Figure D.3.

In this case, the evaluation of data will compare participants' own scores at baseline and subsequently.

Quasi-experimental research designs may look like experimental designs (e.g. they can involve pre/post or only post testing) but although they may involve comparing groups of participants, they do not involve **randomisation** into those groups: this is sometimes known as a non-equivalent groups design. An example would be a quasi-experiment involving a comparison between data from a group of social workers and from a group of nurses – participants cannot self-evidently be randomised into these occupational groups.

APPENDIX D-4

SAMPLING

All researchers need to pay attention to sampling, whatever kind of research design they are using (quantitative or qualitative). Sampling techniques include both probability sampling (capable of statistical representativeness) and non-probability sampling.

Probability sampling

This is when each individual in the 'sampling frame' has the possibility of being sampled; we would therefore need to start with a complete list of all potential participants making up that population, e.g. all the members of an organisation. This method of sampling is best if we wish to describe sample characteristics accurately in order to represent the parameters of that population (e.g. the membership of the organisation).

Randomisation is a key issue here. If we select respondents randomly, we can try to eliminate any bias and get a more precise representation of the specified population. **Randomisation** is the basis of a true experimental research design. This high precision in probability sampling means we can have a low standard error; this standard error can be calculated statistically and relates to how the sample is distributed. The larger our sample from the wider population is, the lower the standard error will be. We have to decide whether it is cost effective to have a large sample from the total population or if we can be less precise. A 'census' covers the whole population but is expensive to carry out. It may aim at complete coverage, but due to non-response from some of those sampled, it may not be able to achieve this. When selecting a sample, we may either randomise our selection of survey respondents from the whole population or from particular strata within it (stratified sampling, see below).

Probability sampling in practice

i) *Simple Random Sampling*: this is the simplest method of random sampling. Subjects are selected either by numbers (e.g. computer generated) or by names or numbers pulled from a box or hat etc..

ii) *Systematic Sampling*: in this case, the researcher knows the number of cases in the sample frame /list (total number of subjects who could potentially be recruited) and the sample size required. S/he then selects systematically, e.g. every tenth case from the list (the sampling interval).

iii) *Stratified Sampling*: individuals are identified as having certain 'target characteristics' (e.g. age, gender, ethnicity) which the investigator wishes to investigate. All those with the target characteristic (in that stratum) are selected (useful if there are few people with that characteristic – e.g. a few male student social workers within a predominantly female class); alternatively, they are then selected either randomly (as above) or according to principles described for systematic sampling.

iv) *Cluster Samples*: when selecting a cluster sample, the researcher draws from a large population, and selects out progressively smaller ones, e.g. samples of hospital-based registered social workers, employed in various settings (i/ii/iii above are not necessarily appropriate for geographically dispersed populations).

The Electoral Register is deficient as an original sampling frame because young people, homeless, transient and ethnic minority groups, especially refugees, are less likely to be included. On these occasions, non-probability sampling may be more appropriate. Probability sampling is particularly problematic with what are termed hard-to-reach or 'deviant' populations, e.g. drug users, sex workers. When behaviour is invisible or illegal, then it may be very difficult or impossible to draw up a sampling frame to ensure all potential subjects could be selected. In such circumstances, non-probability sampling techniques are more appropriate.

Non-probability sampling

When a researcher has used non-probability sampling, no attempt has been made to estimate the probability of an individual being included and no assurance is made that every individual has a potential of inclusion. The main advantages of these sampling methods are that they are cheap, convenient and that the required sample number is usually achieved.

However, there are a number of disadvantages. There is considerable potential for **bias**, and the sample may thus be unrepresentative of the population being sampled. Conversely, we may be interested in well-designed 'naturalistic' studies (those that 'replicate' reality by not pre-selecting participants artificially). The main examples of this are convenience and accidental sampling procedures.

These are the most common forms of non-probability sampling:

a) *Convenience/accidental sampling*:
Here, no sampling frame is required. Cases are selected on the basis of availability for the study, e.g. they may be approached on campus (students) or in the street. There is considerable potential for bias here, but if the sample is focused, e.g. onto one university campus, there may be some value in the resulting sample (especially if it is modified as quota sampling), although it may not be generalisable to other settings.

b) *Quota sampling*:
An addition to the above method. The interviewer/researcher selects a sample that yields the same proportions as the population on easily identified variables (e.g. number of men/women). This methodology is usually employed in market research and a reason why such samples cannot be seen as representative of a wider population.

c) *Purposive sampling:*
The researcher chooses a type of person and/or group that will fit the purpose of the study. This sampling method is often used in qualitative work. For example, if you wish to interview staff in a drug rehabilitation unit, or members of a child and family social work team, you would try to recruit members of those staff groups; this is a 'convenient' way to sample, but is usually more focused than just approaching 'anyone' to take part (as in (*a*) above). If not enough people come forward from the chosen staff team, you can usually increase the sample size by approaching similar staff from a second or subsequent team or unit. This method will ensure that your sample is not excessively biased, and it may be a useful approach for students working in social work placements. In health research, advice is sometimes given to researchers to recruit participants from outside their own work team.

d) *Snowball sampling:*
When using this method of sampling, one individual is recruited and is then asked to nominate others for the researcher to contact. This is particularly useful when researching participants from 'hard-to-reach' groups. This method is also frequently used in qualitative research approaches.

NOTES

Chapter 01

1 A 'one tailed' hypothesis

Chapter 02

1 A well-known exception to this 'pre-reading' approach is **grounded theory**, although, as we will see later, this a not a straightforward issue (see Dunne, 2011; Chapter 4).
2 The Cochrane Library and the Campbell Collaboration are two established online **databases** of systematic reviews in various subject areas.
3 For more on RCTs, see Chapter 6 and Appendix D-3 below.
4 Especially in terms of presenting effect sizes or odds-ratios (see Appendix D-1).
5 These criteria have been adapted from Bowling (1997), ch 6, pp. 118–121 (extract) (on searching literature and reviewing).

Chapter 03

1 See also Appendix D-3 on RCTs and Appendix D-4 on Sampling.
2 These three measures are listed in the paper as 1) a measure of participants' Knowledge of Behavioural Principles as Applied to Children (KBPAC); 2) the Child Behavioural Checklist (CBCL); and 3) a Foster Carer Satisfaction Questionnaire.
3 We return to this example in Chapter 6.

Chapter 04

1 'Lifeworld' is a term coined by the philosopher Edmund Husserl.

Chapter 05

1   Historical 'provenance' relating to archives is a slightly different but related concept that may be defined as the specific place of origin or producer.
2   See also Elliott (2005).
3   See also Elliott (2005).

Chapter 06

1   For more on the importance of randomisation, see Appendix D-4, Sampling.
2   Results for negatively worded statements on attitude measures are often 'reversed' so that when scores are calculated for the measure, negative and positive results are basically going in the 'same direction' and can be totalled accurately to take account of the negativity.
3   See Appendix D-1, Levels of measurement.
4   This includes quantitative methods in particular (one statement is 'I have trouble with arithmetic', for example).
5   There are many textbooks relating to use of SPSS. One I have found particularly helpful is Pallant (2013) – or earlier or later edition – which also links to online statistics support.
6   Students were judged to have had 'previous research experience' if they had previously done a research-based dissertation or if they reported they had had some other primary research experience.
7   The t-test firstly assumes data is parametric (normally distributed) – see diagram in Appendix D-1. The test shows results in a table including equality of means (with significance level), 95% confidence intervals and Levene's test for equality of variances. As in most testing for statistical significance, we judged a p (alpha) value of 0.05 or below to be 'significant'. If data is not normally distributed, a non-parametric test ought to be used instead, e.g. the Mann-Whitney or the Wilcoxon Signed-Rank test.
8   'Quasi-experiments' follow the logic of experimental work, but unlike true experiments (RCTs), they may lack certain aspects such as randomisation, as was the case here.
9   This is a 'directional' hypothesis – stated in a 'positive' direction.
10 If groups are not comparable at baseline, this introduces difficulties later on in any experiment, as you would not know whether it is the intervention or the differences between groups that accounts for any difference in scores.
11 The researchers used the test 2 (group) x 2 (time) mixed-model analysis of variance (ANOVA), with time as a within-subjects factor. Please see the research paper for actual results.
12 'A' represents 'antecedents', 'B' represents 'behaviour' and 'C' represents 'consequences'.

13 Only 9% of participants in the control group mentioned using this strategy, compared with 42% in the training group, and this result was statistically significant.

Chapter 07

1 Six self-report measures were used, including the Parenting Stress Index (PSI), Short form (SF) (see Abidin, 1995) and, to assess child development, the Brief Infant–Toddler Social and Emotional Assessment Scale (BITSEA) (see Briggs-Gowan and Carter, 2001).

2 This contextual aspect of the project was further developed into a second, related project that we called 'Training to Communicate', also using mixed methods (a survey with questionnaires and interviews). For more information on this project, see Bell (2007).

Chapter 08

1 Sure Start began in 1998 as a government-led initiative in the UK; it has led to the development of Children's Centres offering family support, child and family health services and early years provision.

2 'Resilience is understood here as an outcome associated with the capacity to do well despite adverse experiences' (Macpherson, Hart and Heaver, 2016, p. 2).

3 For example: 'following Foucault in understanding visual images as embedded in the practices of institutions and their exercise of power' (Rose, 2007, p. 193).

Chapter 09

1 'Twitter is a web-based Internet chat client (web-based Short Message Service system – "SMS") that provides a social network structure and a medium for information exchange/flow, allowing users to post short messages/updates, called tweets, of 140 characters (similar to SMS messaging but using an Internet browser), and to subscribe to (i.e. "follow") other users to receive postings/updates (tweets)' (Megele, 2014).

2 For example, in the cases Bartlett and Norrie (2015) focus upon, they found men were more likely to 'tweet' than women.

REFERENCES

Abidin, RR (1995) *Parenting Stress Index-Professional Manual*, 3rd edn, Odessa: Psychological Assessment Resources

Achenbach, TM (1993) *Empirically Based Taxonomy: How to use Syndromes and Profile Types Derived from the CBCL/4-18, TRF, and YSR*, Vermont: University of Vermont, Department of Psychiatry

Allain, L, Cocker, C, Hinds, O, Naluwaga, E and Babondock, A (2011) What's important for looked after children? The views of young people leaving care IN Cocker, C and Allain, L (eds) *Advanced Social Work with Children and Families*, Exeter: Learning Matters/Sage

Allen, L (2008) Young people's 'agency' in sexuality research using visual methods, *Journal of Youth Studies*, 11 (6): 565–577, doi: 10.1080/13676260802225744, http://www.tandfonline.com Accessed 20 October 2016

Atkinson, D (2005) Research as social work: participatory research in learning disability, *British Journal of Social Work*, 35 (4): 425–434, doi: 10.1093/bjsw/bch189, http://www.bjsw.oxfordjournals.org Accessed 10th October 2016

Aubrey, C and Dahl, S (2006) Children's voices: the views of vulnerable children on their service providers and the relevance of services they receive, *British Journal of Social Work*, 36: 21–39

Aveyard, H (2007) *Doing a Literature Review in Health and Social Care: A Practical Guide*, Berkshire: Open University Press

Ayling, P (2012) Learning through playing in higher education: Promoting play as a skill for social work students, *Social Work Education*, 31 (6): 764–777, doi: 10.1080/02615479.2012.695185, http://www.tandfonline.com/loi/cswe20 Accessed 1 Feb 2016

Babones, S (2016) Interpretive quantitative methods for the social sciences, *Sociology*, 50 (3): 453–469

Banks, M (2009) *Using Visual Data in Qualitative Research*, London: Sage

Banks, S (2004) *Ethics, Accountability and the Social Professions*, Basingstoke: Palgrave Macmillan

Banks, S (2012) *Ethics and Values in Social Work*, 4th edn, Basingstoke: Palgrave

Banks, S and Gallagher, A (2009) *Ethics in Professional Life: Virtues for Health and Social Care*, London: Palgrave Macmillan

Bartlett, J and Norrie, R (2015) *Immigration on Twitter: Understanding Public Attitudes Online*, London: DEMOS

BASW (2012) *Code of Ethics for Social Work*, Birmingham: British Association of Social Workers

Beauchamp, TL and Childress, J (2013) *Principles of Biomedical Ethics*, 7th edn, Oxford: Oxford University Press

Bell, L (1995) Just a token commitment'? Women's involvement in a local babysitting circle, *Women's Studies International Forum,* 18 (3) (Special Issue: Women in Families and Households; Qualitative Research): 325–336

Bell, L (1998) Public and private meanings in diaries: Researching family and child care IN Ribbens, J and Edwards, R (eds) *Feminist Dilemmas in Qualitative Research: Public Knowledge and Private Lives,* London: Sage

Bell, L (2003) *Survey of a Bereavement Counselling Service* (Thames Valley Hospice) Paper presented at the Middlesex University Cancer and Palliative Care Research Group Workshop, June 2003, London

Bell, L (2007) Training managers constructing their identities in English health and care agencies, *Equal Opportunities International,* 26 (4): 287–304

Bell, L (2012) Public and private meanings in diaries: Researching family and child care IN Goodwin, J (ed) *Sage Biographical Research,* volume 3, London: Sage

Bell, L (2014) Ethics and feminist research IN Hess-Biber, SN (ed) *Feminist Research Practice: A Primer,* 2nd edn, Thousand Oaks: Sage

Bell, L and Allain, L (2011) Exploring professional stereotypes and learning for interprofessional practice: An example from UK qualifying level social work education, *Social Work Education,* 30 (3): 266–280

Bell, L and Clancy, C (2013) Postgraduate students learning about research: Exploring the attitudes of social work and mental health students in an English university setting, *Social Work and Social Sciences Review,* 16 (2): 37–50

Bell, L and Hafford-Letchfield, T (eds) (2015) *Ethics, Values and Social Work Practice,* Maidenhead: Open University Press/McGraw-Hill

Bell, L, Lewis-Brooke, S, Herring, R, Lehane, L, O'Farrell-Pearce, S, Quinn, K, So, T (2015) *Mothers Apart: Working with Birth Mothers Who Have Had Children Successively and Permanently Removed from Their Care* Paper presented at the 5th European Conference for Social Work Research Ljubljana, Slovenia, April 2015

Bell, L, Nissen, MA and Vindegg, J (*forthcoming*) The construction of professional identity in social work: experience, analytical reflection and time IN Blom, B, Evertsson, L and Perlinski, M (eds) *Social and Caring Professions in European Welfare States: Policies, Services and Professional Practices,* Bristol: Policy Press

Bell, L and Nutt, L (2012) Divided loyalties, divided expectations: research ethics, professional and occupational responsibilities IN Mauthner, M et al. (eds) *Ethics in Qualitative Research,* 2nd rev edn, London: Sage

Bell, L and Villadsen, A (2011) *'A sense of belonging': Examining How Social Work Students Acquire Professional Values, Identities and Practice Competence through Group Support* Paper presented at the 1st European Social Work Research Conference, St Catherine's College, Oxford University, March 2011

Best, P, Manktelow, R and Taylor, B (2016) Social work and social media: Online help-seeking and the mental well-being of adolescent males, *British Journal of Social Work,* 46: 257–276, doi: 10.1093/bjsw/bcu130, downloaded from http://bjsw.oxfordjournals.org 15 November 2015

Birch, M (1998) Re/constructing research narratives: Self and sociological identity in alternative settings IN Ribbens, J and Edwards, R (eds) (1998) *Feminist Dilemmas in Qualitative Research: Public Knowledge and Private Lives,* London: Sage

Bisman, C (2004) Social work values: The moral core of the profession, *British Journal of Social Work*, 34 (1): 109–123.

Blaikie, N (1993) *Approaches to Social Enquiry*, Cambridge: Polity Press

Blaikie, N (2007) *Approaches to Social Enquiry*, 2nd edn, Cambridge: Polity Press

Bober, M (2004) Virtual youth research: An exploration of methodologies and ethical dilemmas from a British perspective IN Buchanan, EA (ed) *Readings in Virtual Research Ethics: Issues and Controversies*, Hershey: Information Science Publishing

Boddy, J, Boaz, A, Lupton, C and Pahl, J (2006) What counts as research? The implications for research governance in social care, *International Journal of Social Research Methodology*, 9 (4): 317 –330

Bornat, J, Johnson, J and Reynolds, J (eds) (2013) *Secondary Analysis and Re-using Archived Data in the Context of Ageing and Biography*, Research series – The representation of older people in ageing, number 12, London: Open University, Centre for Policy of Ageing

Boulton, M and Parker, M (2007) Introduction: 'Informed consent in a changing environment, *Social Science & Medicine*, 65 (11) (Special Issue): 2187– 2198

Bowling, A (1997) *Research Methods in Health: Investigating Health and Health Services*, Milton Keynes: Open University Press

Boxall, K and Beresford, P (2013) Service user research in social work and disability studies in the United Kingdom, *Disability and Society*, 28 (5): 587–600, doi: 10.1080/09687599.2012.717876, accessed from www.tandfonline.com 20 October 2016

Brannen, J (2005) Mixing methods: The entry of qualitative and quantitative approaches into the research process, *International Journal of Social Research Methodology*, 8 (3): 173–184

Briggs-Gowan, MJ and Carter, AS (2001) *The Brief Infant-Toddler Social and Emotional Assessment (BITSEA) Manual*, New Haven: Yale University, Department of Psychology

Bryan, K, Axelrod, L, Maxim, J, Bell, L and Jordan, L (2002) Working with older people with communication difficulties: An evaluation of care worker training, *Aging and Mental Health*, 6 (3): 248–254

Bryant, L (ed) (2015) *Critical and Creative Research Methodologies in Social Work*, London: Ashgate

Bryman, A (2007) The research question in social research: What is its role?, *International Journal of Social Research Methodology*, 10 (1): 5–20

Bryman, A (2012) *Social Research Methods*, 4th edn, Oxford: Oxford University Press

Buchanan, EA (2004) *Readings in Virtual Research Ethics: Issues and Controversies*, Hershey: Information Science Publishing

Caelli, K, Ray, L and Mill, J (2003) 'Clear as mud': Toward greater clarity in generic qualitative research, *International Journal of Qualitative Methods*, 2 (2): 1–13

Caldwell, K, Coleman, K, Copp, G, Bell, L and Ghazi, F (2007) Preparing for professional practice: How well does professional training equip health and social care practitioners to engage in evidence-based practice?, *Nurse Education Today*, 27 (6): 518–528

Cantijoch, M, Gibson, R and Ward, S (eds) (2014) *Analysing Social Media Data and Web Networks*, Basingstoke: Palgrave

Carr, S (2007) Participation, power, conflict and change: Theorizing dynamics of service user participation in the social care system of England and Wales, *Critical Social Policy*, 27 (2): 266–276

Cartney, P (2015) Links between reflective practice, ethics and values IN Bell, L and Hafford-Letchfield, T (eds) *Ethics, Values and Social Work Practice*, Maidenhead: Open University Press/McGraw-Hill

Charmaz, K (2006) *Constructing Grounded Theory: A practical Guide through Qualitative Methods*, London: Sage

Chu, W, Tsui, M, and Yan, M (2009) Social work as a moral and political practice, *International Social Work*, 52 (3): 287–298

Clark, C (2006) Moral character in social Work, *British Journal of Social Work*, 36 (1): 75–89

Clarke, AE (2005) *Situational Analysis: Grounded Theory after the Postmodern Turn*, Thousand Oaks: Sage

Cooke, M, Moyle, W, Shum, D, Harrison, S and Murfield, J (2010) A randomized controlled trial exploring the effect of music on quality of life and depression in older people with dementia, *Journal of Health Psychology*, 15 (5): 765–776

Cooper, A (2009) Hearing the grass grow: Emotional and epistemological challenges of practice-near research, *Journal of Social Work Practice*, 23 (4): 429–442

Corbin, J and Strauss, A (1990) Grounded theory research: Procedures, canons and evaluative criteria, *Qualitative Sociology*, 13 (1): 3–21

Corby, D, Taggart, L and Cousins, W (2015) People with intellectual disability and human science research: A systematic review of phenomenological studies using interviews for data collection, *Research in Developmental Disabilities*, 47: 451–465, doi: 10.1016/j.ridd.2015.09.001, accessed from http//www.sciencedirect.com 20 October 2016

Cotterell, S (2014) *Dissertations and Project Reports: A Step by Step Guide*, Basingstoke: Palgrave Macmillan

Craig, C, Chadborn, N, Sands, G, Tuomainen, H and Gladman, J (2015) Systematic review of EASY-care needs assessment for community-dwelling older people, *Age and Ageing*, 44: 559–565, doi: 10.1093/ageing/afv050, http://creativecommons.org/licenses/by/4.0/ Downloaded from http://ageing.oxfordjournals.com September 3rd 2015

Cree, VE, Jain, S and Hillen, P (2016) The challenge of measuring effectiveness in social work: A case study of an evaluation of a drug and alcohol referral service in Scotland, *British Journal of Social Work*, 46 (1): 27–293, doi: 10.1093/bjsw/bcu118, downloaded from http://bjsw.oxfordjournals.org 15 November 2015

D'Cruz, H, Gillingham, P and Melendez, S (2007) Reflexivity, its meanings and relevance for social work: A critical review of the literature, *British Journal of Social Work*, 37: 73–90, doi: 10.1093/bjsw/bcl001, http://www.bjsw.oxfordjournals.org Accessed 10 October 2016

Denzin, N and Lincoln, Y (2000) *Handbook of Qualitative Research*, 2nd edn, Thousand Oaks: Sage

Dey, I (1999) *Grounding Grounded Theory: Guidelines for Qualitative Inquiry*, London: Academic Press

Dickson-Swift, V, James, E, Kippen, S and Liamputtong, P (2009) Researching sensitive topics: Qualitative research as emotion work, *Qualitative Research*, 9 (1): 61–79

Dodsworth, J, Bailey, S, Schofield, G, Cooper, N, Fleming, P and Young, J (2013) Internet technology: An empowering or alienating tool for communication between foster-carers and social workers?, *British Journal of Social Work*, 43 (4): 775–795, doi:10.1093/bjsw/bcs007, http://www.bjsw.oxfordjournals.org Accessed 10 October 2016

Dracopoulou, S (2015) Major trends in applied ethics, including the ethics of social work IN Bell, L and Hafford-Letchfield, T (eds) *Ethics, Values and Social Work Practice*, Maidenhead: Open University Press/McGraw-Hill

Dunne, C (2011) The place of the literature review in grounded theory research, *International Journal of Social Research Methodology*, 14 (2): 111–124

Elliott, H (1997) The use of diaries in sociological research on health experience, *Sociological Research Online*, 2 (2), www.socresonline.org.uk/2/2/7.html

Elliott, J (2005) *Using Narrative in Social Research: Qualitative and Quantitative Approaches*, Thousand Oaks: Sage

Ferguson, H (2016) Researching social work practice close up: Using ethnographic and mobile methods to understand encounters between social workers, children and families, *British Journal of Social Work*, 46 (1): 153–168, doi: 10.1093/bjsw/bcu120, http://www.bjsw.oxfordjournals.org Accessed 10 October 2016

Flick, U (ed) (2014) *The Sage Handbook of Qualitative Data Analysis*, London: Sage

Foster, J, Bell, L and Serasinghe, N (2013) Care, control and collaborative working in a prison hospital wing, *Journal of Interprofessional Care*, 27(2): 184–90, doi: 10.3109/13561820.2012.730073 Accessed from tandfonline.com 22 October 2016, http://dx.doi.org./10.3109/13561820.2012.730073

Foster, V (2012a) What if? The use of poetry to promote social justice, *Social Work Education*, 31 (6): 742–755, doi: 10.1080/ o2615479.2012.695936, http://www.tandfonline.com/loi/cswe20 Accessed 1 Feb 2016

Foster, V (2012b) The pleasure principle: Employing arts-based methods in social work research, *European Journal of Social Work*, 15 (4): 532–545, doi: 10.1080/13691457.2012.702311, http://www-tandfonline-com/toc/cesw20/15/4 Accessed 22 October 2016

Fountain, J et al. (1999) Benzodiazepines in poly-drug using repertoires: The impact of the decreased availability of temazepam gel-filled capsules, *Drugs, Education, Prevention and Policy*, 6 (1): 61–69

Fraser, K. D and al Sayah, F (2011) Arts-based methods in health research: a systematic review of the literature *Arts and Health*, 3 (2): 110–145

Froggett, L and Briggs, S (2012) Practice-near and practice-distant methods in human services research, *Journal of Research Practice*, 8 (2), Article M9, http://jrp.icaap.org/index.php/jrp/article/view/318/276

Frost, N and Elichaoff, F (2014) Feminist postmodernism, poststructuralism, and critical theory IN Hess-Biber, SN (ed) *Feminist Research Practice: A Primer*, 2nd edn, Thousand Oaks: Sage

Gadamer, H (2004) *Philosophical Hermeneutics*, translated and edited by DE Linge, 2nd edn, Berkeley: University of California Press

Garrity, Z (2010) Discourse analysis, Foucault and social work research identifying some methodological complexities, *Journal of Social Work*, 10 (2): 193–210, doi: 10.1177/1468017310363641, accessed from http://jsw.sagepub.com.ezproxy.mdx.ac.uk/content/10/2.toc 22 October 2016

Gill, R (2000) Discourse analysis IN Bauer, M and Gaskell, G (eds) *Qualitative Researching with Text, Image and Sound*, London: Sage

Gillies, V and Lucey, H (eds) (2007) *Power, Knowledge and the Academy*, Basingstoke: Palgrave Macmillan

Glaser, B and Strauss, A (1967) *The Discovery of Grounded Theory: Strategies for Qualitative Research*, New York: Aldine

Gomm, R and Davies, C (eds) (2000) *Using Evidence in Health and Social Care*, London: Sage/Open University

Gomm, R, Needham, G and Boullman, A (eds) (2000) *Evaluating Research in Health and Social Care*, London: Sage/Open University

Goodman, R and Scott, S (1999) Comparing the strengths and difficulties questionnaire and the child behavior checklist: Is small beautiful?, *Journal of Abnormal Child Psychology*, 27 (1): 17–24

Gray, M (2010) Moral sources and emergent ethics theories in social work, *British Journal of Social Work*, 40: 1794–1811

Gray, M, Plath, D and Webb, SA (2009) *Evidence-Based Social Work: A Critical Stance*, London: Routledge

Gribble, K and Gallagher, M (2014) Rights of children in relation to breastfeeding in child protection cases, *British Journal of Social Work*, 44: 434–450, doi: 10.1093/bjsw/bcu004, downloaded from http://bjsw.oxfordjournals.org 15 November 2015

Gringeri, C, Barusch, A and Cambron, C (2013) Epistemology in qualitative social work research: A review of published articles, 2008–2010, *Social Work Research*, 37 (1): 55–63

Grix, J (2010) The Foundations of Research, 2nd edn, Basingstoke: Palgrave Macmillan

Gubrium, JF and Holstein, JA (2000) Analyzing interpretive practice IN Denzin, NK and Lincoln, YS (eds) *Handbook of Qualitative Research*, 2nd edn, Thousand Oaks: Sage

Hafford-Letchfield, T (2013) Funny things happen at the Grange: Introducing comedy activities in day services to older people with dementia – innovative practice, *Dementia*, 12 (6): 840– 852, doi:10.1177/1471301212454357, http://dem.sagepub.com./content/12/6.toc Accessed 22nd October 2016

Hafford-Letchfield, T (2015) Power IN Bell, L and Hafford-Letchfield, T (eds) *Ethics, Values and Social Work Practice*, Maidenhead: Open University Press/McGraw-Hill

Hafford-Letchfield, T and Bell, L (2015) Situating ethics and values in social work practice IN Bell, L and Hafford-Letchfield, T (eds) *Ethics, Values and Social Work Practice*, Maidenhead: Open University Press/McGraw-Hill

Hafford-Letchfield, T, Couchman, W, Webster, M and Avery, P (2010) A drama project about older people's intimacy and sexuality, *Educational Gerontology*, 36 (7): 604–621

Hafford-Letchfield, T, Leonard, K and Couchman, W (2012) Editorial: Arts and extremely dangerous: Critical commentary on the Arts in social work education, *Social Work Education: The International Journal*, 31 (6): 683–690

Halse, C and Honey, A (2005) Unravelling ethics: Illuminating the moral dilemmas of research ethics, *Signs*, 30 (4): 2141–2162

Hammersley, M (2009) Against the ethicists: On the evils of ethical regulation, *International Journal of Social Research Methodology*, 12 (3): 211–225

Harden, A and Thomas, J (2005) Methodological issues in combining diverse study types in systematic reviews, *International Journal of Social Research Methodology*, 8 (3): 257–271

Harris, M and Taylor, G (2014) *Medical statistics Made Easy*, 3rd edn, Banbury: Scion Publishing

Harding, S (ed) (1987) *Feminism and Methodology*, Bloomington: Indiana University Press

Hart, C (1998) *Doing a Literature Review: Releasing the Social Science Research Imagination*, London: Sage

Hatton, K (2001) Translating values: Making sense of different value bases – reflections from Denmark and the UK, *International Journal of Social Research Methodology*, 4(4): 265–278

Hedgecoe, A (2008) Research ethics review and the sociological research relationship, *Sociology*, 42 (5): 873–886

Hedgecoe, A (2016) Reputational risk, academic freedom and research ethics review, *Sociology*, 50 (3): 486–501

Heron, G, McGoldrick, R and Wilson, R (2015) Exploring the influence of feedback on student social workers' understanding of childcare and protection, *British Journal of Social Work*, 45 (8): 2317–2334, doi: 10.1093/bjsw/bcu071, http://www.bjsw.oxfordjournals.org Accessed 10 October 2016

Hesse-Biber, SN (ed) (2014) *Feminist Research Practice*, Thousand Oaks: Sage

Hine, C (2015) *Ethnography for the Internet: Embedded, Embodied and Everyday*, London: Bloomsbury Academic

Hingley-Jones, H (2009) Developing practice-near social work research to explore the emotional worlds of severely learning disabled adolescents in 'transition' and their families, *Journal of Social Work Practice*, 23 (4): 413–428, doi: 10.1080/02650530903374952, http://www-tandfonline-com/toc/cjsw20/23/4 Accessed 22 Ocober 2016

Ho, RTH (2015) A place and space to survive: A dance/movement therapy program for childhood sexual abuse survivors, *The Arts in Psychotherapy*, 46: 9–16

Holland, R (1999) Reflexivity, *Human Relations*, 52 (4): 463–484, doi: 10.1177/001872679905200403, http://hum.sagepub.com/content/52/4.toc Accessed 22 October 2016

Holstein, JA and Gubrium, JF (1994) Phenomenology, ethnomethodology, and interpretive practice IN Denzin, NK and Lincoln, YS (eds) *Handbook of Qualitative Research*, Thousand Oaks: Sage

Hubbard, G, Backett-Milburn, K and Kemmer, D (2001) Working with emotion: Issues for the researcher in fieldwork and teamwork, *International Journal of Social Research Methodology: Theory and Practice*, 4 (2): 119–137

Huss, E (2012) Utilizing an image to evaluate stress and coping for social workers, *Social Work Education*, 31 (6) (Special Issue: Arts in social work education): 691–702, doi: 10.1080/02615479.2012.695154, http://www.tandfonline.com/loi/cswe20 Accessed 1 Feb 2016

Huss, E, Kaufman, R, Avgar, A and Shouker, E (2015) Using arts-based research to help visualize community intervention in international aid International social work, *International Social Work*, 58 (5): 673–688

Ingram, R (2013) Emotions, social work practice and supervision: an uneasy alliance?, *Journal of Social Work Practice*, 27 (1): 5–19, doi: 10.1080/02650533.2012.745842, http://www-tandfonline-com/toc/cjsw20/27/1 Accessed 22 October 2016

Iphofen, R (2009) *Ethical Decision-Making in Social Research: A Practical Guide*, Basingstoke: Palgrave Macmillan

Jaggar, A (1997) Love and knowledge: Emotion in feminist epistemology IN Kemp, S and Squires, J (eds) *Feminisms*, Oxford: Oxford University Press

Jordan, L, Bell, L, Bryan, K, Maxim, J and Newman, C (1998) *Communicate*: Organisational issues and their relevance for clinical evaluation, *International Journal of Language and Communication Disorders*, 33 (S1): 60–65, doi: 10.3109/13682829809179397, http://onlinelibrary.wiley.com/doi/10.1111/jlcd.1998.33.issue-S1/issuetoc Accessed 22 October 2016

Kim, K and Berard, T (2009) Typification in society and social science: The continuing relevance of Schutz's Social Phenomenology, *Human Studies*, 32 (3): 263–289, doi: 10.1007/s10746-009-9120-6, http://search.proquest.com./publicationissue/28E09110D91A4CBDPQ/$B/1/Human+Studies/02009Y09Y01$23Sep+2009$3b++Vol.+32+$283$29?accountid=12441 Accessed 22 October 2016

Kiteley, R and Stogdon, C (2014) *Literature Reviews in Social Work*, London: Sage

Kratochwill, TR, MacDonald, L, Levin, J, Scalia, PA and Coover, G (2009) Families and schools together: An experimental study of multi-family support groups for children at risk, *Journal of School Psychology*, 47 (4): 245–265

Krumer-Nevo, M and Komem, M (2015) Intersectionality and critical social work with girls: Theory and practice, *British Journal of Social Work*, 45 (4): 1190–1206, doi: 10.1093/bjsw/bct189, http://www.bjsw.oxfordjournals.org Accessed 10 October 2016

Leavy, P (2015) *Method Meets Art: Arts-Based Research Practice*, 2nd edn, New York: Guilford Press

Leece, J and Leece, D (2011) Personalisation: Perceptions of the role of social work in a world of brokers and budgets, *British Journal of Social Work*, 41 (2): 204–223, doi: 10.1093/bjsw/bcq087, http://www.bjsw.oxfordjournals.org Accessed 10 October 2016

Leonard, K, Hafford-Letchfield, T and Couchman, W (2013) 'We're all going Bali': Utilizing Gamelan as an educational resource for leadership and teamwork in post-qualifying education in health and social care, *British Journal of Social Work*, 43 (1): 173–190

Letherby, G, Scott, J and Williams, M (2013) *Objectivity and Subjectivity in Social Research*, London: Sage

Lloyd, L (2010) The individual in social care: The ethics of care and the 'personalisation agenda' in services for older people in England, *Ethics and Social Welfare*, 4 (2): 188–200

Ma, A and Norwich, B (2007) Triangulation and theoretical understanding, *International Journal of Social Research Methodology*, 10 (3): 211– 226

McAuley, C, McCurry, N, Knapp, M, Beecham, J, Sleed, M (2006) Young families under stress: Assessing maternal and child well-being using a mixed-methods approach, *Child and Family Social Work*, 11: 43–54

McKeganey, N (1995) Quantitative and qualitative research in the addictions: An unhelpful divide, *Addiction*, 90: 749–751

MacDonald, G and Turner, W (2005) An experiment in helping foster carers manage challenging behaviour, *British Journal of Social Work*, 35: 1265–1282, doi:10.1093/bjsw/bch204, http://www.bjsw.oxfordjournals.org Accessed 10 October 2016

Macpherson, H, Hart, A and Heaver, B (2016) Building resilience through group visual arts activities: Findings from a scoping study with young people who experience mental health complexities and/or learning difficulties, *Journal of Social Work*, 16 (5): 541–560, doi: 10.1177/1468017315581772, http://jsw. sagepub.com./content/16/5.toc Accessed 22 October 2016

Mason, J (1996; 2002) *Qualitative Researching*, 2nd edn, London: Sage

Mauthner, M and Bell, L (2007) Power in research teams IN Gillies, V and Lucey, H (eds) *Power, Knowledge and the Academy*, London: Palgrave Macmillan

Mauthner, NS and Doucet, A (2003) Reflexive accounts and accounts of reflexivity in qualitative data analysis, *Sociology*, 37(3): 413–431

Mauthner, NS and Doucet, A (1998) Reflections on a voice-centred relational method: Analysing maternal and domestic voices IN Ribbens, J and Edwards, R (eds) (1998) *Feminist Dilemmas in Qualitative Research: Public Knowledge and Private Lives*, London: Sage

Maxim, J, Bryan, K, Axelrod, L, Jordan L and Bell, L (2001) Speech and language therapists as trainers: Enabling care staff working with older people, *International Journal of Language and Communication Disorders*, 36 (Supplement): 194–199

May-Chahal, C, Mason, C, Rashid, A, Walkerdine, J, Rayson, P and Greenwood, P (2014) Safeguarding cyborg childhoods: Incorporating the on/offline behaviour of children into everyday social work practices, *British Journal of Social Work*, 44 (3): 596–614, doi: 10.1093/bjsw/bcs121, http://www.bjsw. oxfordjournals.org Accessed 10 October 2016

Mazza, N (2009) The arts and family social work: A call for advancing practice, research, and education, *Journal of Family Social Work*, 12 (1): 3–8, doi:10.1080/10522150802383084, web.a.ebscohost.com/ehost/ results?sid=887cc12f-cfe9-47f8-8edf-23d93c6d59b4%40sessionmgr4010&vid =1&hid=4209&bquery=JN+"Journal+of+Family+Social+Work"+AND+DT+200 90101&bdata=JmRiPWVoaCZ0eXBlPTAmc2l0ZT1laG9zdC1saXZl Accessed 22 October 2016

Mehrotra, G (2010) Toward a continuum of intersectionality theorizing for feminist social work scholarship, *Affilia*, 25 (4): 417–430, doi:

10.1177/0886109910384190, http://aff.sagepub.com/content/25/4.toc Accessed 22 October 2016

Mehrotra, G (2015) Considering emotion and emotional labor in feminist social work research IN Wahab, S, Anderson-Nathe, B and Gringeri, C (eds) (2015) *Feminisms in Social Work Research: Promise and Possibilities for Justice-Based Knowledge*, Abingdon: Routledge

Megele, C (2014) Theorizing Twitter chat, *Journal of Perspectives in Applied Academic Practice*, 2 (2): 46–51

Meyer, J (1993) New paradigm research in practice: The trials and tribulations of action research, *Journal of Advanced Nursing*, 18 (7): 1066–1072

Miller, T and Bell, L (2012; 2002) Consenting to what? Issues of access, gatekeeping and 'informed' consent IN Miller, T, Mauthner, M, Birch, M and Jessop, J (eds) *Ethics in Qualitative Research*, 2nd edn, London: Sage

Miller, T and Boulton, M (2007) Changing constructions of informed consent: Qualitative research and complex social worlds, *Social Science & Medicine*, 65 (11): 2199–2211

Miller, T, Mauthner, M, Birch, M and Jessop, J (eds) (2012) *Ethics in Qualitative Research*, 2nd edn, London: Sage

Moore, T, Noble-Carr, D and McArthur, M (2016) Changing things for the better: the use of children and young people's reference groups in social research, *International Journal of Social Research Methodology*, 19 (2): 241–256, doi: 10.1080/13645579.2014.989640, http://web.a.ebscohost.com/ehost/results?sid=80cd98ba-c25d-4d77-87f5-69ec10f6e3ee%40sessionmgr4007&vid=1&hid=4209&bquery=JN+%22International+Journal+of+Social+Research+Methodology%22+AND+DT+20160301&bdata=JmRiPWJ0aCZ0eXBlPTAmc2l0ZT1laG9zdC1saXZl Accessed 21 October 2016

Morgenshtern, T, Freymond, N, Agyapong, S and Greeson, C (2011) Graduate social work students' attitudes toward research: Problems and prospects, *Journal of Teaching in Social Work*, 31 (5): 552–568

Moxley, DP, Feen-Calligan, H and Washington, OGM (2012) Lessons learned from three projects linking social work, the arts, and humanities, *Social Work Education*, 31 (6): 703–723, doi: 10.1080/02615479.2012.695160, http://www.tandfonline.com/loi/cswe20 Accessed 1 Feb 2016

Munro, E (2004) The impact of audit on social work practice, *British Journal of Social Work*, 34 (8): 1075–1095, doi: 10.1093/bjsw/bch130, http://www.bjsw.oxfordjournals.org Accessed 20 October 2016

Murthy, D (2008) Digital ethnography: An examination of the use of new technologies for social research, *Sociology*, 42 (5): 837–855

Murtonen, M (2005) University students' research orientations: Do negative attitudes exist toward quantitative methods? *Scandinavian Journal of Educational Research*, 49: 263–280

Naples, N and Gurr, B (2014) Feminist empiricism and standpoint theory: Approaches to understanding the social world IN Hesse-Biber, SN (ed) *Feminist Research Practice*, Thousand Oaks: Sage

Nash, JC (2008) Re-thinking intersectionality, *Feminist Review*, 89: 1–15

Needham, C and Carr, S (2009) *Co-production: An Emerging Evidence Base for Adult Social Care Transformation. Research Briefing no 31*, London: Social Care Institute for Excellence

Ney, T, Stoltz, J and Maloney, M (2013) Voice, power and discourse: Experiences of participants in family group conferences in the context of child protection, *Journal of Social Work*, 13 (2): 184–202, doi: 10.1177/1468017311410514, http://jsw.sagepub.com./content/13/2.toc Accessed 22 October 2016

Noaks, L and Wincup, E (2004) *Criminological Research: Understanding Qualitative Research Methods*, Thousand Oaks: Sage

Nowicka, M and Ryan, L (2015) Beyond insiders and outsiders in migration research: Rejecting a priori commonalities (Introduction to the *FQS* Thematic Section on 'Researcher, Migrant, Woman: Methodological Implications of multiple positionalities in Migration Studies'), *Forum: Qualitative Social Research*, 16 (2): art. 18

Oakley, A (1998) Science, gender, and women's liberation: An argument against postmodernism, *Women's Studies International Forum*, 21 (2): 133–146

O'Dell, SL, Tarler-Belolo, L and Flynn, JM (1979) An instrument to measure knowledge of behavioural principles as applied to children, *Journal of Behavioral Therapy and Experimental Psychiatry*, 10: 29–34

Oliver, C (2012) Critical realist grounded theory: A new approach for social work research, *British Journal of Social Work*, 42 (2): 371–387

Oppenheim, AN (1992) *Questionnaire Design, Interviewing and Attitude Measurement*, London: Pinter

Orme, J (2002) Social work: Gender, care and justice, *British Journal of Social Work*, 32 (6): 799–814

Orme, J (2003) 'It's feminist because I say so!' Feminism, social work and critical practice in the UK, *Qualitative Social Work*, 2(2): 131–153

Øvretveit, J (1998) *Evaluating Health Interventions*, Buckingham: Open University Press

Øvretveit, J (2002) *Action Evaluation of Health Programmes and Changes: A Handbook for a User-focused Approach*, Abingdon: Radcliffe Medical Press

Pallant, J (2013) *SPSS Survival Manual*, 5th edn, London: Allen and Unwin

Papadaki, E and Papadaki, E (2008) Ethically difficult situations related to organisational conditions: Social workers' experiences in Crete, Greece, *Journal of Social Work*, 8 (2): 163–181

Papadopoulos, I and Ali, S (2016) Measuring compassion in nurses and other healthcare professionals: An integrative review, *Nurse Education in Practice*, 16 (1): 133–139, doi: 10.1016/j.nepr.2015.08.001, http://www.sciencedirect.com/science/journal/14715953/16/1 Accessed 22 October 2016

Papanastasiou, E (2005) Factor structure of the 'Attitudes Toward Research' scale,6 *Statistics Education Research Journal*, 4 (1): 16–26

Park, Y (2008) Making refugees: A historical discourse analysis of the construction of the 'refugee' in US social work, 1900–1957, *British Journal of Social Work*, 38 (4): 771–787, doi:10.1093/bjsw/bcn015, http://www.bjsw.oxfordjournals.org Accessed 10 October 2016

Parrott, L and Madoc-Jones, I (2008) Reclaiming information and communication technologies for empowering social work practice, *Journal of Social Work*, 8 (2): 181–197

Pawson, R, Boaz, A, Grayson, L, Long, A and Barnes, C (2003) *Types and Quality of Knowledge in Social Care*, London: SCIE

Petersen, A and Olsson, J (2015) Calling evidence-based practice into question: Acknowledging phronetic knowledge in social work, *British Journal of Social Work*, 45 (5): 1581–1597

Phillips, C and Bellinger, A (2011) Feeling the cut: Exploring the use of photography in social work education, *Qualitative Social Work*, 10 (1): 86–105, doi: 10.1177/1473325010361999, http://qsw.sagepub.com/content/10/1.toc Accessed 20 October 2016

Phillips, J, Macgiollari, D and Callaghan, S (2012) Encouraging research in social work: Narrative as the thread integrating education and research in social work, *Social Work Education*, 31(6): 785–793, doi: 10.1080/02615479.2012.695200, http://www.tandfonline.com/loi/cswe20 Accessed 1 Feb 2016

Pilcher, K, Martin, W and Williams, V (2015) Issues of collaboration, representation, meaning and emotions: Utilising participant-led visual diaries to capture the everyday lives of people in mid to later life, *International Journal of Social Research Methodology*, doi: 10.1080/13645579.2015. 1086199, http://dx.doi.org/10.1080/13645579.2015.1086199 Accessed from tandfonline.com 22 October 2016

Pink, S (2003) Interdisciplinary agendas in visual research: Re-situating visual anthropology, *Visual Studies*, 1 8(2): 179–192, doi: 10.1080/ 14725860310001632029, http://www-tandfonline-com/toc/rvst20/18/ 2?nav=tocList Accessed 21 October 2016

Pink, S (2012) *Advances in Visual Methodology*, London: Sage

Plewis, I and Mason, P (2005) What works and why: Combining quantitative and qualitative approaches in large-scale evaluations, *International Journal of Social Research Methodology*, 8 (3) (Special Issue: Combining Qualitative and Quantitative Methods in Educational and Social Research): 185–194

Potter, J (2004) Discourse analysis IN Hardy, M and Bryman, A (eds) *Handbook of Data Analysis*, London: Sage

Prosser, J (1998) *Image-Based Research: A Resource for Qualitative Researchers*, London: Routledge

Rabiee, P, Baxter, K, and Glendinning, C (2016) Supporting choice: Support planning, older people and managed personal budgets, *Journal of Social Work*, 16 (4): 453–469, doi: 10.1177/1468017315581529, http:// jsw.sagepub.com./ content/16/4/453.full Accessed 22 October 2016

Rallis, SE and Rossman, GB (2012) *The Research Journey: Introduction to Inquiry*, New York: Guilford Press

Reynolds, J (2007) Discourses of inter-professionalism, *British Journal of Social Work*, 37 (3): 441–457, doi: 10.1093/bjsw/bcm023, http://www.bjsw. oxfordjournals.org Accessed 10 October 2016

Rhodes, T and Quirk, A (1998) Drug users' sexual relationships and the social organisation of risk: The sexual relationship as a site of risk management, *Social Science and Medicine*, 46 (2): 157–169

Ribbens, J, and Edwards, R (eds) (1998) *Feminist Dilemmas in Qualitative Research*, London: Sage

Ribbens-McCarthy, J, Edwards, R and Gillies, V (2000) Moral tales of the child and the adult: Narratives of contemporary family lives under changing circumstances, *Sociology*, 34: 785–803

Ribbens-McCarthy, J, Edwards, R and Gillies, V (2003) *Making Families: Moral Tales of Parenting and Step-Parenting*, Durham: Sociologypress

Robson, C (1993; 2002) *Real World Research: A Resource for Social Scientists and Practitioner-Researchers*, Oxford: Blackwell

Rogers, C and Weller, S (2013) (eds) *Critical Approaches to Care: Understanding Caring Relations, Identities and Cultures*, London: Routledge

Rose, G (2007) *Visual Methodologies: An Introduction to the Interpretation of Visual Materials*, 2nd edn, London: Sage

Ruch, G (2012) Where have all the feelings gone? Developing reflective and relationship-based management in child-care social work, *British Journal Social Work*, 42 (7): 1315–1332

Ruch, G (2014) 'Helping children is a human process': Researching the challenges social workers face in communicating with children, *British Journal Social Work*, 44: 2145–2162

Rugkåsa, J et al. (2001) Anxious adults vs cool children: Children's views on smoking and addiction, *Social Science and Medicine*, 53: 593—602

Rushton, A (2003) SCIE Knowledge Review 2: The Adoption of Looked After Children: A Scoping Review of Research. London: SCIE

Rutter, D, Francis, J, Coren, E and Fisher, M (2010) *SCIE Systematic Research Reviews: Guidelines*, 2nd edn, London: SCIE

Ryan, P, Edwards, M, Hafford-Letchfield, T, Bell, l, Carr, S, Puniskis, M, Hanna, S and Jeewa, S (2016) *Research on the Experience of Staff with Disabilities within the NHS Workforce*, Project Report, London: Middlesex University

Schon, D (1983) *The Reflective Practitioner*, New York: Basic Books

Scurlock-Evans, L and Upton, D (2015) The role and nature of evidence: A systematic review of social workers' evidence-based practice orientation, attitudes and implementation, *Journal of Evidence-Informed Social Work*, 12 (4): 369–399

Sen, R (2015) Not all that is solid melts into air? Care-experienced young people, friendship and relationships in the 'digital age', *British Journal of Social Work*, doi: 10.1093/bjsw/bcu152, http://www.bjsw.oxfordjournals.org Accessed 10 October 2016

Sevenhuijsen, S (1998) *Citizenship and the Ethics of Care: Feminist Considerations on Justice, Morality and Politics*, London: Routledge

Shakespeare, T (ed) (2015) *Disability Research Today*, London: Taylor & Francis

Shaw, I (1999) *Qualitative Evaluation*, London: Sage

Shaw, I (2011) *Evaluating in Practice*, London: Ashgate

Skehill, C, Satka, M and Hoikkala, S (2013) Exploring innovative methodologies in time and place to analyse child protection documents as elements of practice, *Qualitative Social Work*, 12 (1): 57–72, doi: 10.1177/1473325011416878, http://qsw.sagepub.com/content/12/1.toc Accessed 22 October 2016

Smith, R (2009) *Doing Social Work Research*, Maidenhead: Open University Press

Soydan, H and Palinkas, LA (2014) *Evidence-Based Practice in Social Work: Development of a New Professional Culture*, Abingdon: Routledge

Standing, K (1998) Writing the voices of the less powerful: Research on lone mothers IN Ribbens, J and Edwards, R (eds) *Feminist Dilemmas in Qualitative Research*, London: Sage

Stanczak, G (ed) (2007) *Visual Research Methods: Image, Society and Representation*, London: Sage

Tanner, D (2007) Starting with lives: Supporting older peoples' strategies and ways of coping, *Journal of Social Work*, 7 (1): 7–30, doi:10.1177/1468017307075987, http://jsw.sagepub.com.ezproxy.mdx.ac.uk/content/7/1.toc Accessed 22 October 2016

Thomson, P (2008) *Doing Visual Research with Children and Young People*, London: Routledge

Tight, M (2010) The curious case of case study: A viewpoint, *International Journal of Social Research Methodology,* 13 (4): 329– 339

Verschuren, P (2003) Case study as a research strategy: And some ambiguities and opportunities, *International Journal of Social Research Methodology*, 6 (2): 121–139

Vervliet, M, De Mol, J, Broekaert, E and Derluyn, I (2014) 'That I live, that's because of her': Intersectionality as framework for unaccompanied refugee mothers, *British Journal of Social Work*, 44 (7): 2023–2041, doi:10.1093/bjsw/ bct060, http://www.bjsw.oxfordjournals.org Accessed 10 October 2016

Villadsen, A, Allain, L, Bell, L and Hingley-Jones, H (2012) The use of role-play and drama in interprofessional education: An evaluation of a workshop with social work, midwifery, early years and medical students, *Social Work Education*, 31 (1): 75–89

Wahab, S, Anderson-Nathe, B and Gringeri, C (eds) (2015) *Feminisms in Social Work Research: Promise and Possibilities for Justice-Based Knowledge*, Abingdon: Routledge

Walliman, N (2005) *Your Research Project: A Step-by-Step Guide for the First-Time Researcher*, 2nd edn, London: Sage

Walton, P (2012) Beyond talk and text: An expressive visual arts method for social work education, *Social work Education*, 31 (6) (Special Issue): 724–741, doi: 10.1080/02615479.2012.695934, http://www.tandfonline.com/loi/ cswe20 Accessed 1 Feb 2016

Weinberg, A, Williamson, J, Challis, D and Hughes, J (2003) What do care managers do? A study of working practice in older peoples' services, *British Journal of Social Work*, 33 (7): 901–919, doi:10.1093/bjsw/33.7.901, http:// www.bjsw.oxfordjournals.org Accessed 10 October 2016

White, S et al. (2009) Whither practice-near research in the modernization programme? Policy blunders in children's services, *Journal of Social Work*

Practice, 23 (4): 401–411, doi: 10.1080/02650530903374945, http://www-tandfonline-com/toc/cjsw20/23/4 Accessed 22 Ocober 2016

Whittaker, A (2012) *Research Skills for Social Work*, 2nd edn, London: Sage

Whittington, C and Whittington, M (2015) Partnership working, ethics and social work practice IN Bell, L and Hafford-Letchfield, T (eds) *Ethics, Values and Social Work Practice*, Maidenhead: Open University Press/McGraw-Hill

Wilcke, M (2002) Hermeneutic phenomenology as a research method in social work, *Currents: New Scholarship in the Human Services*, 1 (1)

Wilks, T (2004) The Use of Vignettes in Qualitative Research into Social Work Values, *Qualitative Social Work*, 3 (1): 78–87, doi: 10.1177/1473325004041133, http://qsw.sagepub.com/content/3/1.toc Accessed 22 October 2016

Wilks, T (2005) Social work and narrative ethics, *British Journal of Social Work*, 35 (8): 1249–1264, doi: 10.1093/bjsw/bch242

Williams, M (1998) The social work as knowable IN May, T and Williams, M (eds) *Knowing The Social World*, Buckingham: Open University Press

Williams, M, Payne, G, Hodgkinson, L, Poade, D (2008) Does British Sociology Count? Sociology 42 (5): 1003–1021, doi: 10.1177/0038038508094576, Accessed from http://soc.sagepub.com/content/42/5/ 19 October 2016

Wilson, J and While, AE (1998) Methodological issues surrounding the use of vignettes in qualitative research, *Journal of Interprofessional Care*, 12 (1): 79–86

Wincup, E (2000) Surviving through substance use: The role of substances in the lives of women who appear before the courts, *Sociological Research Online*, 4 (4), www.socresonline.org.uk/4/4/wincup.html

Winter, K, Hallett, S, Morrison, F, Cree, V, Ruch, G, Hatfield, M and Holland, S (2015) *Practice-Near Research: Exploring Insights from Different Degrees of Closeness*, Edinburgh: BASPCAN Congress

Wright, CV, Darko, N, Standen, PJ and Patel, TG (2010) Visual research methods: Using cameras to empower socially excluded black youth, *Sociology*, 44 (3): 541–558

Wright, S and Klee, H (1999) A profile of amphetamine users who present to treatment services and do not return, *Drugs, Education, Prevention and Policy*, 6 (2): 227–241

Yin, R (2014) *Case Study Research: Design and Methods*, 5th edn, Thousand Oaks: Sage

Zeilig, H, Killick, J and Fox, C (2014) The participative arts for people living with a dementia: A critical review, *International Journal of Ageing and Later Life*, 9(1): 7–34

INDEX

academic dissertations 5, 11, 18, 29–30, 34–35, 40, 54, 107, 164, 207

access 46, 57, 88–89, 110, 111, 155, 159–160, 161, 177, 184, 188, 189

accounts (research) 3, 25, 61, 69–70, 80, 94–96, 102–104, 165

alcohol *see* substance misuse

ambiguous contexts 25, 60, 67, 104, 131, 134, 157, 161–162

analytic 'themes' 63, 90, 92, 96, 102–104, 148, 152

anonymity *see also* confidentiality 4, 48, 54, 88, 157

ANOVA (analysis of variance) 124, 174, 180, 207

anthropology 65, 80, 141

archives 19, 89, 207

arguments (reviewing research) 35–36

arts-based research 141–153, 166, 173, 186

arts–therapeutic 142–143

attitude statements 55–56, 112, 115–117, 193, 203

Attitudes to Research measure (ATR) 56, 115, 117–118, 120, 122

audio (digital) recording 3, 19, 58, 78, 84, 94, 96, 177, 179

auditing 5, 12–13, 16, 174

axial coding 102

baseline measures 38, 51, 118, 120, 123, 132, 213, 198, 202, 207

The *Beck Depression Inventory* (BDI) 199

bias 10, 21–22, 33, 77, 131, 132, 136, 174, 179, 180, 203, 205

boundaries–research and practice xi, 143, 145, 150, 166, 173

Brief Infant–Toddler Social and Emotional Assessment Scale (BITSEA) 200, 208

Campbell Collaboration 30–31, 175, 206

Care Act, 2014 7, 10, 187

carers *see also* foster carers 51, 62, 93, 135, 144, 145, 147–148, 161, 176

'caring profession' 67, 176

case study 26, 60, 62, 65, 71–73, 74, 76, 87, 89, 91, 135, 148, 174

causal logic 8, 9, 38, 51, 71, 121–124, 133, 177, 181, 182, 198–199, 201, 202, 207

census 108, 203

change, measuring 51, 52, 55, 80, 107, 114–115, 120–124, 135, 198–199

checklists 83, 122, 133, 200

chi square test 175, 179, 195

Chicago School (sociology) 65

The Child Behavioural Checklist (CBCL) 122, 124, 200, 206

child protection 11, 18, 72–73, 88, 99, 100, 186, 187

children *see* young people

citizenship 67

client *see* service user

CMC (computer-mediated communication) 155, 157, 161, 162, 192

Cochrane Library 30, 31, 32, 175, 182, 206

coding (data analysis) 80, 97, 98, 99, 102, 104, 105, 135, 177

cognitive behavioural therapy (CBT) 51–52, 124

comments (open) on questionnaires 97, 99
Communicate training 53, 89, 133–136, 208
communication 1, 2, 4,15, 135
skills 2, 133
Community Care 17
Comte, Auguste 23
conceptual framework 71, 175
confidentiality *see also* anonymity 48, 54, 78, 91, 149, 151, 157, 159, 160–161,188
consent 44, 46, 48, 51, 56, 57, 58–59, 65,78, 89,148,157, 161, 162, 163, 175
Consequentialism 42, 175
consistency in recording data 19, 75, 116, 176
constant comparative analysis (grounded theory) 65, 101–102, 177
constructionism 25–26, 175, 176
content analysis 97–100, 103, 105, 135, 150, 156
context 4, 6, 7, 15, 22, 25, 38, 65, 67, 71, 72, 83, 104, 131, 134, 135–136, 137, 138, 141–142, 154–158, 161–162, 165, 176, 179, 208
Continuing Professional Development (CPD) x, 14–15
control group or participants 38, 51–52, 121–124, 134, 180, 190, 201, 208
controlled trials, randomized (RCTS) 31, 107, 121, 124, 138, 170, 175, 178, 190, 201, 206, 207
convenience sampling *see* sampling
co-production 18, 19, 61, 136, 138, 141, 143, 145, 149, 150, 176
courts 66
covert research 78, 81
creativity 136, 142, 143–147, 151
criminology *see also* courts 65
criteria, inclusion or exclusion 10, 20, 21, 28, 31, 33, 38, 51, 90, 175–176

critical appraisal *see also* literature reviewing 34, 35–39, 111–112
Critical Appraisal Skills Programme (CASP) 39
critical rationalism 24
critical realism 64
critical theory 67
critical thinking skills 4, 15
Cronbach's alpha coefficient 116, 117, 176
cross-national studies 131
Cumulative Index to Nursing and Allied Health Literature (Cinhal) 18

data analysis, qualitative 15, 39, 63, 64, 80, 98, 100–105, 129, 135, 142, 146, 150, 170, 177
data analysis, quantitative *see also* statistics 38, 39, 56, 118–121, 122–124, 129, 135
data archives 19, 207
data sources 17–19, 27–29, 72–73, 87–89, 154–155, 181
deduction 24, 176, 177
dementia 11, 143, 147, 148, 158, 186
demographics 75
DEMOS 4, 156
Deontology 42, 176
dependent variable *see* variable
Derrida, Jacques 97–98
descriptive/ exploratory research design *see also* survey 6, 9, 10, 26, 38, 39, 56, 157
descriptive phenomenology *see* phenomenology
diaries *see also* field notes/diary 52, 82, 83, 87, 89, 92–94, 96, 102, 105, 143, 165, 177, 190
digital media 18, 28, 150, 155, 156
dilemmas in research 41–44, 46, 48–50, 67, 75, 93
disability research 70, 133, 136, 137, 160
discourses 97, 101, 151, 155
discourse analysis 90, 97–98, 150, 176

doctoral students 138, 164

documents 17, 19, 29, 34, 71, 72–73, 82, 83, 87–94, 98, 113, 165, 177

documentary analysis 65, 66, 98–99, 135, 181

drugs *see* substance misuse

effect size 120, 196–197

Electronic Theses Online Service 18

embodiment 68

emotions xi, 14, 15, 16, 49, 62, 68, 73, 74, 79, 81, 82, 93, 94, 145, 165, 181, 190, 200, 208

empathy 146

epistemology 8, 15, 20–21, 23, 40, 49, 128, 164, 176, 181

ESRC 18

ethical codes 43

ethics 3, 9, 15, 35, 37, 41–59, 67, 68, 88,

   see also dilemmas in research 141, 142, 148, 165, 166, 167, 170, 172, 176, 183, 187–189

ethics, professional 41–42, 48, 58, 172

ethics approval (research) 3, 37, 45–47, 79, 81, 114, 120, 156, 166, 172, 180, 182, 184

ethics committees 3, 45–47, 77, 78, 89, 114,120, 157

ethics of care 68, 176

ethnography 26, 60, 65–66, 71, 73, 74, 81, 82, 85, 87, 92, 135, 141, 176

European Monitoring Centre For Drugs and Drug Addiction (EMCDDA) 18

evaluation 3, 5, 12, 13, 19, 26, 42, 45, 72, 133–135, 136, 137, 145, 150, 158–160, 176, 202

everyday concepts 25, 60, 61, 62, 66, 69, 74, 93, 144, 175

evidence 1, 7, 8, 9, 10, 24, 30, 33, 36, 46, 55, 71, 88, 107, 143, 165,172, 177, 190

Evidence based practice (EBP) 31, 32, 109–112, 165

Evidence informed practice 31

experimental research design 13, 26, 38, 51–53, 71, 107, 120, 121–125, 174, 176–177, 180, 190–191, 199, 201–202, 203, 207

Facebook 2

factor analysis 116–117, 195

FAST programme 121

feminist ethics 57, 68, 177

feminist research 20, 21, 23, 25, 26, 56–58, 60, 66–69, 70, 82, 176

field notes/ diary 81, 92–94, 96, 105, 155, 177, 179, 190

field work 81–83, 131, 137

focus group(s) 6, 50, 60, 72, 83–84, 94–95, 99, 101, 136, 138, 159, 178, 186, 188,

foster carers 51–52, 121–124, 158–160, 186

Foster Carer Satisfaction Questionnaire 122, 206

Foucault, Michel 98, 208

Gadamer, Hans-Georg 69, 70

gate-keeper 177

gender 21, 67, 89, 91, 96, 111, 118, 175, 194, 204

generalizability 38, 39, 170, 177, 182

'generic' qualitative research 26, 60–62

Gilligan, Carol 103

Glaser & Strauss (grounded theory) 62, 63, 177

Government publications (UK) 17, 18, 29, 34

grey literature 18–20, 34, 177

grounded theory 26, 60, 62–65, 74, 75, 77, 85, 99, 101–102, 105, 129, 160, 169, 177, 178, 206

group dynamics 61, 83

'hard to reach' participants 146, 160, 161, 204, 205

Health & Care Professions Council (HCPC) 17, 18, 43, 108

Health Research Authority (HRA)   44, 45
Heidegger, Martin   70
hermeneutic phenomenology *see* phenomenology
historical analysis   70, 89, 98, 207
holistic approaches   103, 142
Home-Start (UK)   132, 134
hypothesis
   see also research question,null hypothesis   8, 9, 10, 11, 24, 26, 31, 38, 118–119, 123, 124, 169, 175, 177, 179, 181, 187, 196, 206, 207
hypothetico-deductive reasoning   23, 24, 31, 176, 177

identifier, participant   56, 96
identity/ies   12, 21, 31, 102, 142, 143
independent variable *see* variable
infant observation   73
information   1–4, 17–19, 29, 45, 46, 48, 51, 52, 57, 78, 79, 81, 88, 89, 90–91, 100, 108, 109, 154, 156, 164, 175, 180
informed consent *see* consent
insider/outsider perspectives   42, 62, 131, 132, 136
insurance   45
Integrated Research Application System (IRAS)   45
integrative reviews   31
integrity   103–104, 164–165, 166, 172, 191
international social work   67, 121, 143, 144
internet   3, 151, 154–163, 208
interpreting data   62, 65, 97–105, 117–120, 131
interpretivism   25, 26, 60, 71, 74, 92, 107, 131, 177
interprofessional   117, 155
intersectionality   67
interview guide or schedule   46, 77, 171, 177, 178, 185, 189
interviews   6, 7, 11, 33, 50, 52, 56–58, 60, 61, 69, 70, 72, 74–80, 83,
   85, 94–96, 100–101, 104–105, 132–133, 134, 136, 146, 149, 150, 159, 169, 184, 186, 187, 189
   structured   76
   semi-structured   66, 68, 70, 76, 160,
   unstructured   76
interviews, telephone   2, 70, 75, 79, 187

Joseph Rowntree Foundation (JRF)   18

keywords   27–29, 156, 169, 187
knowledge   1, 8, 12, 13, 17, 18, 20–22, 27, 30, 31, 49, 60, 113, 123, 130, 160, 166, 176
Knowledge of Behavioural Principles as Applied to Children (KBPAC)   122–123, 200, 206

language   28, 36, 61, 69, 96, 98, 142, 150, 175, 180, 181, 189
Law Reports, All England   17
learning difficulties   33, 70
Likert scale   111, 112, 114–116, 118, 178, 193
line numbers (transcription)   95
literary arts   142
literature reviewing   6, 11, 30, 31, 34–35, 37, 110, 111,137
   see also secondary research   143, 167, 175, 181,182, 206
literature searching   17–20, 27–29, 175, 178
local authorities (UK)   xi, 11, 12, 14, 18, 45, 46, 51, 56, 57, 93, 122, 158–160, 174

masters students   30, 55, 169
'matched pairs' (in sampling)   77, 121, 204
measurement   13, 26, 106–126, 178, 182, 191, 193, 194, 199–200, 201, 202
measurement– levels (statistics)
   Categorical or nominal   118, 175, 178, 179, 193
   Ordinal   115, 116, 178, 179, 193

measurement– levels
  (statistics)–continued
  Interval   178, 193
  Ratio   178, 194
media   2, 17, 18, 19, 150, 155, 156, 164
  see also social media
mental health   11, 77, 88, 117, 133,
  148–149, 186
meta-analysis   34, 178
methodology xi, 4, 15, 23- 27, 30, 34,
  36–39, 53, 62- 63, 66, 69, 71, 108,
  128, 138, 166, 170, 178
methods   xi, 4, 7, 12, 13, 23, 26,
  32, 36–39, 60, 71, 80- 85, 90–93,
  106–108, 124, 127, 128, 132- 137,
  142, 144, 145–146, 147–149, 150,
  151, 152, 155–156, 162, 165, 166,
  168, 170, 178, 186, 190, 191, 192
Mill, J.S.   23
minutes of meetings   19, 88, 90, 92
mixed methods   6, 7, 37, 53, 65, 67,
  68, 72, 127–140, 149, 178–179,
  191, 208
morality   49
mothers   56–57, 68, 73, 75, 104,
  132–133, 145–146
multilogues *see also* Twitter   156
multiple readings
  (transcripts)   102–104

narrative   64, 76, 82, 90, 98, 99, 101,
  102, 103, 105, 142, 145, 151, 152
National Archives (UK)   19
National Health Service (NHS)   12, 45,
  133–134, 137, 138, 189
National Statistics, Office for (ONS)
  [UK]   3, 18
naturalistic enquiry   63, 81, 205
negotiation   61, 88, 179
networks   102, 159, 208
non-parametric   121, 179, 195–196,
  207
null hypothesis   8, 24, 118–119, 177,
  196

objectivity   10, 22, 65, 81, 179, 180,
  181, 182

observation   3, 4, 24, 25, 64, 73, 74,
  80–83, 84, 92, 177, 179
  see also participant observation
official documents   17, 18
online methods   3, 28, 29, 154–163,
  165, 166, 192
  see also CMC, internet
ontology   20–22, 25, 60, 128, 179
organisations   12, 18, 19, 27, 44, 52,
  54, 58, 62, 71, 78, 84, 87, 88, 89,
  92, 133–135, 154, 162, 172, 176,
  184–185, 188, 192, 203
outcomes   10, 11, 29, 38, 51, 72, 121-
  123, 129, 132, 135, 136, 138, 147,
  150, 151, 152, 158,159, 169, 199,
  201, 202, 223

paradigm   8, 9, 64, 92, 164, 165, 179
parametric   121, 174, 179–180,
  195–196, 207
Parenting Stress Index (PSI)   200, 208
participant   4, 6, 10, 21, 25, 37, 38,
  43, 46, 48, 51–53, 54, 57–58, 62,
  64, 70, 82, 84, 92, 121, 138, 143,
  145–146, 151, 160, 175, 176, 177,
  180, 188, 189, 203
participant observation   65–66, 69,
  71, 72, 81–82, 92, 96, 135, 176,
  179
participatory research   58, 143, 144,
  145, 152, 166, 186
  see also co-production
partnership   x, 11, 56–58, 147, 148,
  172, 186
performance (arts)   142, 150
performance measurement   13, 44,
  100
phenomenology   26, 69–70, 74, 168,
  180
philosophy   14, 20, 21, 23, 25, 42, 69,
  82, 128, 175, 176, 180, 206
photographs   2, 3, 87 92, 141, 143,
  144, 148, 149, 152, 191
  see also visual methods
piloting   39, 78, 85, 112, 114, 156
politics   21, 62, 67, 68, 72, 82, 172
Popper, Karl   23, 24

positionality (researcher) 61
positivism 23–24, 25, 67, 71, 72, 98, 100, 106–107, 131, 180
postmodernism 67
postpositivism 129
post-structuralism 67
power 15, 60, 61, 68, 82, 92, 143, 146, 158, 160, 165, 172, 189, 208
power calculation (statistics) 38, 119
practice educator 14
'practice-near' research 73–74, 180
practitioner researchers 54, 62, 74, 145, 164, 166
pre- and post-tests design 120–121, 122, 124, 135, 201- 202
primary research 6, 17, 29, 37, 128, 175, 180, 207
problem solving skills x, 2, 4, 15, 49, 58
professionals xi, 2, 3, 9, 12, 14–15, 16, 17, 18, 21, 28, 31, 32, 41–42, 43, 48, 78, 79, 81, 85, 109–112, 133, 136, 147, 148, 155, 164–166, 171
project examples: Project
attitudes to research C
bereavement counselling B
breast feeding/ children's rights J
child protection/ safeguarding D, Q
community arts T, U
evidence based practice P
family wellbeing Q
foster carers A, W
health & social care practitioners P
internet W, X
mental health V
mothers D, Q, T
older people O, U, X
people with disabilities K, R, S, X
personalisation X
refugees G, M
role play T, U
student social workers C, N
substance misuse E, F, H, L
visual arts V
women migrants G
women substance misusers F
workforce development P, R, S
young people K, V
protocol 30, 46, 164, 166, 182
provenance 88, 89, 105, 207
psycho-analytically informed observation
see practice near research
purposive sampling see sampling

qualitative research–generic 26, 60–62
quantitative methods 26, 54–56, 71, 72, 83, 90, 106–126, 133- 135, 165, 190–191, 193–197
quasi-experimentation 120, 132, 134, 176, 190, 202, 207
question wording 53, 54, 110, 112–114
questionnaire
design 39, 53, 110–112, 114–115, 116–117, 122, 191, 198–199

randomisation 38, 51, 121–122, 134, 177, 180, 190, 191, 202, 203
Randomised Controlled Trials (RCTs) 31, 107, 121–125, 138, 175, 190, 201, 202, 207
records see documents
referencing (bibliographic) 34, 169
reflectivity/ reflexivity 15, 16, 21, 62, 68, 72, 73, 81, 92, 93, 100, 103, 105, 132, 136, 138, 141, 143, 164, 165, 172, 181
relationship-based research approaches 60–62, 68, 73–74
relationships 14, 16, 20, 22, 60–62, 65, 68, 80, 85, 104, 105, 144, 148, 165, 166
reliability 20, 33, 37, 114, 116, 117, 170, 181, 198
see also validity and trustworthiness
representation 9, 65, 82, 88, 92, 98, 99, 103, 142, 189
representativeness (statistics) 38, 39, 76, 184, 203, 205
R&D departments 45

research design *see* methodology
research governance   43, 44, 45, 50, 57
   see also ethics committees
research mindedness   x, 1–4, 5, 154,
   164, 172
research processes   42, 62, 76–79, 99,
   102, 103, 116, 122, 124, 130, 134,
   139, 146, 167
research proposal   169–172
research question   5–10, 23, 31, 37,
   127, 131, 133, 134, 135, 138,
   165,169, 170, 172, 175, 181, 192
   predictive research question *see*
   hypothesis
resilience   148–149, 208
rigour   12, 13, 54, 63, 64, 90, 107,
   117, 127, 129, 133, 142, 166, 176,
   200
risk assessment   33, 42, 43, 44, 46, 48,
   76, 80, 160

safeguarding   11, 160, 166, 178, 187
   see also child protection
Sampling   22, 35, 37, 39, 63–64, 71,
   76, 77, 78, 88, 89, 90, 98, 108,
   110, 125, 152, 170, 180, 190,
   203–205
sampling, theoretical (grounded
   theory)   63–64, 77
Schutz (phenomenology)   69
'scoping' study   29–30, 44, 148, 156,
   181
scriptwriting and data analysis   146
secondary research   6, 29, 128, 181
semiotics (language)   150, 181
sensitive questions /research   14, 53,
   54, 63, 78, 79, 111, 114
Serious Case Reviews   18, 90
service outcomes *see* outcomes
service users   x, xi, 2, 6, 22, 60, 61, 72,
   77, 81, 85, 87, 93, 97, 104, 113,
   135, 144, 145, 152, 155, 158, 160,
   161, 172, 186, 188–189, 191, 192
service user involvement

   see also co-production   14, 18,
   19, 50, 53, 133, 137, 141, 172,
   188–189, 192
service user records   87, 89, 90, 91
sexualities   21, 67, 143
Signs of Safety   178
situational analysis   64
Skype   60, 79
'snowball' sampling
   see sampling
social justice   47, 57, 58, 67, 68, 143,
   144, 155, 173
social model of disability   133, 137
Social Research Association
   43, 48
sharing information   4, 160
Social Care Institute for Excellence
   (SCIE)   18, 20, 28, 30, 31, 44
social media   2, 4, 6, 61, 83, 89, 154,
   157, 173
social work education   50, 56,
   118–121, 143–145, 147, 150
social work practice   xi, 2, 4, 5–6, 10,
   11–16, 20, 21, 27, 31, 41- 42, 48,
   49, 50, 58, 61, 62, 64, 67, 68, 73,
   74, 77, 94, 99, 107, 109–112, 113,
   130, 142, 143, 144–145, 150, 157,
   161, 162, 164, 166, 169, 172, 180,
   181, 187, 190, 191
'solicited diaries' *see also* diaries   87,
   92, 93
stakeholders   13, 72, 134, 136
statistics   18, 38, 39, 106, 111–112,
   115–120, 125, 193–197
*The Strengths and Difficulties
   Questionnaire (SDQ)*   121, 200
student projects   14, 58, 76, 107, 128,
   138, 139, 144, 166, 172, 187
   see also academic dissertations
subjectivity   4, 10, 21, 25, 38, 39, 67,
   69–70, 116, 151, 177, 179, 181
substance misuse   7, 8, 18, 24, 64–65,
   66, 72, 76, 77, 80, 83–84, 94,
   135–137, 198, 204, 205

see also European Monitoring Centre For Drugs and Drug Addiction (EMCDDA)
supervision 5, 6
Sure Start (UK) 145–147, 208
survey 3, 4, 6, 11, 26, 37, 38, 39, 53–54, 55–56, 65, 97, 107–121, 125, 146, 150, 155, 156, 158, 159, 181, 187, 193, 199, 208
symbolic interactionism 63
(being) systematic 4, 12, 23, 27, 29, 35, 37, 63, 64, 101, 106, 109, 176, 204
systematic review 30–33, 70, 80, 97, 128, 142, 174, 175, 182, 206

teaching quantitative methods 55–56, 115–121
techniques *see* methods
technological changes 4, 154, 155, 156, 158–160, 161–162
texting 60
thematic analysis 148
theoretical saturation 63–65, 102, 161
theory/practice (social work) 62
therapeutic interviewing 78, 79
therapeutic approaches 142, 143, 150, 152, 160, 166, 173
theses *see Electronic Theses Online Service*time xi, 4, 6, 51, 53, 57, 62, 65, 66, 73, 75, 79, 81, 82, 93, 95, 96, 101, 104, 111, 112, 115, 121, 124, 130, 132, 135, 136, 156, 159, 175, 176, 181, 190, 198, 202, 207
time management 4, 47, 54, 79, 101, 188, 190
timetable (research proposal) 13, 169, 171
transcription 95, 102
transcripts 3, 82, 92, 96, 103, 104
transparency (methodological) 20, 152, 166, 188

triangulation 72, 127, 129, 130, 138, 182
trustworthiness 37, 72, 92, 98, 170, 182, 190
see also reliability and validity
Twitter 2, 4, 154, 156, 157, 208
Type 1 / Type 2 errors 119, 121
typifications *see* Schutz

unconscious 61, 74
unobtrusive methods 93

validity 20, 36, 37, 38, 39, 114, 115, 116, 117, 132, 133, 147, 149, 156, 170, 180, 182, 198, 199, 200
see also reliability and trustworthiness
values 15, 21, 31, 41, 42, 63, 83, 165, 172, 173, 180, 181
variable 8, 56, 63, 90, 91, 103, 110, 111, 116, 118, 120, 121, 174, 175, 177, 182, 193, 195, 196, 205
video 3, 83, 84, 133, 137, 141, 144, 145, 146, 150, 151
vignette 85
virtue ethics 42, 182
visual analog scale 133, 182
visual research methods 18, 19, 25, 61, 64, 83, 87, 97, 141–145, 146, 147–152, 154, 162, 179, 208
'voice-centred' relational method (analysis) 103–105
vulnerable participants 48, 53, 57, 79, 151, 157, 163

young people 11, 13, 14, 24, 26, 30, 51, 58, 70, 72–73, 79–80, 82, 88, 91, 112, 121, 122, 123, 124, 144, 145–146, 148–149, 155, 157, 162, 163, 186, 187, 200, 206, 208